The Cinematic Jane .

CW01023864

The Cinematic Jane Austen

Essays on the Filmic Sensibility of the Novels

by DAVID MONAGHAN,
ARIANE HUDELET, *and*
JOHN WILTSHIRE

McFarland & Company, Inc., Publishers
Jefferson, North Carolina, and London

LIBRARY OF CONGRESS CATALOGUING-IN-PUBLICATION DATA

Monaghan, David.
    The cinematic Jane Austen : essays on the filmic sensibility of
the novels / by David Monaghan, Ariane Hudelet, and John
Wiltshire.
       p.   cm.
    Includes bibliographical references and index.

    ISBN 978-0-7864-3506-7
    softcover : 50# alkaline paper ∞

    1. Austen, Jane, 1775–1817—Film and video adaptations.
2. Film adaptations—History and criticism. 3. English
literature—History and criticism. I. Hudelet, Ariane, 1975–
II. Wiltshire, John. III. Title.
PR4038.F55M66 2009
791.43'6—dc22   2008050262

British Library cataloguing data are available

©2009 David Monaghan, Ariane Hudelet and John Wiltshire.
All rights reserved

*No part of this book may be reproduced or transmitted in any form
or by any means, electronic or mechanical, including photocopying
or recording, or by any information storage and retrieval system,
without permission in writing from the publisher.*

On the cover: *Pride and Prejudice*, 2005, with: Matthew
MacFadyen (as Mr. Darcy) and Keira Knightley (as Elizabeth
Bennet) ©Universal/Photofest; background images ©2009 Shut-
terstock.

Manufactured in the United States of America

McFarland & Company, Inc., Publishers
  Box 611, Jefferson, North Carolina 28640
  www.mcfarlandpub.com

Table of Contents

Table of Contents

Preface

The authors of *The Cinematic Jane Austen* share certain assumptions. For instance, we all have an understanding of Austen as cinematic that is succinctly expressed by John Wiltshire in the first chapter: "my intention here is not to show how Jane Austen mysteriously anticipated the techniques of cinema, but informed and influenced by the study of cinema, to consider whether some of the terms and approaches developed in film criticism can offer helpful ways to increase awareness of the distinctive qualities of Austen's art." More broadly, the theoretical assumptions about the adaptation process developed in the introduction by David Monaghan are ones that inform the work of each author, although with some variations, most notably in John Wiltshire's discussion of the vexed question of fidelity in chapter 9. Finally, and most crucially, we all believe that, besides making it possible to cast fresh light on her achievement in the art of fiction, an approach that emphasizes Austen's visual and auditory dimensions will open up the way for productive new readings of films adapted from her novels.

However, in moving from shared assumptions to analyses of specific texts, the authors of this book follow directions entirely of their own choosing. Although ideas and drafts have passed back and forth across three continents throughout the development of our project, we have followed the principle that each chapter will ultimately be the responsibility of a single author. *The Cinematic Jane Austen* is therefore a collaborative, but also an individual endeavor. Consequently, the authors adopt quite different vantage points necessitating a wide range of cinematic vocabulary in their explorations of audio-visual aspects of Austen's art. Equally varied are the interpretations and estimations of Austen film adaptations that flow from these initial cinematic framings of her novels.

When this book was first conceived, there was already a significant body of criticism inspired by the explosion of Austen film and television adaptations of the 1990s, most of it produced by scholars with more expertise in literary than film studies. Inevitably, in approaching visual texts, these scholars have tended to emphasize the presence (or more usually lack) of literary characteristics long considered fundamental to Austen's achievement as a novelist but which, in this new context, were all too often unhelpfully reformulated as barriers to the successful adaptation of her works into a new medium. Perhaps because critical interest cooled off with the commercial failure of Patricia Rozema's subversive and expensive version of *Mansfield Park* (1999), Austen adaptation studies did not develop very far beyond this theoretically unsophisticated approach during the period when this book was in preparation. Neither has there been much serious attention given to the many films and television adaptations that have continued to be produced in the post–Austenmania period. Opportunities thus exist for new approaches to the relationship between Austen's novels and their film adaptations and for discussions of recent additions to the Austen adaptation oeuvre. It is the goal of its authors that *The Cinematic Jane Austen* will make a significant contribution in both of these areas.

This book has its origins in a serendipitous meeting between the three authors at the Women's Writing in Britain, 1660–1830, Conference in July 2003, where events were divided, most appropriately from our perspective, between Winchester and Chawton, two iconic Austen locations. Each of us came to the conference confident that our papers would be unique in proposing that, contrary to conventional wisdom, Jane Austen does indeed possess cinematic qualities similar to those associated with other great nineteenth-century novelists such as Hardy, Conrad and Flaubert. Having discovered, however, that, in our examinations of light, the body and movement, we were working along parallel if not identical lines, it did not take long for us to decide that we should cooperate on a book devoted to our shared interest in the cinematic aspects of Austen's art. Given that *The Cinematic Jane Austen* has its origins in this specific occasion, it is appropriate that the authors give particular thanks to Cora Kaplan and Jennie Batchelor, the organizers of the Women's Writing conference, for inviting us to present papers on lighting, the body and movement, longer versions of which can be found in chapters 2, 3 and 6.

Ariane Hudelet thanks Professor Frédéric Ogée for his precious advice and counsel, and priceless friendship, as well as Professors Catherine Bernard, Marc Porée, Peter Sabor and Dominique Sipière for their close reading and generous remarks. Warmest thanks also to Shannon Wells-Lassagne whose benevolent reading has always been a great help, and above all for the fun they've had working together. Her gratitude also goes to Jean-Loup Bourget and the Arias research group at Paris 3–Sorbonne Nouvelle for providing the means to carry out her research at home and abroad. David Monaghan thanks Mount Saint Vincent University for the research grants and sabbatical leaves that have facilitated his research efforts and the staff of the Mount Saint Vincent and British libraries for their assistance in locating secondary sources. He is particularly grateful to Kamilla Elliott for her always illuminating responses to my questions, and to Noreen Hartlen for her ruthless but always judicious editing. John Wiltshire thanks the members of the Jane Austen Society of Melbourne and the Jane Austen Society of Australia, based in Sydney, to each of which he presented an earlier version of chapter 5. He would also like to thank Laura Carroll for helpful conversations about adaptation, Ruth Wiltshire for trenchant comments on a draft of chapter 9, and Mercia Chapman for coming to the rescue with DVD versions of recent films. Finally, the authors are grateful to each other for their mutual support, encouragement and helpful critiques. The whole, in this instance, at least, has truly been greater than the sum of the parts.

Earlier versions of chapters 3, 6 and 7 have been previously published as "Incarnating Jane Austen: The Role of Sound in Recent Film Adaptations," *Persuasions* 27 (2005): 175–84; "Reinventing Fanny Price: Patricia Rozema's Thoroughly Modern *Mansfield Park*," *Mosaic* 40, 3 (2007): 85–102; and "'A Cheerful Confidence in Futurity': The Movement Motif in Austen's Novel and Dear/Michell's Film Adaptation of *Persuasion*," in *New Windows on a Woman's World: A Festschrift for Jocelyn Harris*, ed. Colin Gibson and Lisa Marr, 2:69–92 (*Otago Studies in English* 9, Dunedin, NZ: Department of English, University of Otago, 2005). The authors are grateful to the editors of these publications for permission to reprint this material.

Throughout this book, quotations from Jane Austen's novels are taken from *The Cambridge Edition of the Works of Jane Austen*, general editor Janet Todd, and are cited parenthetically within the text. Citations include the following abbreviated titles, *NA*, *SS*, *PP*, *MP*, *E*, *P*, where the identity of the work might otherwise be unclear, as well as volume, chapter and page number(s).

Readers are encouraged to refer to www.cinematicjaneausten.com, the companion web site to *The Cinematic Jane Austen* for a comprehensive selection of illustrative film stills.

Introduction.
Jane Austen, Adaptation and the Cinematic Novel: Theoretical Considerations

David Monaghan

The purpose of this book, as its title suggests, is to explore the various ways in which Jane Austen can be described as a cinematic novelist. For the casual observer, such a proposition might seem self-evident. After all, beginning with the 1940 MGM version of *Pride and Prejudice*, Austen's novels have been adapted for film or television over thirty times.[1] Nevertheless, to describe Jane Austen as cinematic is to challenge two theoretical positions, both semiotically based, that have exercised a substantial influence on the field of adaptation studies. Proponents of the first position consider the very term "cinematic novel" to be an oxymoron because, for them, novels and films employ distinct semiotic systems and are therefore divergent forms of artistic expression with "different capabilities and limitations."[2] Those who favor the second usually acknowledge the importance of the image/word divide but nevertheless propose a degree of cross-fertilization between the novel and film genres. However, the definitions of "cinematic novel" that this group of critics has developed in studies of authors such as Dickens, Hardy, Conrad, Flaubert, and Joyce exclude the type of fiction that Austen writes. In preparing for the fresh readings of Austen's relationship to film developed in the main body of *The Cinematic Jane Austen*, my introduction will begin with a review of, and recent correctives to, the semiotic approach. It will then move on to outline an understanding of Austen's novels that draws attention to some important visual and auditory—and hence cinematic—dimensions that have hitherto been rarely acknowledged.

The Semiotic Approach to Adaptation

George Bluestone's *Novels into Film*, written in 1959, has been enor-
mously influential in disseminating the view that the novel and film are fundamentally incompatible forms of media.[3] The basis of Bluestone's argument
is that the novel is a linguistic medium while film is visual (the binary nature
of the comparison necessitates reducing dialogue and sound to subsidiary
roles). He concludes that novels are conceptual while films are perceptual.
Implicit in the semiotic distinction created by Bluestone is the traditional
logocentric proposition that words communicate better than images. Thus,
while he acknowledges that novels and films have their own capacities, Bluestone repeatedly dwells on the superiority of the discursive form in creating
metaphors and in rendering thought; mental states such as memory, dream
and imagination; and past, present and future tenses. Chatman, Bluestone's
most important disciple, supplements this catalogue by commenting on the
problems created by film's lack of a narrative voice, particularly in the areas
of description, summary, and abstract comment. The fact that Bluestone and
Chatman take typical features of prose fiction as their starting points fur-
thers the subordination of film to novel in the adaptation process by valoriz-
ing the original over the copy.

As postulated by Bluestone, the semiotic distinctiveness of film and its
implicit inferiority to the novel means that filmmakers should regard their
novelistic sources as nothing more than raw material for "new cinematic
entit[ies]."[4] For him, to do otherwise would be to engage in an inevitably
doomed attempt to split content from form. As an acerbic Kamilla Elliott
notes, theories based on "word/image and form/content dogmas ... conspire
to render adaptation a theoretical impossibility" even though "adaptation ...
is culturally ubiquitous."[5] Bluestone's position is thus fundamentally unten-
able, as his own analyses of specific film adaptations frequently reveal. For
instance, having proposed that the scope for transfer between novel and film
is limited to "subject, story and plot,"[6] Bluestone then demonstrates that the
1940 film version of *Pride and Prejudice* is successful in approximating both
Austen's narrative focalization and her dance-like rhythms.[7] Ultimately,
immersion in the specifics of film adaptation leads Bluestone far away from
his theoretical foundations, with the result that he speaks of both *Pride and
Prejudice* and *Madame Bovary*—in which Flaubert exploits the structural and
symbolic potential of buildings and objects—as "cinematic" novels.[8]

Although published nearly fifty years ago, *Novels into Film* continues to
exercise a considerable influence on thinking about the relationship of fiction,
and by implication other literary forms, to film. Willemen, for instance, writing in 1994, argues that language and images should be regarded as entirely

separate and that "language is the symbolic expression *par excellence,*"[9] while, as recently as 2003, Gard redeploys the Bluestone/Chatman catalogue of cinematic inadequacy in decrying attempts to adapt Austen's novels for that medium.[10] Nevertheless, and not surprisingly given Bluestone's own equivocation on the subject, most theorists—although continuing to insist on the separation of word and image—now reject the hierarchy implicit in this binary opposition.[11] McFarlane, for example, states that the concept/percept distinction between novel and film is "all but axiomatic."[12] At the same time, he advises scholars involved in the literature/film field to reject the original/copy model in favor of a "more productive invoking of intertexuality" and to pay attention to "what makes for such qualities as subtlety and complexity in film, rather than complaining of the loss of what is peculiar to literature."[13]

In rejecting hierarchy, theorists are also expressing their uneasiness with the unbridgeable gap between the novel and its film adaptation created by the semiotic approach. The plethora of terms now used to describe the process by means of which one form emerges out of a creative engagement with the other pays tribute to efforts to overcome this scholarly discomfort. A list of such terms put together by Robert Stam includes "reading, rewriting, critique, translation, transmutation, metamorphosis, recreation, transvocalization, resuscitation, transfiguration, actualization, transmodalization, signifying, performance, dialogization, cannibalization, reinvisioning, incarnation, or reaccentuation."[14] However, regardless of the number of paths that are established across the novel/film divide, and how decisively the elitism implicit in Bluestone and explicit in fidelity criticism is challenged, the two mediums will never share enough common ground to place the term "cinematic novel" on a sound theoretical footing unless alternatives can be found to the semiotic approach to adaptation.

Some Alternatives to Semiotics

One alternative to the semiotic approach to adaptation is offered by narratologists who propose that actions and events—what Barthes calls "functions proper"—are "directly transferable from one medium to another."[15] The work done by Propp and Campbell on the universality of plot and character functions deriving from fairytale and myth also provides evidence that, at their most basic level, narrative elements are independent of the conventions of specific media.[16] At the same time, however, narratology is too narrow in scope to provide a sufficient theoretical base because discussions of the "cinematic novel" are generally as much—if not more—concerned with questions of literary technique as they are with elemental narrative structures.

An acknowledgment of the fact that words and sound have a vital role
to play in both novels and films offers a second, but also incomplete way of
drawing the two mediums closer together. As Kamilla Elliott points out in
the course of her comprehensive analysis of the subject, the word/image
divide upon which Bluestone bases his theories creates a false binary opposition because film is actually an audio/visual medium.[17] Films sometimes
make use of narrators and written texts, and almost always employ dialogue;
thus, in this area at least, there is a direct (and obvious) conceptual link
between film and prose fiction. Unfortunately, while this observation helps
to close the gap between film and novel and encourages skepticism about the
validity of the semiotic distinctions upon which Bluestone bases his approach
to the issue of adaptation, it does not bring us any closer to a definition of
the cinematic novel. Words play a part in film, but they are everything in the
novel. It would therefore be unhelpful to describe a novel as cinematic
because of its linguistic features alone. However, because sound—which
properly includes not only diegetic and nondiegetic music and noise, but
also non-conceptual aspects of spoken narrative commentary and dialogue
such as volume, tone, and pitch—is a much more fundamental aspect of film
than of the novel, it would seem reasonable to allow space for novels that
cultivate such sensory auditory effects in a comprehensive definition of the
cinematic novel.[18]

Helpful as they are in erasing rigid distinctions between novel and film,
neither a narratological approach nor a consideration of the overlapping
conceptual/perceptual roles played by language and sound in the two mediums fully addresses the problem introduced at the beginning of this discussion. A possible answer has in fact been available since at least 1927 when,
rather than dwell on distinctions that emerge once words and images are
abstracted from their functions, Levinson considered the cognitive processes
involved in actual book reading and film viewing. As a result, he was able to
identify an inverse inherence between linguistic and visual sign systems: "In
the cinema, one extracts the thought from the image; in literature the image
from the thought."[19] Over the years, a number of theorists have made similar statements. Dudley Andrew, for example, comments that "generally film
is found to work from perception towards signification, from external facts
to interior motivations and consequences, from the givenness of a world to
the meaning of a story cut out of that world. Literary fiction works oppo-
sitely. It begins with signs (graphemes and words) building to propositions
which attempt to develop perception."[20]

The most comprehensive and intellectually rigorous discussion of this
alternative way of viewing the relationship between words and images is provided by Kamilla Elliott's *Rethinking the Novel/Film Debate*. She identifies her

approach as in one sense old—dating back at least as far as Sir Richard Blakemore and the beginnings of the sister-arts tradition.[21] At the same time, Elliott is able to describe it as new because she is one of the first scholars to bring to bear on the subject developments in cognitive linguistics and neuropsychology which have been responsible for "largely erod[ing] the categorical differences between mental and perceptual images prevalent in Bluestone's day."[22]

At the core of Elliott's extended questioning of the Bluestone approach to adaptation is a metaphor based on the "endlessly inverting mutual containment of facing mirrors," which she employs in developing a "verbal-visual looking-glass analogy ... predicated on the reciprocal power of words to evoke mental images and of pictures to evoke verbal figures in cognition."[23] For Elliott "looking glass analogies maintain oppositions between the arts, but integrate these oppositions as an inextricable secondary identity." As she puts it, the arts of fiction and film "contain and invert the otherness of each other reciprocally, inversely, and inherently rather than being divided from the other by their otherness."[24] Thus, "a film of a novel reduces the novel's words and realizes its implied images; a novelization of a film turns perceptual and auditory images into verbal signs."[25] Elliott neatly summarizes her disagreement with Bluestone and his followers when she states, "I want to modify Bluestone's famous maxim [i.e., "between the percept of the visual image and the concept of the mental image lies the root difference between the two media"[26]] to argue that between the concept evoked by pictures and the percept evoked by words lies a root connection between novels and films."[27] Adaptation under looking glass analogies is, as a consequence, "excess rather than reduction."[28]

Far from being isolated into their separate semiotic spheres, as Bluestone would argue, novels and film are closely related because of their transferable narrative functions and, more importantly, their ability to integrate the conceptual and perceptual (specifically, visual and auditory) aspects of cognition. We can, therefore, now be confident that in proceeding to a discussion of the cinematic novel we are not yoking together dissonant terms.

The Cinematic Novel

Although it has become "a rhetorical commonplace," the term "cinematic novel" has never been defined very precisely.[29] Nevertheless, in practice, those who refer to novels as cinematic have generally focused, as have the theorists discussed above, on the transferability of plot and character functions between genres and on the visual potential of language. The sensory dimension of words has not usually been included in attempts to identify the cinematic aspects of novels because very little critical attention has been paid to the aural dimensions of film (see note 19). However, this ability is integral to the definition of the cinematic novel being proposed here.

The kind of novel generally considered cinematic from a narratological perspective is one that develops patterns of action and character types similar to those employed in mainstream commercial cinema. Thus, it typically makes use of a self-effacing narrator to tell an uncomplicated and chronologically linear story that includes more action than introspection and develops vivid but straightforward characters. In her study of novel/film relations, Judith Mayne identifies the nineteenth-century novel in particular and, more generally, the middle-class realist "readerly" text, as the type of fiction that most closely approximates the norms of classic cinematic narration.[30]

For other critics, the cinematic novel is one in which the writer either exploits the ability of words to "arouse mental images"[31] or utilizes techniques more usually associated with film in order to present his or her material in primarily visual terms. This definition of the cinematic novel is sufficiently broad (or perhaps vague) to embrace a remarkably wide range of fiction written during the last two centuries. It is not surprising that cinematic terminology has been applied to authors writing in the twentieth and twenty-first centuries because most of them are or were, of course, familiar with and many have admitted their indebtedness to the film medium. Writers as different as Hemingway and Robbe-Grillet have thus been described as cinematic because they seek the visual immediacy made possible by dwelling, as the camera does, on surfaces.[32] Similarly, Cohen argues that Joyce, Faulkner, Woolf and Proust developed techniques comparable to film montage in order to express the fragmented experience and intense subjectivity and multiplicity of vision that are, from a Modernist perspective, characteristic of twentieth-century life.[33]

However, awareness of the film medium is not a prerequisite for authors to be described as cinematic. Thus, although they had either reached artistic maturity or ceased to write before the birth of the film industry in the early twentieth-century, Conrad, Dickens, Hardy, James and Flaubert have all been termed cinematic because of the strong visual element in their work and because the methods employed in their descriptive passages seemingly anticipate a wide variety of film techniques. The most significant contribution to this line of argument is provided by the great film theorist and practitioner Sergei Eisenstein who not only claims that Dickens anticipates film but identifies a direct influence on D. W. Griffith, the inventor of close up and cross-cutting techniques.[34] Lodge follows Eisenstein's lead by analyzing Hardy's use of descriptive techniques analogous to the long shot, close-up, wide angle and zoom, and heavy reliance on detached observing eyes that function like camera lenses.[35] Spiegel, in his turn, describes Flaubert's method of isolating individual objects and showing them close as "cinematographic," while McFarlane argues that Conrad and James "anticipate the cinema" in two ways: by stressing "physical surfaces and behaviors of objects and figures," thereby "de-emphasiz[ing] the author's personal narrating voice," and by "fragmenting" the visual field through shifts in point of view.[36]

Kellman and Elliott share a concern about the attribution of cinematic qualities to novels written before the invention of the movie camera.[37] For Elliott, an over-emphasis on the influence of nineteenth-century novels on filmmakers also serves to obscure the importance of theater and, to a lesser extent, painting, as a source for film. While such reservations cannot be ignored, the authors of this book believe that the cinematic designation is appropriate not only when applied to a number of nineteenth-century novelists but also to Jane Austen, who is not typically described in this way. The next section of the introduction will address the issue of Austen as a cinematic novelist but, first, three reasons of a more general nature will be presented as justification for using the term when discussing authors who could have known nothing about film.

First, whatever the development of film might owe to arts such as theater and painting, there can be little doubt that nineteenth-century novelists have provided important models for cinematic practice. Eisenstein's argument regarding the influence of Dickens on Griffith is particularly compelling because of its origin in Griffith's own acknowledgment of an indebtedness to the novelist.[38] While lacking direct verification, the case that Lodge and Spiegel develop through detailed analyses of selected passages from works such as *Tess of the D'Urbervilles* and *Madame Bovary* is plausible because of their success in demonstrating strong similarities between the descriptive techniques of Hardy and Flaubert and the storyboards prepared by filmmakers.[39] Turning to the area of narrative transfer, it seems indisputable that mainstream cinema owes far more to the well-rounded and relatively linear plots of nineteenth-century novels than it does to the complexly structured and "writerly" fiction developed by Modernist novelists and their successors in the twentieth century. Thus, McFarlane argues that film's "*embourgeoisement* inevitably led it ... towards that narrative representationalism which had reached a peak in the classic nineteenth-century novel. If film did not grow *out* of the [nineteenth-century novel], it grew *towards* it."[40]

Second, we do not need to postulate the nineteenth-century novel as a direct influence on film in order to justify the claim that, in some important respects, the two arts use similar techniques. Artists working in both novel and film mediums are concerned to realize the visual potential of their chosen forms; consequently we should not be surprised when they arrive at similar technical solutions to the challenges facing them. Hardy, Flaubert and other nineteenth-century novelists would obviously have been unfamiliar with concepts such as editing and mise en scène and could not have known anything about a moving camera's ability to pan and track. Nevertheless, they were well aware of how much more effective it is to construct descriptive passages out of fragments of the whole scene and with changes in distance and angle than to provide one-directional "scenographic" overviews.[41]

Third, to comprehend techniques such as those described above as cinematic may be anachronistic; but to do so can be justified by reference to Umberto Eco's concept of "open work," in which texts take on new meanings, new aspects, every time they are read in a new manner.[42] Once we have become aware of the medium of film and the technical means by which it shapes its raw visual material into artistic form, it is almost inevitable and potentially very productive for us to bring this fresh perspective to bear as we engage with the visual aspects of other creative media, including the pre-cinematic novel.

Jane Austen as a Cinematic Novelist

As we have already seen, Jane Austen is not typically included amongst the nineteenth-century novelists judged to be cinematic. However, when critics have considered the relationship between Austen's novels and films based on them, they have often addressed the closely related—but not always identical—issue of her adaptability.[43] Broadly speaking, there seems to be fairly widespread agreement that Austen lends herself to both film and television adaptation because her plots are well constructed, her casts of characters and settings are relatively limited, and her subject matter is archetypal or romantic—characteristics that accord with definitions of the cinematic based on narratological criteria. It is other aspects of her work that are seen to pose problems rather than possibilities for filmmakers.

Much of the discussion of the adaptability—or, we are safe to say in this case at least, the cinematic nature—of Austen's main narrative features is fairly cursory and impressionistic. For instance, in explaining why it was so easy to transform the early nineteenth-century novel *Emma* into a 1990s high school movie, both the critic Hoberg and Heckerling, the writer/director of *Clueless*, take the universal nature of Austen's plots as self-evident: Hoberg's argument amounts to the statement that "Austenites ... view [*Clueless*] as a version that validates the universality of the original" while Heckerling is content with the statement, "I loved *Emma* in college. The plot is perfect for any time."[44] However, there are a handful of more substantial studies. Lauritzen, employing a methodology derived from the narratologist Todorov, uses the example of the 1972 BBC adaptation of *Emma* to demonstrate the relative ease with which Austen's plot and characters can be reshaped according to the conventions of the television classic drama serial.[45] In their essays, both Kaplan and Richards discuss how what may be seen as the simple love stories underpinning Austen's novels provide more than adequate structures for films that resemble Harlequin or Regency romances more than they do their "culturally and linguistically complex" sources.[46]

However, once analysis goes beyond plot and character functions, Austen is only occasionally described as cinematic. One of these exceptional critics is Gay who offers the brief, but telling, observation that "Austen's liberal stage directions [during the concert scene in *Persuasion*] regarding characters' movements towards and away from each other ... , glances, blushes, averted eyes, offer the sort of detail that only in the twentieth century was it possible to represent theatrically, in the realistic formats and observant lenses of film and television." Others include Sutherland, who also argues for the cinematic potential of Austen's details, and Pucci, who suggests that country houses acquire "a dominant visual presence" in film adaptations as reflections of the important domestic contexts they provide in her novels.[47]

More typically, scholars dwell on three aspects of Austen's art that supposedly make her novels difficult to adapt to a visual medium: her use of a pervasive and ironic narrative voice, her emphasis on the inner lives of her characters, and her spare descriptions of characters and places.[48] An approach to adaptation that is not hindered—as is so much of the criticism that deals with film versions of Austen's novels—by nostalgia for the novelistic original, and a lack of awareness of the artistic resources available to filmmakers, would regard these problems as more illusory than real.[49] Here, though, one must separate the adaptable from the cinematic because, in so far as her novels are dominated by their narrators, have an interior focus, and lack descriptive fullness, Austen cannot be accommodated within conventional understandings of the term "cinematic novelist."

A quite different picture emerges once we expand our understanding of Austen's artistic repertoire beyond the narrow terms in which it has been defined by most critics. Far from being disembodied and abstract, Austen's novels prove to be powerfully visual and auditory, and hence cinematic. The narrator, for instance, is not omnipresent but frequently withdraws to allow for scenes that are developed through unmediated dialogue and action. As a result, we come to know the characters not just through their rich inner lives but also through their dramatized interactions with others. Furthermore, while it is rare for Austen to fully contextualize her action, such scenes frequently make telling use of descriptive and auditory detail.

Ironically, some of the most effective demonstrations of the visual and auditory dimensions that allow us to define Austen's work as cinematic are provided by recent critical studies that are completely unconcerned with her relationship to film. Their authors cover a wide variety of topics, including the movement motif, most notably stagnation and restless energy as forms of evil in *Mansfield Park*[50]; the role of physical objects, such as the solitary candle in the Prices' sitting room in *Mansfield Park*[51]; the function of natural and human spaces and places, including Fanny Price's creation of free space in *Mansfield Park*, Bath as an urban/consumer location in *Persuasion*, the interaction between inner and outer space in *Persuasion*, and nature as a reflector of character in *Mansfield Park*[52]; group interactions during the dinners and balls that play a prominent role in all of the novels[53]; the body as carrier of meaning, whether it be Elizabeth Bennet's blushing, Anne and Wentworth's communicating through touch, Mary Crawford's posing by her harp like an art object, or Henry Crawford's pressing Fanny Price's hand in precisely the manner he previously employed with Maria Bertram[54]; and the pervasive role of noise and quiet in *Mansfield Park* and *Persuasion*.[55]

Because their focus is entirely on the novels, these critics do not make any attempt to identify similarities between Austen's techniques and those that filmmakers employ in creating the audio-visual dimensions of their work. Nevertheless, such similarities occur to us almost immediately if we keep in mind Austen's cinematic potential as we read the various analyses, whether it be in the form of close-ups or shallow focus to isolate details, such as candles, blushes or hands; long shots to introduce rural or urban locations; tracking and panning to communicate movement; crosscutting to establish contrasts between locations; montage sequences and changes of distance and angle to create appropriate rhythms and emphases during group scenes; or modulations in the sound track to emphasize noise/quiet contrasts. The point at which this group of critics comes closest to directly communicating a cinematic understanding of Austen occurs when John Wiltshire compares "the way in which Austen controls her reader's attention to her text to the way in which Rembrandt controls the viewer's attention" by painting certain areas of his canvas such as "a face, glove or lace with great vividness and detail" while others "are merely sketched."[56] Although Wiltshire turns to painting for his metaphor, his account of Austen's characteristic descriptive technique can easily be reframed in the cinematic language of selective focus. From here, it is a short step to grouping Austen with novelists such as Hardy and Flaubert who have been praised for their ability to describe in a cinematic way.

In addressing Austen as a cinematic novelist, the main body of this book cultivates a receptiveness to her visual and auditory qualities that is similar to the works cited above but which is curiously absent from most studies that consider her novels in relation to their film adaptations. In addition, it pays some attention to the one area of Austen's art that has been widely described as cinematic: the archetypal or universal nature of her basic plot and character functions. The first five chapters are concerned with issues relating to mise en scène.[57] Thus, chapter 1 argues that, while Austen is not a particularly visual novelist, she generates a sense of spatial relationships akin to the planes, or mise en scène, of a visual medium through the motif of overhearing. Chapter 2 examines the role of Austen's occasional, but highly significant, use of lighting—always a key element of frame composition in film—and more specifically of candle or gas light, both of which play a fundamental part in creating the typical style of heritage cinema. Chapters 3 and 4 are concerned with some of the details that comprise Austen's mise en scène, including body language, facial expression and non-verbal sound. In the course of the two chapters Ariane Hudelet demonstrates how these audio-visual elements provide Austen, as they do the filmmaker, with alternatives to linguistic forms of communication. She also argues in chapter 4 that problems facing her characters in judging the meaning of body language and facial expression strike the modern reader as particularly cinematic because they raise questions about perception and interpretation that are also related to the reception of the film form itself. Chapter 5 continues the topic of body language by examining how Elizabeth's failure to recognize Darcy's smile serves as an indicator of her broader misperceptions about him. Chapters 6 and 7 identify significant differences in the thematic roles played by patterns of movement and stillness in *Mansfield Park* and *Persuasion*, respectively. By so doing, they shift the book's emphasis away from mise en scène to techniques broadly analogous to editing and camera movement, and hence from the spatial to the temporal. Chapter 8 refocuses discussion once again, this time towards narratological issues through an analysis of the broad mythological structures that underpin Austen's socially specific plots and that make her novels cinematic in the sense of being a prime target for appropriation by filmmakers working in very different cultural/social circumstances from her own. Finally, chapter 9 is titled "Afterword" because it both offers a new definition of the term fidelity and considers the new conceptual questions opened by the appearance of Austen film adaptations that owe as much to previous films in the genre as to their source texts. These "hybrid" films, as Wiltshire calls them, greatly complicate what Monaghan describes in chapter 7 as the "stereoscopic" vision that can emerge from the interplay between novel original and film adaptation, and offer fresh challenges for the next generation of Austen-adaptation studies.

Although this introduction has been preoccupied with problems arising from the concept of the cinematic novel and its application to Jane

Austen, the chapters that follow not only move inwards to examine the cinematic ways in which her novels develop their audio-visual aspects and narrative framework, as indicated above, but they also move outwards to consider the interplay between the novels and their film adaptations. It should be noted, though, that in approaching the relationship of novel to film from a perspective provided by an understanding of Austen as cinematic, the authors of this book are not practicing a form of fidelity criticism. Thus, estimates of the success of adaptations will not be based on the degree to which their creators have proven willing or able to identify and incorporate the audio-visual cues provided by the novels. On the contrary, as is demonstrated throughout the book, attention to differences in technique can provide significant insights into some of the more elliptical and, not coincidentally, productive relationships that exist between adaptations and source texts. For example, in Chapter 5, Wiltshire points out the contrast between the frequently smiling and always smoldering Darcy, revealed by close-ups in novel and film versions of *Pride and Prejudice*, respectively, as a preamble to a discussion of significant differences in Austen's and filmmaker Joe Wright's approaches to the theme of appearance. Similarly, in chapter 6, a comparison of the very dissimilar patterns of movement developed in Austen's *Mansfield Park* and the adaptation written and directed by Patricia Rozema provides Monaghan with a basis for exploring the ideological gulf that separates novel and film.

Just as we earlier rejected the idea that the non-audiovisual aspects of Austen's artistic practice cause problems for filmmakers, so we authors of *The Cinematic Jane Austen* are not claiming that her novels are more easily adapted than others because, in certain respects, they are cinematic. To do so would be to deny the close relationship between the cognitive processes involved in novel reading and film viewing established by Kamilla Elliott in *Rethinking the Novel/Film Debate* and subsequently used by her to argue for the adaptability of even the most apparently "unfilmable books."[58] What we are claiming is that, by going beyond the lopsided accounts of Austen's formal characteristics provided by adaptation critics, we have opened up the way for some productive readings of the complex interrelations between her novels and the many films based on them. While the emphasis of this introduction has been theoretical and general, the success of our endeavor will depend on the quality of the close analyses conducted in the chapters that follow.

1

Jane Austen: Sight and Sound

JOHN WILTSHIRE

Jane Austen is a famously (or notoriously) unvisual novelist. George Henry Lewes even speculated that she might have been shortsighted, for "the absence of all sense of outward world—either of scenery or personal appearance—is more remarkable in her than any writer we remember."[1] She was, as he declared in his mid–nineteenth century appraisal, an unacknowledged "artist of the first rank," and above all, a "dramatic" novelist. "So entirely dramatic, and so little descriptive, is the genius of Miss Austen, that she seems to rely upon what her people say and do for the effect they are to produce on our imaginations," he wrote. Austen's achievements, then, being "dramatic," would seem to involve limitations, or exclusions—the visual most of all.

The Box Hill chapter in *Emma* might be a good example of what Lewes meant. The editors of the Cambridge edition of the novel cite Gilpin's *Observations of the Western Parts of England Relative Chiefly to Picturesque Beauty* (1798) on "that boast of Surrey, the celebrated Box Hill; so called from the profusion of box which flourishes spontaneously upon it," to illuminate the sequence. "This hill," Gilpin wrote, "from its downy back to and precipitous sides, exhibits great variety of pleasing views into the lower parts of Surrey; and the higher parts of the neighbouring counties."[2] Jane Austen had read "Gilpin on the picturesque," but there is nothing picturesque about her chapter. Nothing about the picnic (so elaborately presented in both movies so far made of the novel), no description of the hill, or vistas, or the nature of the "explorations" that might be made, except in Mrs. Elton's comic use of the word. The only indication of the location, though it is a precise one, comes in Frank's histrionics: "I saw you first in February. Let every body on the Hill hear me if they can. Let accents swell to Mickleham on one side, and Dorking on the other" (III, 7, 401). But this speech evokes not the scene but the speaker's forced high spirits.

It can be argued that both novel and film have their ultimate roots in the drama; and it is probable, as Lewes and other critics imply, that the Austen narrative's closest affinities are with the dramatic script.[3] But the skimpiness of the visual in Austen's novels obviously poses a challenge to any reading which considers them in the light of film and film theory. This however is the project—the experiment—of this chapter. "The cinematic Jane Austen" may well be an anachronistic absurdity[4]: my intention here though is not to show how Jane Austen mysteriously anticipated the techniques of the cinema, but informed and influenced by the study of cinema, to consider whether some of the terms and approaches developed in film criticism can offer helpful ways to increase awareness of the distinctive qualities of Jane Austen's art. Thus I seek to perform a kind of reverse epistemology, traveling not "from page to screen," as is common in adaptation studies, but from "screen to page."[5] Ultimately, I shall suggest that we need to think of Austen's achievement not in terms of visuality but of spatiality, revealed not in description but in the structuration of her narratives. In the second part of this chapter, I shall offer a reading of her final completed work, *Persuasion*, in which spatial relationships are particularly important, and in which hearing, rather than seeing, plays a key role.

The experiment is not without other challenges. Many aspects of film may have no equivalent or analogy in the novel. And many terms in film criticism have been developed to isolate features specific to the cinema. "Mise en scène" is an important concept for anyone trying to think about the role of the visual in narrative art, but mise en scène is associated with the emphasis on the director as "auteur" that flourished in the nineteen-sixties and which in effect relegated the screenplay to a minor role in film production, and the criticism that followed. The term often functions then as a way of disassociating cinematic art from literature. "It is this that makes film, as an art, so much closer to music than to literature," Robin Wood declared.[6] Or as a recent guide puts it, "Mise en scène is unique to the cinema, and it is the way in which cinema is uniquely expressive."[7] Nevertheless, I want to see how far the conception of mise en scène will take us in reading Austen's novels. Reading them "with the eye of a stranger," turning to them from film, may at least sharpen our understanding of the unique qualities, and limits, of Austen's narrative art.

Film critics, like narratologists, often dispute the meaning of the terms they use. One of these, common to both fields, is "point of view."[8] It is clear that some sequences in film, like some in novels, rely upon the viewer or reader identifying the material they are presented with as subjective experience. In a film there are various means by which this is achieved—voice over, the tracking shot, the inclusion of the character from within a shot framed from their angle of vision. Austen's novels are commonly distinguished from those of her contemporaries by the pervasiveness of techniques which allow the reader to associate what they are reading with a specific character—most famously in *Emma*, but also in the other novels. This association is what facilitates her irony—the recognition that the material being presented may be ascribed to a consciousness not quite identical with the author, often called the "omniscient narrator," who like god, sees into the soul, and can move at will between the thoughts of one and another imagined figure.[9] The narrator in Jane Austen's novels has some of the characteristics, though, of a participant in the world her characters inhabit, and this complicates the whole question of point of view: "About thirty years ago," begins *Mansfield Park*, "Miss Maria Ward of Huntingdon, with only seven thousand pounds, had the good luck to captivate Sir Thomas Bertram" (I, 1, 3). A conventional opening, supposedly the neutral report of history. But in the second sentence (if not in the first) something more than impersonality appears. "All Huntingdon exclaimed on the greatness of the match, and her uncle, the lawyer, himself, allowed her to be at least three thousand pounds short of any equitable claim to it." The superfluousness of the adverb "himself" to the information given, that slightly surprised lifting of the voice which the insertion mimics, displaces external, objective definition into something like a neighborly knowingness. So that the "omniscience" is paradoxically and inconveniently registered as culturally sited. "Point of view" in the novels is consequently often difficult to identify. And while point of view (however defined) in the film has an obvious relevance, there is an endemic confusion in the criticism of the novel because terms implying visuality are used of material which (except in the act of reading) is scarcely visual at all.

Visuality in the Novels

"Emma had not another word to oppose. She saw it all" (II, 6, 394). In English the verb "to see" can and often does mean "to understand," or here, when Emma is responding to Jane Fairfax's distress at Donwell Abbey, "to perceive and sympathize." Or it can mean "to appraise" as in "Mrs. Elton was first seen at church" (II, 14, 291). It is common to find literary critics using "to see" to mean "to know" or even "to read." In an early narratological analysis of point of view in *Emma*, Wayne Booth handles it with a flourish: "But Jane Austen never lets us forget that Emma is not what she appears to be. For every section devoted to her misdeeds—and even they are seen for the most part through her own eyes—there is a section devoted to her self-reproach. We see her rudeness to Miss Bates, and we see it vividly. But her remorse and act of penance in visiting Miss Bates after Knightley's rebuke are experienced even more vividly. We see successive attempts to mislead Harriet, but we see at great length and in high color her self-castigation."[10] Booth's famous analysis of "Control of Distance" in *Emma* turns on the notion of "double vision": the simultaneous "inside view" of Emma, and the "objective view" of the narrator.[11] He does not use the verb metaphorically, despite that last phrase in my quotation. For him, as for many readers, "seeing" is tantamount to "experiencing" or perhaps "reading imaginatively." Evidently then "seeing" need not involve the exercise of the eyes, except in so far as these are engaged in reading the text. But even if it refers to the imagination, confusion still remains, since that very word—imagination—and its cognates implies visuality.

How far attentive reading involves the reader's imagination and how far imagination involves visualization is a phenomenological issue which can only be assessed through introspection. It is plausible to suggest that it will vary from reader to reader, and from moment to moment, or from phrase to phrase, of the text. Most importantly, the prompting towards the reader's visual imagination is married to or blended with the specifically intellectual or at least non-visual pleasure provided by other "information" carried in the prose—by means of its rhythm, for example. An instance occurs in *Mansfield Park* when Tom Bertram is drumming up reasons why the theatricals should go ahead in his father's absence. For one thing, he tells his brother Edmund, they will divert his mother, since "It is a *very* anxious period for her":

> As he said this, each looked towards their mother. Lady Bertram, sunk back in one corner of the sofa, the picture of health, wealth, ease and tranquility, was falling into a gentle doze, while Fanny was getting through the few difficulties of her work for her.
> Edmund smiled and shook his head [I, 13, 148].

Though the reader's attention is certainly directed towards the "picture" it is important that the description is not literal. The phrase is idiomatic (Emma, says Mrs. Weston, is also "the picture of health") and means the epitome, the absolute embodiment. The joking informality inherent in the use of idiom contributes to the accolade's forming a kind of back-handed compliment. As the sentence creates the picture, the reader enjoys this as a specifically verbal wit, capped by the way the upbeat rhythm bathetically tails off into the rueful reference to Fanny's role as her aunt's support system. Fanny has only the most fleeting visual presence. The whole quick comic vignette passes through the reader's imagination in a moment, before the focus returns to Tom and Edmund: "'By Jove! This won't do—cried Tom, throwing himself into a chair with a hearty laugh. To be sure, my dear mother, your anxiety—I was unlucky there.'"

If we were to conceive of the reader's imagination as a camera, what happens here is a quick succession of distinct foci—first the men, agents who look, then dwelling for a moment on the object of their gaze, widening to include Fanny, and then returning to Edmund, and finally Tom. One might guess that if a camera did replicate the speed or smoothness with which these adjustments are made it would be contributing a salience to the moment which in Austen's text it does not possess. This is a brief comic diversion from a serious quarrel between the brothers, which besides characterizing, as here, Tom's insouciance, underlines the rather ugly domestic politics of the Bertram family. The moment of visuality passes, and the argument resumes, presented without commentary, as if being performed on a stage.

The antecedents of the kind of reversal epitomized in this moment certainly also lie in stage comedy. A similar effect (in a novel usually thought of as grimly humorless) occurs when Fanny receives an invitation to dine at the Grants.' Pages are occupied by Mrs. Norris's attempts to strip from Fanny any pleasure or gratification at the invitation, culminating in her saying that of course Fanny mustn't expect the use of the family carriage. Soon afterwards (more or less instantly in reading time) the door opens and Sir Thomas offers it to her: "'My dear Sir Thomas!' cried Mrs. Norris, red with anger, 'Fanny can walk.'" (II, 5, 258). Other signs of the influence of the theater on Austen's imagination are everywhere. When Emma Woodhouse, for example, steps out of Ford's shop to survey the village street, there is an illuminating usage of the word "scene." At first Emma observes only miscellaneous small activities, which amuse her enough, "quite enough still to stand at the door." In the next paragraph, though, "She looked down the Randalls road. The scene enlarged; two persons appeared; Mrs. Weston and her son-in-law; they were walking into Highbury" (II, 9, 251–2). A reader used to the cinema might think of a camera dollying back, to disclose more visual material, but the word "scene" in fact picks up the older theatrical usage, in which "scene" meant not a discrete section of a play, but rather marked the entry of new personages. "Scenes or set pieces are units of action built around exits and entrances."[12] Thus, one might say, not a visual but a formal point is being made.

Another example of apparent visuality occurs in Chapter 16 of the second volume of *Emma*. The topic of the chapter is the heroine's welcoming dinner for the Eltons. It begins with paragraphs which seem to represent Mrs. Elton's opinions, but with a clearly indicated transition—"Emma, in the meanwhile"—moves towards her, and begins to pick up her characteristic inflections. The focus on Emma continues, though with variations of technique, for two pages. For one paragraph (II, 16, 315) Emma apparently talks to herself: "'This is very true,' said she, 'at least as relates to me,'" etc.

This paragraph represents her not only acknowledging Mr. Knightley's criticisms, but speaking aloud—which suggests a full and conscious admission culminating in resolution. The plans for the dinner party are upset by the unexpected visit of Mr. John Knightley, but eventually "the philosophic composure of her brother on hearing his fate, removed the chief of even Emma's vexation."

So at the end of the paragraph, the reader is still "with" Emma. This paragraph follows:

> The day came, the party were punctually assembled, and Mr. John Knightley seemed early to devote himself to the business of being agreeable. Instead of drawing his brother off to a window while they waited for dinner, he was talking to Miss Fairfax. Mrs. Elton, as elegant as lace and pearls could make her, he looked at in silence—wanting only to observe enough for Isabella's information—but Miss Fairfax was an old acquaintance and a quiet girl, and he could talk to her. He had met her before breakfast as he was returning from a walk with his little boys, when it had been just beginning to rain. It was natural to have some civil hopes on the subject, and he said....

(And a page and a half of dialogue between John Knightley and Jane Fairfax ensues.) From the cue in the previous paragraph, the reader may assume the continuance of Emma's point of view (she may still have a few apprehensions about John's behavior, and therefore be watching him). The phrasing of "he was talking to Miss Fairfax," rather than, say, "he talked" designates an observation made apparently by Emma, rather than a diegetic "fact." The next sentence can also be read as Emma's—its wit, rather like "the business of being agreeable" in the sentence before, seeming consonant with her style, and her previous opinion of Mrs. Elton. It is even possible that the interpolated phrase "wanting only to observe enough for Isabella's information" is Emma's hypothesis. "Mrs. Elton ... he looked at in silence—wanting only to observe enough for Isabella's information—but Miss Fairfax was an old acquaintance, and a quiet girl, and he could talk to her." But the narrative has imperceptibly segued from one point of view to another—from Emma to John Knightley. The sleight of hand is performed through the previous sentence. "As elegant as pearls and lace could make her" is not so much a visual image as a witty flirtation with the visual, which—momentarily enticing the reader—covertly allows the switch to John Knightley's thoughts. Certainly by the phrase "quiet girl," we are securely within his orbit.

Staying with this chapter, one can examine some aspects of Jane Austen's management of the group scene, which becomes increasingly central to her achievement in the last three novels. There are ten people in the Hartfield drawing room. The duologue between John Knightley and Jane Fairfax which follows this paragraph is offered as if between two isolated voices: there is no indication of the speakers, their position or their relation to others in the room. The dialogue is "dramatic" in the sense that only the words spoken are given, and the reader's imagination is relied on to supply the rest. And there is no "Emma observed" or "Emma could not help but overhear." So it is slightly surprising that after the dialogue is completed Mr. Woodhouse, "making the circle of his guests, with all his mildest urbanity, said 'I am very sorry to hear, Miss Fairfax, of your being out this morning in the rain'" (I, 16, 318). How he has got to hear of it and how it reaches Mrs. Elton, whose interferences now occupy two more pages of dialogue, is anyone's guess (even if one guesses Emma). The omission of the connection generates a significant point: what has seemed an intimate, exclusive exchange is not; nothing, the reader learns, can be kept private in this circle. Perhaps this cut, or omission of connection, is tantamount to the filmic "montage." Eisenstein's historic insistence was that montage (or the assemblage and editing of images) constitutes the basic "language" of film which generates or produces "meaning" for the spectator. In a parallel fashion, one can argue that Austen's narrative here, leaving out information, generates a sense of the close gossipy confines of the room.

The conversation culminates in a discussion of handwriting; even letters, folded and sealed, are not immune from neighborly speculation, for handwriting itself, we learn, betrays secrets. John Knightley and Jane Fairfax have spoken to each other in accents of people who know something of the world. Their dialogue's insertion into the a setting in which Mr. Woodhouse, politely going his rounds, can assure Jane Fairfax that "Young ladies are sure to be cared for" and that her grandmother and aunt are "some of my very old friends," weaves potential isolation and estrangement into, and therefore momentarily chills or distances the coziness of which the scene is otherwise brimful. The word "friend" so important in Jane and John Knightley's conversation means something different in the closed community of Highbury's genteel. The narrative's movement from one figure to another, from Mrs. Elton to Emma, from Emma to John Knightley, then back to the conversational group, is surely akin to one conception of mise en scène, in which directional control is an important generator of meanings not obviously present in dialogue.

Mise en scène

But mise en scène, though much used, is a not an entirely transparent term in film criticism. The Oxford English Dictionary, behind the times, defines the phrase as the staging of a play, or "the settings and surroundings of an event or action." But as used of a film, it has many meanings, from the workaday "contents of the frame and the way they are organized" to such aspects of visuality as camera movement, and can even broaden out to encompass the whole tone or mood of a film. James Monaco, for example, begins his extensive interpretation of the term with a discussion of the various planes by which we make sense of visual material.[13] If however the notion of variation between various planes of awareness or recognition is transferred to the discussion of Jane Austen's novels, it may contribute to an awareness of her "control of distance" more complex and precise than in Booth's famous article. The notion of planes (or levels of attention) is especially pertinent to an author whose commitment in the later novels is increasingly to group scenes, and to the isolation of exchanges which occur within the inevitable social constraints of public places.

If there are exceptions to the notion of Jane Austen as a predominantly dramatic novelist, with little interest in the visible scene, they would be those scenes of apparent interest in landscape. One obvious example is the chapter immediately before the Box Hill episode, the visit to Donwell Abbey. Here, Emma, escaping from the rest, regales herself with a survey of the house and grounds ("respectable" here means "venerable"):

> She felt all the honest pride and complacency which her alliance with the present and future proprietor could fairly warrant, as she viewed the respectable size and style of the building, its suitable, becoming characteristic situation, low and sheltered—its ample gardens stretching down to meadows washed by a stream, of which the Abbey, with all the old neglect of prospect, had scarcely a sight—and its abundance of timber in rows and avenues, which neither fashion nor extravagance had rooted up.—The house was larger than Hartfield, and totally unlike it, covering a good deal of ground, rambling and irregular, with many comfortable and one or two handsome rooms.—It was just what it ought to be, and it looked what it was [III, 6, 388–9].

This is one of those passages where the reader might assume that the narrator is standing back from the character for a moment, painting the scene, but this not the case. The word "fairly" is not the narrator's sympathetic assessment but Emma's own self-complacency. The clue is in "her alliance with the ... future proprietor," in other words, John Knightley's eldest son. Marriage for herself is far from Emma's mind, and part of the comedy of this appraisal is that she admires Mr. Knightley's house without a clue as to why she really does so. This passage, far from being a "picturesque" view, divorced from character, is in fact telling the reader as much about Emma's social priorities as it is about the scenery. Nevertheless it is reasonable to say that this paragraph, including the detailed description of the avenue of limes with its abrupt termination, corresponds to one definition of mise en scène, since in effect it reflects and—for the reader—deepens understanding of Mr. Knightley, if not his personal "character," in the modern sense, his public standing and role, in the eighteenth-century one.

This is only one mode of representation in the chapter. Earlier, there has been a dialogue between Mr. Knightley and Mrs. Elton, which is presented in the familiar bare mode—without any indication of how and where it takes place—and Mrs. Elton (hardly "of such true gentility") is thus in the background of the reader's as well as Emma's mind in this passage. Mrs. Elton then comes to the fore, without a break in the paragraph, in the famous passage about strawberry picking. There then follows one of Jane Austen's very few genuine descriptive paragraphs, and not a very successful one at that, the description of the gardens of Donwell Abbey, and the lime walk, culminating in the "favourably placed and sheltered" Abbey-Mill farm. Is it Emma or the embedded narrator who thinks or pronounces the famous praise of an England "seen under a sun bright, without being oppressive" (391)? The imperceptible modulation from one narrative mode to another makes it hard to tell.

The East Room

Another apparent exception is the East room to which Fanny Price repairs in *Mansfield Park*. Sotherton might come to mind, but Sotherton is described with a cursory carelessness more akin to Mary Crawford's boredom than Fanny Price's virginal wonder, and the anomaly of a "mere, spacious, oblong room" doing duty as a chapel in an Elizabethan manor house is disarmingly unexplained. As with the Elliots' smart residence in Bath (*P*, II, 3) Austen is not interested in the details, and only gestures at the way they might reflect the character of its occupants. But the concept of mise en scène may be helpful in the discussion of the East Room. "It is his [the director's] business to place the actors significantly within the decor, so that the decor itself becomes an actor"—this fragment of Robin Wood's account of mise en scène is perhaps helpful.[14] The East Room is an interesting innovation since a room is presented as identifiable with a person. Introduced into the text for the first time in Chapter 16, as "now considered Fanny's" it is accompanied with the important rider of Mrs. Norris's "having stipulated that there should never [be] a fire in it on Fanny's account."

> The aspect was so favourable, that even without a fire it was habitable in many an early spring, and late autumn morning, to such a willing mind as Fanny's and while there was such a gleam of sunshine, she hoped not to be driven from it entirely, even when winter came. The comfort of it in

> her hours of leisure was extreme. She could go there after any thing unpleasant below, and find immediate consolation in some pursuit, or some train of thought at hand.—Her plants, her books—of which she had been a collector, from the first hour of her commanding a shilling—her writing desk, and her works of charity and ingenuity, were all within her reach;—or if indisposed for employment, if nothing but musing would do, she could scarcely see an object in that room which had not an interesting remembrance connected with it.—Every thing was a friend, or bore her thoughts to a friend [I, 16, 177–8].

The presence of William Cowper, Fanny's favorite poet, hangs over this passage. She retreats from suffering to her room, just as Cowper in *The Task* (1785) retreats from unspoken psychological sufferings to the "soothing" compensations of the countryside or the comforts of the sofa and the fireside. But behind this need for refuge lies pain:

> Every thing was a friend, or bore her thoughts to a friend; and though there had been sometimes much of suffering to her—though her motives had been often misunderstood, her feelings disregarded, and her comprehension undervalued; though she had known the pains of tyranny, of ridicule, and neglect, yet almost every recurrence of either had led to something consolatory; her aunt Bertram had spoken for her, or Miss Lee had been encouraging, or what was yet more frequent or more dear—Edmund had been her champion and her friend.

It is evident that when the writing seems to turn more explicitly to a description of the room, it is under the aegis of Fanny's needs—needs to make the best of things, to perform acts of innocent self-deception which convert instances of neglect or indifference into evidence of her belonging. The words "suffering," "tyranny," and later, "affliction" are allowed into the text, and into her thoughts, only to be denied or passed over, yet they are strong words and register the depth of the misery the compensation seeks to hide. So that the room and its furnishings scarcely exist as an objective setting which she inhabits: instead this is a psychological "nest of comforts," fabricated out of yearning for the warmth of family and maternal love. This is then, it might be argued, a kind of mise en scène, since "the decor itself becomes an actor," the room introduced into the novel and later reintroduced, to instate Fanny as displaced and refugee person, whose transient accommodations are perpetually under siege. But the fact remains that what is registered as seen is through its psychological meaning for the character.

A reader may have the impression, then, that he or she has seen Donwell Abbey and its surroundings, but what they have really "seen" is Emma's thoughts. A reader may remember the appearance of the East Room, but they have "seen" this through the lens of Fanny Price's psychology and mood.

But it can be argued that in one instance, at least, Jane Austen utilizes verbal information so as to produce a necessary prompting of the visual imagination.

Overhearing

"For the impressionists, light was not simply the revealer of the external world but the founder of spatial relations as well."[15] In the film, as in painting, objects gain their solidity from the play of light upon them, and thus their distance from, proximity to, and relations with each other within space also depend upon how they are lit. No form of the photographic reproduction of light can be achieved though the printed word, and therefore a character's position in space in the novel is normally described, rather than left to be intuitively understood though the play of light. In Jane Austen's novels, as we have seen, positions are often minimally indicated, and dialogues appear to take place in a flat plane, with each speaker within the same range of the reader's attention, and other information about other persons in the room simply left out (or retained residually in the reader's mind). But in her later novels Jane Austen develops techniques by which aural material (that which can be reported, or described in words) is made to produce or register specific spatial relationships, and at the same time, reproduce aspects of the psychology of attention. One way in which this occurs is through the motif or topos of overhearing, which culminates in *Persuasion*.

The most famous moment of overhearing in Jane Austen's novels is certainly the one that occurs at the Netherfield ball in *Pride and Prejudice*: "Elizabeth Bennet had been obliged, by the scarcity of gentle-men, to sit down for two dances; and during part of that time, Mr. Darcy had been standing near enough for her to overhear a conversation between him and Mr. Bingley" (I, 3, 11). The exchange between the two men is then presented, including the moment when Darcy looks at Elizabeth "until catching her eye, he withdrew his own, and coldly said, 'She is tolerable'" (I, 3, 11). In *Northanger Abbey*, Catherine sits down with Isabella on a bench between two doors of the Pump Room in Bath. Three pages of duologue are then given, until Isabella catches the eye of Captain Tilney, who "took the seat to which her movements invited him." This is presumably between the two young women, since "his first address made Catherine start. Though spoken low, she could distinguish, 'What! always to be watched, in person or by proxy!'" (II, 3, 149). A flirtatious exchange follows, conducted in half-whispers, which the reader is given in full, and which shocks Catherine, who evidently overhears every word.

The origins of such incidents are evidently in the theater. In Sheridan's

The School for Scandal, for example, Lady Teazle enters the stage in time to indignantly overhear Joseph Surface's lovemaking with Maria (2. 2). Occasions of overhearing are common in other plays which Jane Austen knew well—the most famous being the comic scene in which Sir Toby and his fellow conspirators, hiding in the box-tree, overhear Malvolio's private musings over the fake letter (*Twelfth Night*, 2. 5). More pertinent perhaps is Romeo's standing in the darkness in the Capulets' garden and witnessing Juliet's declaration of love (2. 1)—a scene which, transmuted, will play its role in *Persuasion*. But the stage origin of the incidents in these two early novels limits their effectiveness. Is Darcy aware that Elizabeth is within hearing range? This is an important question, since it bears a good deal on his reputation for arrogance and aloofness. Does Elizabeth assume that he knows she can hear? Different readers give different answers to these questions but the text will not underwrite them. We would need to know more about the positions of the characters and possibly about Elizabeth's interest in the dialogue, to be sure.

Listening in on the conversation of others is common in *Mansfield Park*. But Fanny is "a by-stander" as she calls herself (III, 4, 404) rather than an overhearer. She is treated as an attendant or servant whose witnessing of others' conversations can be disregarded, since the invisible barriers of class mean that whatever she thinks (or conceivably might say) does not matter. Thus the quarrel of Edmund and Tom over the theatricals is presented to the reader as a dramatic dialogue with Fanny only incidentally mentioned, until the narrator returns to her with the reminder that she "had heard it all, and borne Edmund company in every feeling throughout the whole" (I, 13, 150). The memorable quasi-seduction before the iron gate at Sotherton between Maria and Henry is presented with no registration at all of Fanny Price's presence, until, when directly appealed to, she makes an effort to stop Maria from escaping through the fence (I, 10, 116). In other scenes she is "the silent observer of the whole," the listener or witness whose "position" is analogous to the reader's, and thus, to all intents and purposes, invisible.

"Witness," though, is a difficult and contradictory term to use in this context since it is another word that refers primarily to visual information— "to see with one's own eyes." (In contemporary usage, to be a witness of another's illness, however, is to participate in their suffering. The term's elevation into a more privileged ethical domain builds on what was always implicit, that a witness was engaged with, and responsive to, what they saw.) Emma Woodhouse is notoriously often present at exchanges or conversations to which she does not attend: that's to say the narrative presents material to which we presume she is witness (and thus "hears") but without registering its import—her mind often being full of her own ideas and schemes. An example is the passage at Donwell about strawberry-picking, which follows her absorbed appraisal of the house and its grounds. "The best fruit in England—every body's favourite—always wholesome": the implication being that Emma's contempt for Mrs. Elton does not allow her to notice more than the banality and fatuousness of the "conversation" (III, 6, 390). Soon she is "obliged to overhear what Mrs. Elton and Jane were talking of" (though where she is sitting is unclear) and the same condensation into ridiculousness continues ("Delightful, charming, superior, first circles, spheres, lines, ranks, every thing") until—a complete contrast—the narrative finally "tunes in" and gives Jane Fairfax's pointed request to move as a full speech.

Though Jane Austen is a novelist whose focus on the visible scene is limited, she is also a novelist who increasingly shows interest in the distinct phenomena of aural attentiveness. *Emma* is a novel that continually registers the shifting, and sifting, of aural focus: Emma giving all her attention to Frank Churchill at the Coles' dinner, for example, until catching the name "Jane Fairfax," she starts to listen to Mrs. Cole at the other end of the table (II, 8, 232). What in fact one attends to, rather than being present at, or merely hearing, is of key importance in the novel. Often Emma does not listen to what she (apparently) hears. Having deduced that Mr. Dixon is the donor of the pianoforte, she is not startled by Frank Churchill's declaration to Jane that he "would have given worlds—all the worlds one ever has to give—for another half hour" of dancing with her the previous evening. Veiled as this is, that it has a hidden meaning for Jane is communicated to the reader by the instant and wordless response, given a paragraph to itself: "She played." It is not surprising, perhaps, that Emma's preoccupations make her deaf to Frank's speech, which certainly has the earnestness of a lover (II, 10, 261). Full of her own confused emotions, she does not regard, or perceive, or understand, that when Jane Fairfax at Box Hill at last breaks out into speech before herself and Frank, she speaks to bring the engagement to an end (III, 7, 405).

In *Persuasion* this interest in the psychology of attention is developed further, and the conventional use of overhearing to further a plot, or provide comedy, becomes a vital part of the novel's artistic structure. In this novel, the instances of overhearing also generate a sense of spatial relationships, and thus indicate one aspect of visuality.

Overhearing in Persuasion

To overhear one must be in the vicinity of the speaker, but conversationally, or culturally distinct. Overhearing is a phenomenon of the group occasion which Jane Austen became increasingly adept at representing—the outings, picnics, drawing rooms, ballrooms and (in *Persuasion*) walks and public places in which numbers of people are gathered together, but which consist of little distinct affective or conversational worlds. To register overhearing, then, is to imply spatiality, or to imply distinct narrative planes. It is a way in which some of the sense of depth which is germane to representational visual art can be brought into an art which is inevitably serial or sequential—one "object" apparently succeeding another in the reader's attention.

In *Persuasion* overhearing develops from that occasional or incidental registration of a social fact which Jane Austen deploys in *Pride and Prejudice* or *Emma* into something like a structural component of the narrative. The resemblance to visual art or film lies not in the novel's descriptive passages, like the one about Lyme, which are certainly incidental, and even superfluous, but in its rigorous deployment of the aural sense—to be specific, in its handling of Anne Elliot's position as listener. This is not "position" as role or function alone, but material or actual physical position (at the piano, on the other side of the sofa, or on the other side of the room), which has also—and this is where the resemblance to film is strongest—ideological or perhaps political implications. In *Persuasion*, positionality becomes, as in a film frame, not an aesthetic matter, but a means for the furtherance of the work's overall purpose and argument, its intellectual design.

Outwardly, the heroine is an extreme version of the ideal of genteel femininity propagated by pre–Victorian arbitrators of social ideals. "This modesty, which I think so essential in your sex, will naturally dispose you to be rather silent in company," John Gregory, for example, advised his daughters.[16] For much of the novel Anne Elliot is indeed silent in company, or if not silent, unattended to. As an unmarried woman approaching her thirties, she has little social status in her circle. She occupies the traditional female roles of confidante, companion, accompanist, baby-sitter, and nurse. Above all, she is a listener.

And for the first three chapters of the novel, her presence, though noted, is negligible. Even when the narrative turns towards her, denoting her as the heroine, the writing does not allow her full dramatic presence. Anne's point of view is represented, not like Elizabeth Bennet's, Fanny's or Emma's, as transcriptions of her thoughts, but veiled, held at a distance from the reader by the narrator's own sympathetic mediation. "How eloquent could Anne Elliot have been—... She had been forced into prudence in her youth, she learned romance as she grew older—the natural sequel of an unnatural beginning" (I, 4, 32). Existing somewhere between character and narrator, these expressions subdue her even as they bring her forward. This merging of narrator and character is not, as D. A. Miller, argues, a surrender of Austen's ironic privilege: instead it is a vital element within the novel's innovative procedure.[17] And this recession of the character in the narrative plane continues in another form throughout the first volume.

The notion of distinct planes of conceptualization, in fact, essential in the discussion of mise en scène, is helpful in understanding the novel's technique. Roughly speaking, Anne occupies the foreground, since she is the figure to whom the speech of other characters is often addressed, but the novel characteristically suppresses her own replies in return. Like a chair or a balustrade, set before the main plane of the action in a film, Anne's presence is necessary to the scene, but her presence as actor is minimized. (This wholly textual effect is not replicated in the films, where Anne as listener is necessarily an embodied presence.) She attempts to advise her sister Elizabeth about the encroachments of Mrs. Clay on her father's affections, but her words are merely reported as "She spoke, and seemed only to offend" (I, 5, 37). Manifest rather is Elizabeth's long, rude, and indignant reply. Anne's response to this is again left oblique and unrecorded, the technique itself seeming to collaborate with her own lack of self-esteem, as if endorsing her non-importance. And this effect is repeated in exchange after exchange, with speeches to Anne given in full, her responses given only in indirect speech or the barest summary. In Chapter 2 of the second volume, for example, only one short speech of hers is allowed into a dialogue between Charles, Mary and Lady Russell, even though Anne is the apparent subject. In other words, the relegated and inferior position in the social hierarchy she inhabits is replicated in the hierarchy of narrative presence.

Anne's role then is listener, confidante, silent observer. But more significantly for the novel's enterprise, she overhears rather than merely listens. This important structural feature is introduced in the adeptly handled group scene that takes place in the drawing room at Uppercross in the eighth chapter. This is turned into a dinner-party scene in the 1995 Michell/Dear film, but it is crucial to the novel's presentation that the sequence of events takes place in the drawing room, with people sitting or standing at some small distance from each other, because the informal spatial disposition of characters is part of the psychological drama. Jane Austen does not specify each figure's position, yet it is evident that she has imagined the chapter as a largish communal gathering—the Hayter cousins, who never appear elsewhere, are included. Wentworth entertains the party with his experiences, and Anne, at some distance, listens in, until she is "roused by a whisper of Mrs. Musgrove" (who must be close to her) suddenly recalling her lost son. Suppressing a smile (thus indicating that the mind is in two places at once) Anne listens kindly, and this effectively prevents her from attending to the others' talk. "When she could let her attention take its natural course again"

(I, 8, 69–70), she is witness to a conversation between Wentworth and the others, including Admiral Croft, which Austen presents as a full dramatic dialogue for two pages. The Admiralty assigns unseaworthy vessels to its young captains, Wentworth declares. Anne is reintroduced (presented once more to the reader's own attention) with the sentence "Anne's shudderings were to herself, alone," before Mrs. Musgrove, "beckoning" to her son, brings him across to her. Charles shortly after walks away again, thus again defining the main group's separation. Mrs. Musgrove intervenes with her reminder to Wentworth of his acquaintance with her son. "There was a momentary expression in Captain Wentworth's face" at her speech, detected only by Anne, a "transient ... indulgence of self-amusement" which she knows how to read, but "almost instantly" afterwards he comes up to the sofa "on which she and Mrs. Musgrove were sitting" and talks to her just as Anne had, but sits on the other side (I, 8, 73). The shifting positions around Anne and the directions of her attention are thus quietly choreographed, but the point is a psychological one—her thoughts occupy two realms at once. Physical distance (however small) works to indicate emotional or affective separation. Later in the scene, Wentworth puts an end to a dispute with his sister about married women on board ship by getting up and moving away—natural enough in a drawing room, but when transferred to the dining table in the film, arbitrary and even rude.

The chapter, having presented a lively and varied group scene, culminates with a focus on Anne sitting solitary at the piano. Now physically quite detached from the others, who are dancing, she is even more distant aurally, "while her fingers were mechanically at work, proceeding for half an hour together, equally without error and without consciousness":

> Once she felt that he was looking at herself—observing her altered features, perhaps, trying to trace in them the ruins of the face that had once charmed him; and once she knew that he must have spoken of her;—she was hardly aware of it, till she heard the answer; but then she was sure of his having asked his partner whether Miss Elliot never danced? [I, 8, 77–8].

When Elizabeth Bennet, sitting out for two dances, overhears Darcy, who is standing up, the text makes it appear that she hears every word. In this moment in *Persuasion*, the conception of aurality is more complex. Whilst our eyes can direct their attention and can focus on successive objects, hearing is more dependent on what is available to be heard. But hearing, or over-hearing, as Jane Austen represents it here, also depends upon emotional receptivity. "Sunk in thought," one hears nothing: the listener's capacity to hear ambient sounds, or to distinguish voices, is dependent upon their mood and internal disposition. This psychological fact and its implications is crucial to the novel's unfolding drama. Its first appearance is earlier still in the novel, when Anne and Wentworth meet again: "Her eye half met Captain Wentworth's; a bow, a curtsey passed; she heard his voice—he talked to Mary; said all that was right; said something to the Miss Musgroves, enough to mark an easy footing: the room seemed full—full of persons and voices" (I, 7, 64). Overwhelmed with emotion Anne is not able to see or to hear distinctly. This suspension of receptivity to the outer world is not quite what is captured in the rendering of this moment (a slight jolt in focus, a hand twisting a chair spindle) in Michell's direction of the equivalent scene.

But although I have been led to use visual terms like "focus," all this happens in aural terms. The reader is not asked to visualize the characters, only to recognize their spatial relationships, and the small distances between figures, and to read emotional significance into them. The effect is that dialogues presented directly to the reader in dramatic and quasi-theatrical form acquire a distinct depth and coloring from the assumed presence of a third person, the silent overhearer who is Anne. Meaning does not simply inhere in the dialogues, but in their effect on the overhearer. This is notably the case during the walk to Winthrop in Chapter 10, when hidden by the hedgerow, Anne overhears Wentworth and Louisa talking about her. But more importantly, Jane Austen records how Anne's receptivity to the outer world varies with its impingements upon her emotional life, as when, just before, she cannot but overhear Wentworth and Louisa celebrating all-out commitment:

> "Had you? cried he, catching the same tone; "I honour you!" And there was silence between them for a little while.
>   Anne could not immediately fall into a quotation again. The sweet scenes of autumn were for a while put by—unless some tender sonnet, fraught with the apt analogy of the declining year, with declining happiness, and the images of youth and hope, and spring, all gone together, blessed her memory. She roused herself to say, as they struck by order into another path, "Is this not one of the ways to Winthrop?" But nobody heard, or, at least, nobody answered her [I, 10, 91].

One understands, reading such passages, why Miller calls this "the sentimental favorite" among Austen's novels.[18] But the recording of Anne's response as a negative sentence captures the occasion's disabling of her capacity to attend—the sinking into the desolate self of all energy directed to the outside world. By withdrawing its energy from the character, the following sentence performs a narrative analogy of her own sunken depths, as if in such distress a faint hope coming from some far distant side of the self were all that could be heard. Only its vague, sweet, sad, gesturing phrases could do that. A smaller effect of self obliteration occurs once more in the same chapter, when Anne, handed into the carriage by Wentworth, is so emotionally overcome that it is a while "before she was quite awake" to what her companions, the Crofts, are saying: "She then found them talking of 'Frederick'" (I, 10, 98). This contrasts with the more theatrical moment, later in the novel, when Anne, coming down to breakfast at Bath, catches her sister and her father praising Mrs. Clay (II, 4, 157). Anne's marginal or liminal social status position is overtly registered here though the trope of overhearing.

Gradually Anne does come to occupy a more dominant position in the text. In small increments, her opinions, now more decisive, are represented to the reader directly. She is gradually given more initiative, more authority, more independent presence and volition. Here, obviously, the scene of Louisa's fall on the Cobb (I, 12) is critical. Rather overtly and illustratively, her steadiness during the incident (in which the males collapse into "female" behavior, Charles crying and Wentworth staggering against the wall in hysterical distress) alters her position within the group. Whilst still functioning in the characteristic female role of nurse or caretaker, Anne's presence of mind in a crisis elevates her into a position of importance. This is ratified by another incident of overhearing—this time validating her rather than plunging her into isolated depths. Anne, acting as nurse, and "coming quietly down from Louisa's room, could not but hear what followed, for the parlour door was open." She catches Wentworth and the others speaking "warmly" of her—"No-one so proper, so capable as Anne!" "She pause[s] a moment to recover from hearing of herself so spoken of" before she appears (I, 12, 123). It is more than approbation: Wentworth's impetuous, unguarded calling of her "Anne" rather than "Miss Elliot," recalls the past. Another important moment in her trajectory towards authority and independence occurs in her defiance of her family and her visits to her old friend Mrs. Smith at an unfashionable address in Bath. The reader has earlier heard Wentworth protest his freedom to do services for his friend Harville, and defy convention (even perhaps naval rule) to do so. When later he again visits his now disabled friend in Lyme, the parallel with Anne's visiting her disabled friend is clear. The implication is now that Anne is moving towards that independence of action or initiative that had belonged pre-eminently to the male sphere.

The culmination or apotheosis of this movement is the scene at the White Hart. Chapter 11 of the second volume, bringing the Musgroves and Mrs.Croft back into the narrative, is also a recapitulation of the earlier group scenes that have taken place at Uppercross. Here, though, the precise domestic geography of the room is laid out with clarity: Mrs. Musgrove and Mrs. Croft talking at a table; Anne there too, at first, feeling "that she did not belong to the conversation," yet (again) overhearing it, though hoping that "the gentlemen might each be too much self-occupied to hear" (II, 11, 250); Captain Wentworth "nearly turning his back on them all ..., engrossed by

writing," at another table, with Harville sitting at first apart and later beckoning Anne to a window. (In the 1995 film this arrangement is carefully
adhered to, with Wentworth placed in the foreground of the action.)[19] The
women's talk takes an unexpected turn when they discuss unwise engage-
ments, and Anne finds herself once more physically overcome, so much so
that attending to the rest of their conversation becomes impossible. She hears
"nothing distinctly; it was only a buzz of words in her ear, her mind was in
confusion" (II, 11, 251). Once again, Anne hears material that comes home
to her, that seems to externalize issues of her own internal life. And on this
occasion she sees that Wentworth is listening too.

Harville invites her to join him standing at the window, which is at the
other end of the room from the ladies, nearer to Captain Wentworth's table,
"though not very near." Harville opens their conversation with a long speech,
and Anne merely assents, "in a low feeling voice"—as we might expect her
to do. Soon though the two of them are engaged in an equal match, arguing
each with equal firmness, equal authority and conviction, until they are
momentarily interrupted:

> "We shall never agree upon this question"—Captain Harville was begin-
> ning to say, when a slight noise called their attention to Captain Went-
> worth's hitherto perfectly quiet division of the room. It was nothing more
> than that his pen had fallen down, but Anne was startled at finding him
> nearer than she had supposed; and half inclined to suspect that the pen
> had only fallen, because he had been occupied by them, striving to catch
> sounds, which yet she did not think he could have caught [II, 11, 254].

Without the slightest trace of over-conscious art, this moment takes the
reader back to the scene at the Cobb. That accident has been a graphic
demonstration that Wentworth and Louisa are not in complete accord. She
has happily jumped into his arms once, but he disapproves of her second
jump, tries to talk her out of it, his disapproval leading to his momentary
hesitation or unpreparedness. She impetuously jumps, he misses her, and she
falls. He fails to catch her—to catch her physically, but by implication, to be
with her emotionally. It is only after her collapse onto the ground that he
"caught her up" and knelt with her in his arms. Despite being "not very
near," and despite the noise in the White Hart room, in contrast Wentworth
does indeed "catch" Anne, catch the sounds of her voice. He reaches across
to her psychologically as he had not reached to Louisa. Both occasions involve
grasping meaning or understanding across space. "You sink your voice, but
I can distinguish the tones of that voice, when they would be lost on others," his letter, written simultaneously with her speech, asserts. "With love's
light wings did I o'erperch these walls/ For stony limits cannot hold love
out" (2. 1.108–9), Romeo declares from the darkness of the Capulets' gar-

den. Metaphorically, too, that is what has happened here. The preternatural receptivity of his love enables Wentworth to hear what others cannot hear, to understand implications others cannot divine.

The interruption of the dialogue by the slight noise of his dropping pen allows it to modulate into another key, to become less abstract and more distinctly personal. Harville, speaking of the heart, and "pressing his own with emotion," leads the way for Anne to express, more explicitly, more at length, and with even an aria-like eloquence, her protestation of faithfulness: "'All the privilege I claim for my own sex (it is not a very enviable one, you need not covet it) is that of loving longest, when existence or when hope is gone'" (II, 11, 256). It is surely mistaken to assume, as Tony Tanner wrote, that "this is all said for the benefit of the apparently preoccupied but all-attentive Wentworth."[20] On the contrary, this is an instance of wholly indirect communication, and its structural function in the novel as well as its poignancy depends on this. Jane Austen makes it clear that Anne speaks to Harville in a low voice, and has to compete with Mrs. Musgrove's "powerful whisper." One would not be moved by the purity of her sincerity were one to feel that she was covertly aiming at her lover. The point, rather, is that this is both the summation and reversal of those moments of overhearing that have played such an important role in the novel. Anne, the unregarded, unlistened-to female, has lived her emotional life through overhearing, but it is now Wentworth, the active, dominant, assertively story-telling male who occupies the position of listener. Anne is eloquent as she has never been: Wentworth, the man of action, silent at the table, is dependent on what he can hear. Narratively, the novel has allowed them to change places, gender attributes have been reassigned. The structure of *Persuasion*, built on Anne's silence and now capped by her eloquence, is completed with this reversal— the motif of overhearing, with all that it implies about the impingement of the social world, and the interference of others in the lives of the lovers— now being resumed in a triumphant moment of romantic reconciliation.

The aim of the film-maker, Victor Perkins wrote, "is to organize the world to the point where it becomes most meaningful but to resist ordering it out of all resemblance to the real world which it attempts to evoke."[21] Whilst still remaining within the conventions of realism, likewise, *Persuasion*, whose narrative trajectory appears to depend upon chance events, is sustained by a barely perceptible, or even hidden, structural coherence.

The Cinematic Jane Austen?

Jane Austen is not an especially visual artist. In comparison with the novels of her contemporaries, such as Charlotte Smith, Ann Radcliffe or Walter

Scott, for all of whom the appearance of things is the stuff of fascination and romance, Austen's citations of the visible are just that—citations, indices or outlines to be filled in, or not filled in, by the reader's imagination. Though much has been written about landscapes, and especially the artificial landscape of the estate, in her books, these descriptive passages remain special occasions, moments when a different modality takes over—if not the less significant for that. But the sparseness of information about characters' appearances, their clothing, their gestures, the rooms they occupy, the scenes they walk through, is more than a release for the reader's imagination. The omission of what is unnecessary is essential to what is: the strength of each novel's formal organization.

The absence of visual description does not mean neglect of spatial relationships. Jane Austen has imagined her characters within social space, and in her later novels she gives this social space a tangible quality through the movement of her narrative from one figure to another. The narratives' focus on her heroines' attentiveness generates a sense of spatiality even more effectively. Listening to others, and more particularly overhearing, delineates separation and contingency, proximity and apartness. Especially in the group or assembly scenes of her later novels, this generates a sense of different planes of attention, akin to the cinematic frame.

Like much art, and certainly like the classic narrative film, the workings of these novels are not overt. Entertainment at one level, intellectual structure at another: the novels, like the narrative film, employ analogies, parallels, perceived correspondences and distinctions, to generate meanings which are not obvious or made apparent in the action or dialogue. Dramatic presentation (or "realism") is at the forefront, but—again like the cinema—hidden meanings and significances lie in what the reader derives by inference from what is overtly shown. To read Jane Austen with the cinema in mind is not then to affirm her as a visual writer, but to uncover some of the hidden sources of her art.

2

By Candlelight: Jane Austen, Technology and the Heritage Film

JOHN WILTSHIRE

Light largely creates our knowledge of the physical world. But our experience of light—and of darkness—differs radically from our ancestors'. During the later eighteenth and early nineteenth centuries a series of scientific inventions transformed both the availability and the quality of man-made light. These new technologies of light presented challenges as well as opportunities for visual artists and writers. Paradoxically, the new currency of light invested darkness with new significance, a significance bound up with the cultural phenomenon we know as Romanticism. At this moment when light was ceasing to be a precious, fugitive and friendly thing, and becoming instead a taken-for-granted aspect of modernity, Jane Austen was writing her novels. These fictions, in which the rendering of the experience of light belongs wholly to the old world, are now presented to the public in a cultural form that is the ultimate expression of modern industrialized light. The moving picture could not exist without powerful electric lighting in both its production and consumption phases. Yet this "language in light" speaks, in films made from Austen's novels, in the idiom of the old illumination, recreating a time in which firelight, candles, oil lamps and candelabra defined the world after sunset.[1] This contradiction, or inauthenticity, is germane to the genre to which Austen adaptations belong—the so-called "heritage" film.

This chapter considers light (or lighting) in two of the late twentieth-century film versions of Jane Austen's novels within this context. It firstly examines how light is represented in the era before Austen, using the work of the painter Joseph Wright of Derby (1734–97) as a guide. Because artificial light is so ubiquitous in the modern world, so instantly available, it can be difficult to appreciate how darkness was almost universally felt as engulfing and how the available illumination was correspondingly precious.[2] Wright's painting does not so much display old lighting as study its various forms and the different visual effects they produced. He is especially interesting because of his connections with the pioneers of modern science and industry, whose portraits he painted, and one of whom—James Watt—was to give his name to the units of electric power. The chapter then briefly discusses how light and darkness were perceived in the literature of Jane Austen's period. Darkness was to "become a distinctive and conscious experience when it ceased to be the only option at night,"[3] but even before the invention of gas lighting in the first years of the nineteenth century, poets had dwelt on the half-light of dusk, and Gothic novelists had exploited the terrors of darkness or the fascination of flames. In contrast, one hardly notices the representation of lighting in Jane Austen's novels. In the realm of film criticism, Austen adaptations are assigned to the (often despised) genre of "heritage film." Though lighting is rarely mentioned in the analyses of this genre, in fact effects of old or pre-industrial light are important to the films' location of their action in its period setting, and contribute to their possibly "romantic" atmosphere and nostalgic mood. Whether in fact the artificial representation of the world lit by old light necessarily fosters a sentimental or romantic response is one of the questions that run through this discussion. It is approached through an account of the techniques used in Stanley Kubrick's *Barry Lyndon* (1975), which pioneered the use of period lighting in the period film. This in turn leads to a discussion of two more recent movies in which old lighting takes a major affective role. Ang Lee's *Sense and Sensibility* (1995) has significant connections with the eighteenth-century evocations of light. In Roger Michell's *Persuasion* (1995) technologies of lighting form a key part of the cinematic means by which some of the techniques of Austen's prose narrative are reinvented by a distinctly different medium.

Painter of Lighting

Joseph Wright is probably the most significant eighteenth-century painter to represent the varieties of illumination that then defined the physical world. The first authoritative study of his work, published in 1968 by Benedict Nicolson, was in fact called *Joseph Wright of Derby, Painter of Light*. Many other painters from George de la Tour to Chardin could have earned that title, and it might have been more exact to call Wright *Painter of Lighting*. It is the distinct qualities of illumination that emanate from a candle, an oil-lamp, the sun, the moon, an erupting volcano, the glow of molten metal, or a burning torch that Wright painted, sometimes in concert with each other. His works range from "The Alchymist," the ancient figure lit by the bright phosphorescence of his retort, to a view of Thomas Arkwright's cotton mill at night, its rows of factory windows seen from afar dimly lit by candles.[4] Many of his canvases represent only one mode of light, but others are rather complexly lit, and feature the contrast or liaison between two or more forms of illumination. Often his paintings show groups in darkness, gathered around an object, their faces half in shadow; most often, and most compellingly, with the source of the illumination masked by a figure in the foreground. Wright's first exhibited picture is known as *Three Persons Viewing the Gladiator by Candlelight*. This canvas is especially significant for my argument because a work of art resides within the work of art. If we look at this painting now we participate in an experience of light that belongs to a lost age; within the painting itself the connoisseurs are sharing an aesthetic experience that similarly belongs to a civilization remote from their own. The Borgese Gladiator is the focus of the rapt attention of the three men. As Nicolson puts it, "The nobility of the antique statue fills their minds, and justifies their earnestness. Its grace has lifted them above the pettifogging concerns of everyday life, and from its contours their own features have borrowed refinement."[5] In return, the carbon particles of the burning candle emit a reddish glow and bestow flesh tints on the marble statue. It also falls on the faces, and through this linkage by light, the whole group is given some of the significance that earlier painters invested in pictures of religious contemplation. Like Wright's best known picture, the "Experiment with an Air Pump," in the London National Gallery, the supernatural radiance that once emanated from the Holy child in paintings of the nativity is recreated as radiance from a natural source, and in this picture perhaps invests the progress of scientific experiment with a quasi-sacred aura.

Industrialized Light

Wright was associated with members of The Lunar Society, that remarkable association of British eighteenth-century scientific pioneers whose meetings were held on the night of the full moon, so that the gentlemen could ride across country by its light.[6] It included Arkwright, Erasmus Darwin, the grandfather of Charles, and an early advocate of evolutionary ideas, Mathew Boulton and Watt, inventors and industrialists, and the radical physicist Joseph Priestley, the discoverer of oxygen. What they had in common was a passionate interest in scientific experimentation, and in its practical application. They were businessmen at the same time as they were explorers of new technology. In fifty years their work and the work of others like them was to make relying on the moon for light by which to travel almost a thing of the past. The Lunar Society was formally constituted in 1775, the year that Jane Austen was born.

In the early 1780s Ami Argand put Priestley's discovery and Lavoisier's subsequent observation that flames are fed by oxygen to practical use by surrounding the hollow wick of an oil lamp with a glass tube. This produced a brighter, more stable (and sootless) light and, it has been claimed, "represents nothing less than the birth of modern artificial lighting."[7] Finding little encouragement in his native Switzerland, Argand sought out Boulton and Watt, whose factory started producing his burners, which soon became widely adopted in England. By 1797 the firm had developed a new form of lighting: gas. In 1805, gas lighting was installed in a cotton mill in Manchester, and at first its use was confined to factories, where the open flames and sparks of candles had presented constant dangers of fire. These were the first installations of what Wolfgang Schivelbusch calls "industrialised light."[8]

Jane Austen would have seen the beginnings of this shift from individualized to industrial light. In the years after settling in Chawton in 1809, she visited her brother in London regularly. Staying with Henry in Sloane Street and Hans Place, and paying dinner visits, she must have traveled down Pall Mall, the first street in the world to be lit by gas lights in 1808.[9] By 1814, when she was there to negotiate the publication of *Emma*, the main streets of the West End and Mayfair boasted gas-lights that contemporaries always described as "dazzling" (they were about 40 watts). Rudolph Ackermann (1764–1834) whose "Repository of Arts" in the Strand was known in every genteel household (he would have supplied the Bertram sisters in *Mansfield Park* with their paints and gold paper) was an enthusiastic proponent of the new forms of lighting. His well-known publication *The Microcosm of London* (1808–11) displayed the lighting of many famous venues, including the magnificent chandelier with fifty patent lamps at Astley's Amphitheatre, visited by Jane Austen in 1796, and the John Knightleys, Harriet Smith and Robert Martin in *Emma* (III, 18). Ackermann had installed a gas-lighting system in his home, workshop and London print gallery by 1811, testifying in the *Microcosm* that the new lights were cleaner, brighter and cheaper than candles or lamps.

Ackermann's gas plant, built by the gas engineer, Samuel Clegg, gave a strong impetus to the fledgling London Gas-Lighting Company.[10] At first gas was generated by machines attached to the factory or workshop, but the London company and its competitors centralized supply, and piped gas to distant users. This made a difference in the whole experience of lighting. Adequate light was now not only much more available, but drew on sources outside the home, and as gas lighting came to supersede the oil lamp and the candle, the individual household became linked to, and dependent upon a public supply. This, as Schivelbusch argues, was a portent of modernity, a first breaching of the sanctity and self-sufficiency of the home. Gaston

Bachelard called it "administered light": power, in one of its forms at least, now reached into the private domain.[11]

Just as significantly, the whole visual experience of light was changing. Light had been a prized, fugitive possession. After the sun went down, the sources of illumination were all forms of the flame, living things that needed to be continually tended, fed by the wick or the oil, creatures that ultimately dwindled and died. They shed an unsteady, wavering, inconstant light, which fell in pools, leaving the rest of the world in encircling and encroaching darkness. But the revolutionary inventions of nineteenth-century lighting changed that: with gas, and then electricity, light became brighter, steadier, a taken-for-granted, publicly supplied background to life after dark. With modern electric lighting, light is paradoxically often invisible, and artificial light becomes a condition of vision, not a feature of sight. Modern light is available at the flick of a switch—the only flickering thing about it. Old light was close light, drawing workers and families together, to sit at the same table on which the candle or the oil-lamp stood, or to gather around the fire. Modern light is distant, drawn from afar, and often positioned high in the ceiling. In offices, airports, hospitals, light comes from above, and this light, unflattering and cold, can carry a subliminal suggestion of surveillance. And so old light acquired a new value, as the accompaniment and condition of intimacy, privacy, and shared experience. Revived, continued, or recreated in the home, it remains the sign of a refusal of modernity, a refuge, perhaps a romantic dream.

If, with the advent of gas, lighting had been revolutionized, so had darkness. In a parallel development the later eighteenth century poets had become fascinated by dusk, half-light, and night itself, and were drawn to the occlusion of rational thought that twilight or darkness might foster. "Now fades the glimmering landscape on the sight"—ushering in his poetic meditations in a country churchyard, Thomas Gray ushered in the eighteenth-century preoccupation with conditions of half-darkness.[12] In later poems set by the fireside, Cowper and Coleridge could allow their thoughts to wander, and present the results in a form—apparently shapeless, ruminative, episodic, reminiscent—which contradicted the edicts of an earlier poetic of rationality and order.[13] In still later instances such as Wordsworth's recreation of his nocturnal boyhood experiences in the first books of *The Prelude*, and for Keats and Shelley, night is a setting for poetic contemplation, an environment that is both promising and enticing. In Byron's "Darkness" (1816) it is a realm of apocalyptic terror. Romanticism can be understood, in fact, as a discovery of the potentiality of darkness. For the Enlightenment, the sun had been the literal emblem of rationality and the power of thought; night, in contrast, meant fear, superstition and madness. But as Enlightenment met its Other, Romance, darkness became the site of imagination, mystery, release. And this cultural development alongside scientific progress would invest the forms of old lighting, which had made darkness real, with retrospective magic.

At the same time, the Gothic novelists, telling tales with settings far in the past, often evoked the terrors of night-time without even the oil lamp. Ann Radcliffe (1764–1823) became a virtuoso of effects of light and darkness. The covers of the Oxford Classics editions of Radcliffe's *A Sicilian Romance* (1790) and *The Romance of the Forest* (1791) rightly link her work with paintings by Joseph Wright.[14] Throughout Radcliffe's novels, her affiliations with the late eighteenth-century cult of darkness are everywhere evident. *The Romance of the Forest*, for example, contains two poems to "Night," as well as one to "The Nightingale." Throughout the novels, scenes are set at dusk, or at night, when mysterious music is heard from the dark woods, or the stars glimmer upon the heroine lost in sublime meditation. In the "Gothic" sequences, the play of different illuminations against encroaching night is everywhere: subterranean passageways, half lit halls, flickering torches, the eruptions of Etna sending fire into the darkness in *The Italian* (1797), the lights that gleam fitfully in the deserted and ruined part of the castle in *A Sicilian Romance*. Radcliffe writes this material with especial potency, but except in the burlesque parts of *Northanger Abbey* there are few signs that Jane Austen was touched by it. In fact, as in *Northanger*, Austen's novels turn their back on the romantic investment in darkness.

Jane Austen and Light

William O'Dea remarks on the paucity of documentation available to the historian of lighting. "It is obvious ... that light—or the absence of it after dark was a most important fact in social history," he writes, "it is however one that has been almost completely ignored. This is no doubt due to the scarcity of references to lighting in both literature and art, and the fact that most of the references that do exist are to the unusual rather than the ordinary."[15] An example of the unusual occurs in the chapter "A Masquerade" of Frances Burney's second novel, *Cecilia*, published in 1782 (I, 3). During the party described in the chapter the heroine is pursued by a man in fancy-dress. Suddenly a Harlequin attempts to leap over a small table, but instead "finding himself falling, imprudently caught hold of the newly-erected awning, and pulled it entirely upon his own head, and with it the newly-contrived lights." "Splinters of the glass" fly everywhere and Harlequin is "covered with glass, papier-mâché, lamps and oil," the crowd screams and the room falls into darkness.[16] The accident is not important, merely an incidental narrative contrivance to get the heroine away from her pursuer. Burney's "new-contrived lights" could not be Argand lamps, but there were various patent modifications of the oil lamp current in London at the time. Previous to this incident, though, no mention has been made of this mode of lighting. Suddenly the modern reader of the novel is made aware that the whole festive scene takes place under the fitful and unreliable illumination of pre-industrial light.

In the provincial, genteel world of the early nineteenth century which Jane Austen depicts, lighting by candles and oil-lamps was so ordinary that it would be no more likely to be recorded than other features of that world, like servants waiting at table. Nevertheless, lighting in the broadest sense does play an imperceptible role in the novels. Available light was dependent largely upon the seasons and the time of day, and this determined behavior. Throughout the novels, the calendar and time of day are carefully registered, whilst the results of these on social customs are left to be assumed. The Watsons, obliged to live "in a very humble stile,"[17] dine just after three P.M. in October. Austen's first readers (had there been any of this unpublished work) would know that this is to avoid the need for expensive candles, as they certainly understood how cruel it is of Mrs. Norris in *Mansfield Park* to deny Fanny Price the use of the carriage, when she needs it, to get across the park for a late dinner at the Grants (II, 5, 258). It is November: at that time of the year evening would be descending.

Such implications are sometimes missed by modern readers. Assemblies and balls, though, are perhaps an exception to Austen's general unconcern with lighting effects. Emma Watson passes through a corridor to the "Assembly room, brilliant in lights" before her, and Miss Bates is overcome by the dazzle of the usually shabby Crown Inn. "'Well!—(as soon as she was within the door) Well! This is brilliant indeed!—This is admirable!—Excellently contrived, upon my word. Nothing wanting. Could not have imagined it.—So well lighted up.—Jane, Jane, look—did you ever see anything? Oh! Mr. Weston, you must really have had Aladdin's lamp'" (III, 2, 348). "This is meeting quite in fairy-land!—Such a transformation" she gushes later in the same speech to Emma herself. "I never saw any thing equal to the comfort and style—Candles every where" (III, 2, 356). Schivelbusch writes of "the outpouring of ecstasy as everyday constraints were suddenly lifted"[18] at the spectacle of festive lighting, and Austen captures something of this in Miss Bates's raptures. But the focus is not on the lighting in itself, but on her speeches' disclosure of how rare such pleasures as the ball are in her experience. The Bates, poor like the Watsons, would be very careful in their use of candles at home.

A moment with interesting implications occurs in *Emma*, however, when the point of view shifts to Mr. Knightley in Chapter 5 of Volume III. On a "dull-looking evening" in June, the party repair to Hartfield and Frank proposes the word-game. Looking on, Knightley perceives secret communications passing forth between Frank and Jane Fairfax, but he cannot be sure of what he sees, partly because of the gathering dusk. When he remains behind at Hartfield after all the rest, Austen renders his thoughts through the stylistic retinue (such as repetitions and dashes) that she had learned from the novelists of sensibility and that here characterize Mr. Knightley's "free indirect speech": "His thoughts full of what he had seen; so full, that when the candles came to assist his observations, he must—yes, he certainly must, as a friend,—an anxious friend—give Emma some hint" (III, 5, 379). It is as if the tenebrific quality of the light infuses his thought processes, which barely achieve the clarity of resolution. "His observations" become both what he sees and what he thinks, perception and perception inextricably linked. Mr. Knightley then would be, as one might expect, a son of the Enlightenment.

There are other passing mentions of candles, such as "the solitary candle" that Mr. Price in *Mansfield Park* holds between himself and the newspaper in Portsmouth, leaving his newly arrived daughter to sit in darkness (III, 7, 442). The circumscribed light of the candle is registered, but when, later in the scene, Fanny is able to admire the Lieutenant's uniform her brother has donned, by what magic it has become visible is not mentioned, (though presumably more candles are supplied as darkness deepens). The social effects of old lighting can be detected more precisely though in an earlier sequence from *Mansfield Park*.[19] Sir Thomas Bertram arrives home unexpectedly, late on an October evening, when the rehearsal of *Lovers' Vows* is in full swing. Fanny Price, left alone with Mr. Rushworth when the rest of the family flee to welcome him, eventually decides that she too must go to the drawing room: "after pausing a moment for what she knew would not come, for the courage which the outside of no door had ever supplied to her, she turned the lock in desperation, and the lights of the drawing-room and all the collected family were before her" (II, 1, 208). We know that the drawing room is grand, and therefore that there will be several centers of illumination. But are these "lights" single candles, or candelabra? In 1809, the time of the action, in a house like Mansfield, they might well be Argand lamps. After a moment Sir Thomas, perceiving her, leads Fanny "nearer the light," observes her face, and speaks kindly to her; after a moment she in turn, "having courage to lift her eyes to his face" (II, 1, 208), discerns how worn and haggard he has become in his years away. The reader must imagine them standing in a pool of light, thrown by candles or the oil lamp. This is an intimate and touching moment of rapprochement, in which the light, gathering them together, plays a creative role. Shortly afterwards, Sir Thomas brings his family to the fireside, and looks "with heartfelt satisfaction on the faces around him" (II, 1, 209). The novelist again does not specify that he sees them by the firelight, but her early readers would probably have understood this intuitively. In this short sequence, then, faces are brought to life, as it were, by the light of flames, themselves alive in their animation and warmth. As in the Wright painting, the incandescence of moving light communicates affect, and here briefly generates these moments of harmony and reconciliation. But lighting is not, as it is for Wright, Jane Austen's subject.

Barry Lyndon *and Its Heritage*

If lighting and the forms of light have been neglected in social history, they are also neglected in the history of the cinema. Yet it was the constancy of administered, industrial, invisible light that made the effects of the cinema possible. In the history of cinematic lighting, and in heritage film, the critical moment is Stanley Kubrick's Metrocolor *Barry Lyndon* released in 1975. Adapted from Thackeray's satiric historical novel *The Memoirs of Barry Lyndon* (1844, 1852), this is the story of an eighteenth-century Irish adventurer who comes to no good. According to his biographer, Kubrick wanted to re-invent the period film, which had been routinely photographed under multidirectional electric light, filling in and illuminating scenes that were supposedly lit by candles or oil-lamps, and thus destroying their "warm, modulating glow."[20] To recreate the world of the eighteenth century he planned to use natural light for outdoor scenes, and candle-light for interiors. But the film stock available at the time did not have the latitude to allow the emulsion to be lit by the low light of a candle. How this problem was solved is a notable chapter. Kubrick obtained (there are different accounts how) very fast 50mm still-photography lenses from the German Zeiss company, which had been developed for use on the Apollo space program. The aperture was f 0.9, "while the fastest lenses then in general use in cinematography were f1.2" (LoBrutto, 378): Kubrick's lens thus admitted twice as much light as the standard lens.[21] Mounted on a specially modified camera, this lens was used for virtually all the medium and close shots, but since it had very little depth of field, focus had to be monitored constantly, and actors were often constrained in their range of movement.

Many sequences in *Barry Lyndon* are lit only by tall windows, sometimes throwing the grand interiors which dominate the second half of the film into half-light. Two important early scenes feature conversations at a table, with a candelabrum at center providing the only light. When Lyndon takes to high life, scenes are often lit by spectacular candelabra — one containing seventy-five lights. But the technical challenges imposed by the film stock and lenses available meant that compromises with "the painterly documentary reality" (LoBrutto, 380) that Kubrick and his art designer had aimed for by using "natural" light needed to be made. Light filtering from high windows was augmented by extra exterior lighting. In the gambling sequence featuring Lord Ludd, metal reflectors were used to keep the heat of the candles from damaging the ceiling and to provide overall illumination of top light for the scene. The chandeliers in this scene held seventy candles each. Even this amount of illumination was low in relation to conventional filming, and "the negative was pushed one full stop in development to pump appropriate amount of light into the overall image" (LoBrutto, 387). In some cases, the necessity to light the shots with large numbers of candles produced incongruities. In an early scene, Barry sits at a table with the German girl Lischen, a large candelabrum of four candles blazing between them. A single tallow would be more likely in the cottage of a poor woman during the Seven Years' War, but then, it would not have given the camera enough light.

According to his art director, Kubrick wanted to base the look of *Barry Lyndon* on eighteenth-century paintings. Gainsborough, Hogarth, Reynolds, Chardin and Stubbs are often mentioned (LoBrutto, 382) but rarely Joseph Wright.[22] In Wright's paintings, the subject is thrown into relief by the light, and the obscuring of its source is what bestows on the human scene something of the awesome concentration of older religious paintings. In Jane Austen's novels, lighting itself, when it is incidentally mentioned, is always in service to character and action.[23] In Kubrick's film, by contrast, the light source is on display. Found in a peasant's cottage as well as at the bedsides of the great, the candelabra, alive, flickering, manifestly an ethereal form of fire, is close to becoming the real subject, the icon of the film. It is a cinematic homage to past light, an incarnation of the past now made miraculously present. At the same time, the shooting of the scenes in which, for technical reasons, the actors remain almost still and the camera is unmoving, increases the sense that the viewer is observing figures lifted out of past time. The reverse zoom shots which are such a conspicuous feature of Kubrick's style in *Barry Lyndon* (the focus on a face, or an object, gradually widening to display the whole scene or setting in which it occurs) increase the sense that what is being observed is a composition, or a spectacle, akin to a still picture, the portrait of a by-gone age, reanimated.

In *English Heritage, English Cinema* (2003), Andrew Higson describes the aesthetic of the genre of the "heritage" film, and its difference from the Hollywood norm:

> The decoupage and the camerawork tend towards the languid. There is a
> preference for long takes and deep staging, for instance, and for long and

medium shots, rather than for close-ups and rapid or dramatic cutting. The camera is characteristically fluid, but camera movement often seems dictated less by a desire to follow the movement of characters than by a desire to offer the spectator a more aesthetic angle on the period setting and the objects which fill it. Self-conscious crane shots and high-angle shots divorced from character point of view, for instance, are often used to display ostentatiously the seductive mise-en-scène of the films.[24]

This account of the "aesthetics of display" as Higson calls it, applies quite well to the Austen adaptations, but it also describes *Barry Lyndon*'s visual style. Kubrick's film is sometimes extraordinarily slow moving; "landscape shots" repeatedly establish locations, whether it be the German countryside, Belgian spas or the Irish country house and estate; a crane shot gratifies the spectator with the spaciousness and formality of the garden in which Barry first sets his sights on Lady Lyndon.[25] But *Barry Lyndon*, for all its stylistic opulence, suggests at least some qualifications to the assumption that a film set in the past and using old lighting is necessarily romantic. The mood tends towards elegy rather than nostalgia; as Thomas Allen Nelson writes, "the pace of the film resembles a stately procession moving through vanity fair on its way to tragic pageantry."[26]

With the development of much faster film, better lenses and lighter, far more mobile cameras in the thirty years since *Barry Lyndon* was shot, the candle-lit scene or sequence has become much easier to produce. Candle-light features so commonly in the Austen adaptations of the last fifteen years that it might qualify as a defining characteristic of these films. The oil-lamp, which might have stood on a table, or be hung from the ceiling, is nearly as absent from them as it is from Kubrick's film. Night scenes are however an important component of their aesthetic style, and within the night scene, the play of light and shadow, darkness and illumination, can generate powerful effects. In Joe Wright's *Pride and Prejudice* (2005) for example, the vividly filmed Longbourn Assembly is made exotic by the background of candles, flaming sconces and firelight, and other sequences are dramatized by single flares and swaying candle-light. The mobile camera co-operates with the lighting to generate excitement and mystery. On the other hand, in sequences possibly influenced by *Barry Lyndon*, middle-distance shots initially frame the scenes of the action, displaying elegant or picturesque settings, and portraying the figures, for a few moments, as actors in a tableau which comes to life. There are passages in Wright's film which share some of Kubrick's artistic purity, but his use of old light is obviously supplemented by studio lighting; faces in the foreground are always strongly lit, and the ball at Netherfield is filmed in impossibly bright ambient multidirectional lighting.

More recently, old lighting, and the golden or roseate glow of flames have become more or less ubiquitous markers of the genre. *Miss Austen Regrets* (2008), though not a version of any of the novels, identifies itself as belonging to the same world in its opening, pre-credit sequence. Establishing shots show Manydown House with the dying light of an orange sunset behind. The film continues before the credits with a scene in which Harris Bigg-Wither proposes to Jane Austen in a room dimly lit by candelabra and a roaring fire. Later sequences employ candles repeatedly, notably a scene of gentlemen playing cards indoors, seen through a window. *Sense and Sensibility* (2008) opens with the flames of a fire, against which a seduction is being conducted in darkness, the flames casting a reddish light over exposed flesh and exploring hands. Both films thus designate the world the viewer is invited to enter as other to the modern world—an effect accidentally increased by the searchlights that feature as part of the logo of the DVD distributor. In *Sense and Sensibility* the motif of firelight is continued in scenes which show Brandon and Marianne linked through their mutual love of music. Filmed in a darkly wainscoted manorial chamber, apparently lit only by candelabra and the fire, faces are burnished with the reddish-golden light that belongs to flames rather than candles. The dramatic content of the scene presents Brandon as attracted to Marianne, but critical or reserved in his response to her playing. The script conceives him as the mentor lover, like Mr. Knightley in *Emma*. But the closely filmed shots, with faces beautifully glowing and mysterious against the darkness, bestow a form of romantic intimacy on the scene, and invest it with an emotional coloring the script does not necessarily suggest. In a brief later scene Brandon is seen turning the pages of her music for Marianne, and their eyes meeting, as her playing now meets his approval. Candles light the scene. The sequence culminates as the camera withdraws, literally framing the moment on each side by their flickering light.

Sense and Sensibility *(1995) and* Persuasion *(1995)*

A comparison of two earlier films, the Ang Lee/Emma Thompson *Sense and Sensibility* and Nick Dear and Roger Michell's *Persuasion*, however, will demonstrate clearly how different can be the results of the use of old lighting in the "heritage" genre. In *Sense and Sensibility*, despite the film's polish, period lighting is used to conventional effect; in *Persuasion* it is an essential part of the film's expressive language.

In an early scene in the film of *Sense and Sensibility*, Edward Ferrars is reading aloud. The script runs:

Int. Norland Park. Drawing Room. Eve....

EDWARD:
No voice divine the storm allayed
No light propitious shone,
When snatched from all effectual aid
We perished each alone:
But I beneath a rougher sea,
And whelmed in deeper gulfs than he.

Marianne jumps up and goes to him.

MARIANNE: No, Edward! Listen—

She takes the book from him and reads the stanza with passionate brio.

MARIANNE: Can you not feel his despair? Try again.

Rather mortified, Edward starts again, but not before receiving a sympathetic look from Elinor which seems to comfort him a little.[27]

The scene is based on a mention in the novel of Edward reading Cowper, and Marianne's disappointment that he turns "those lines which have frequently driven [her] almost wild" into something "spiritless and tame" (I, 3, 20). "The Castaway" (1799), the poem he reads in the film, is not named (though Mary Lascelles gave reasons for thinking that Austen would indeed have these verses in mind).[28] Beginning with the line "Obscurest night involved the sky," and set in darkness, this is certainly a proto-romantic poem, likely to appeal to Marianne, but the expression of anguished personal experience is held in and mediated by the narrative of disaster at sea by which it is contained.

From pre–Romantic restraint to Victorian saturation: in Charlotte Brontë's *Shirley* (1849) these very lines from "The Castaway" are used to signify the quintessence of poetry, and by implication the quintessence of romanticism.[29] One dark night, whilst a tempest rages outside, Caroline Helstone, standing in the gloom of the room, "her figure just discernible by the ruby shine of the flameless fire," recites the very stanza that Edward Ferrars reads in the film. Caroline, unlike Edward, "went through it as she should have gone through it" (177), with passionate feeling, recognizing that it is the "true ore" (175) of poetry. This was precisely what Brontë found missing in Austen, who "being ... without 'sentiment,' without *poetry*, maybe is sensible, real (more *real* than *true*), but she cannot be great," as she had informed G. H. Lewes in 1848.[30] What one might call the mise en scène—the storm raging in the darkness outside, the firelight and darkness inside—envelope the reading in an aura that is the essence of the romantic. A later novelist, more in sympathy with Jane Austen, treated the poem differently. In Virginia Woolf's *To the Lighthouse* (1927) the bereaved Mr. Ramsay's compulsive declamation of these lines signals not only his grief, but his self-pity. Cam, his daughter, is "outraged" by this melodramatic display of sorrow.[31]

As filmed Thompson's script becomes a candle-lit group round a blazing fire. It seems to recall those paintings of Joseph Wright in which figures of assorted ages, and always including a child, witness a scientific wonder. The family, including the youngest, Margaret (not in the script) is gathered in a loose circle whilst Edward reads. In Wright it is the spectacle of experiment, or the "performance" of a sculptured Roman athlete. The apparatus, the orrery, the air-pump, the molten iron of the forge, draws from spectators the same awe as the gentlemen give to the specimen of antique art. At the center here is another artifact, a poem whose latent individual passion, as in Brontë's scene, is intensified and corroborated by the darkness, candlelight and firelight of its setting. Merging Brontë with Austen, the film, despite the attention given to Elinor's amusement, here necessarily aligns itself with Marianne's incipient romanticism.[32]

Many other scenes in *Sense and Sensibility* feature candle-light. The night-time bedroom sequences between the sisters are apparently lit by candles, often supplemented by the flickering live light of a fire. In one of these the candle is encased in a glass bowl. But unlike *Barry Lyndon*, *Sense and Sensibility* does not rely on candlelight to illuminate the scene, and the presence of candle flame is often deceptive. When Marianne is lying on her sickbed at Norwood, for example, a candle stands at the bedside, but when she is filmed dramatically from above, the source of the light that falls on her white-sheeted figure comes from the opposite direction, and must be artificial studio light. Nor is there any focus on faces illuminated by the light of a candle: instead the film uses candles and firelight very much as props, blurred (and suspiciously unwavering) in the background whilst faces in close-up are in fact lit by ambient lighting. It seems fair to say that this film's use of pre-industrial light is more conventional than Kubrick's, so that lamps, candelabra and firelight here feature as tropes of the heritage genre.

Roger Michell's *Persuasion* (1995) is a rather different matter. The first extended sequence in this film is set in the library or drawing room at Kellynch House, a spacious, grand, elaborately furnished apartment. Sir Walter Elliot holds forth before the mantelpiece mirror, whilst Elizabeth, Mrs. Clay, Lady Russell and Mr. Shepherd look on. Light comes from high windows on the right, and this appears to be the only source of illumination, since the book-lined shelves in the background disappear into darkness. The moribund isolation of the family is captured in the abyss that seems to surround them, intensified by the sound of a clock ticking away in the emptiness. The setting resembles similar scenes in which formal apartments are lit only by high window-light in *Barry Lyndon*. Since this and later scenes set in this room emphasize the uncaring formality of this upper-class family, it is even possible that an allusion to the earlier film is intended.

For it is certainly true that candlelight and natural light are used creatively here in the way pioneered by Kubrick. In other scenes set in this same apartment, figures are lit against a cavernous blackness. Filtered light appears to illuminate Anne Elliot's face, itself blanched in frozen sadness. In a subsequent sequence the camera, moving from right to left, finds Anne and Lady Russell conferring in the library, darker than ever now, the furniture draped in dust-sheets, mysterious white masses all the lighter against the surrounding gloom, their folds suggesting the mourning robes of women in Greek statuary and neo-classical art.[33] The obscured shapes of the furniture read as a metaphor or symbol for the cloaked and buried nature of Anne's feelings of loss and regret. In this exchange near the window, her dress white, her face lit by cold light like the sheets, Anne does attempt to speak of her regrets to Lady Russell, only to be cut short by her friend's dismissive reference to "these Romantics," the poets Lady Russell has been lately reading. Nor is this a romantic scene: the austerity of the setting and the bleakness of the conversation deny that impulse.

This is an instance of the film's employment of the cinematic means of lighting, mise en scène, and camera movement to communicate, and in some degree to replicate, the submerged narratives of Austen's text. Another compelling scene occurs in the darkness of an attic, in which Anne and a bonneted servant are sorting through clothes and dusting away books. A candle burns between them. Anne's attention is gripped as she takes a book from a box. In close-up, lit by the golden-roseate glow of the candle, it is seen to be the paperback Navy List. Anne's hand slips between the pages, and finds a folded paper boat, which her fingers hold delicately as one holds a treasured object. In extreme close-up, the candle blurred on the right of the screen, her face in half darkness, Anne looks briefly across, her face intent, then she appears to put the volume back. Without a word being spoken, this brief sequence fills in and communicates the character's inner life: specifically, it enables the viewer to enter into Anne's memories.[34]

Darkness here signifies both secrecy and deprivation. The letter, folded, is nested within the pages of the pamphlet. The Navy List itself contains messages in print; the letter made into a boat inside it communicates meaning; the copper-plate writing on the boat then adds a third level of suggestion— the personal, intimate, residing within the official life. Made into a toy boat, the folded paper implies an earlier time of fun and happiness, now only a memory. The presence of words on the screen, on the object in Anne's hand, and in the book in which it has lain, invites the viewer to simultaneously become a reader—that is, imaginatively to impute words and the thoughts they carry to the silent image of Anne's face. "How eloquent could Anne Elliot have been" (I, 4, 32) declares the narrator in one of the most memorable passages of the novel, finding a way to express by indirection what the character cannot express, and possibly cannot even allow herself to feel. Here, through visual means, silence is made to "speak."

In the second half of Kubrick's film, in which Redmond Barry has succeeded in marrying Lady Lyndon and become the owner of a great estate, an elaborate formal dinner party is filmed from above, the camera moving transversely down the long table, candelabras aglow, whilst the narrator's voice-over comments sardonically on the trouble Lyndon takes to establish himself in high society. Such candle-lit dinners are one of the commonest features of the Austen films, a stale heritage trope which might justify the scorn many cinema-goers feel for this genre. But in *Persuasion* these dinner parties are filmed creatively, differently each time. In one sequence a still camera placed at a slight distance shows the table at which the Elliots dine, the candelabra lights reflected in its highly polished surface. Unmoving, the camera once again states the formality of this family party. In another sequence, Anne, left behind to care for the sick child in the cottage, is seen in front of a dying fire, and the camera moves into darkness; the dinner party from which she has excluded herself glides into view, brightly-lit squares against the blackness outside. The viewer is invited to imagine that he or she is seeing the scene from within Anne's longings—the dinner party from which she is debarred seen through the windows, its warmth and hilarity glimpsed, or imagined, from outside. Anne's pangs, only half acknowledged in the text, are conjured here only by montage in the film.

More interesting still is the filming of the dinner party at Uppercross in which Captain Wentworth regales the company with his naval experiences. Now the darkness is filled with laughter as the bright and flaring candle-flames light up the various faces, all with different investments in his talk. The scene is filmed from slightly above, with a hand-held camera, hovering near, and almost engaged in, the animation of this extended-family party. And if the slight unsteady movement of the camera partakes in the liveliness of the scene, it also registers Ann's underlying tension, and perhaps even evokes, subliminally, the motion of a ship at sea.

This movement of the camera in *Persuasion* is a contrast with the tableau-like framing of *Barry Lyndon*'s candle-lit sequences. At Lyme, Anne falls in with Captain Benwick, and the two share some moments of friendship as they discuss their interest in poetry. In another night-time party scene, the camera follows as a servant moves to serve, and slows down as it views Anne and Benwick across from each other at the end of the table, a roaring

fire on the left, the flames of a candelabra at the right. As it moves in towards
Benwick, he recites the final lines from Byron's poem on his final estrangement from Lady Byron:

> Fare thee well!—thus disunited—
> Torn from every nearer tie—
> Seared in heart—and lone—and blighted—
> More than this, I scarce can die.[35]

In the half darkness, the two figures engage in an exchange whose intensity
is captured by the closeness of the camera. The candles that light the faces
disappear, and Anne's figure momentarily masks the view of Benwick. Their
isolation from the main party's festivities is registered by the subduing of
other conversation on the sound track and the blurred focus on figures
behind. "I don't know that one," Anne says, and goes on to suggest that "too
much poetry may be unsafe" for a man suffering from grief. "You cannot
know the depths of my despair," Benwick soon responds. The melodrama is
immediately slaked as the camera moves to Anne, the frame half filled by the
blocking of his figure. In the darkness she says simply, "Yes I can."

In the novel "Benwick is silenced by grief—we never hear him speak,"
as Jocelyn Harris has noted.[36] In the novel Anne herself never articulates her
own passionate regrets. The invention of this scene in which Benwick—himself borrowing another man's words—expresses despair allows Anne's own
grief to find displaced (doubly displaced) and disguised expression. It recreates the tone of a novel in which feeling is always implicit, or, if expressed,
or allowed to come into consciousness, quickly repudiated. A restrained or
elegant surface is not incompatible with depth of feeling in either medium.
The camera moves to the face of Wentworth, pipe in hand, contemplative
in the darkness: a movement of his eyes downward registers the implication
of Anne's words.

In these films, then, old light conjures up the past, or rather a dream of
the past. But this form of lighting, its illumination endlessly shifting, its presence tentative and kindly, may be capable of another, more subliminal effect.
It may suggest that what is shadowed or occluded may be as potent, as what
is said or displayed. It conjures up a world in which layers or depths, of
shadow and brightness, but also of feeling, are to be registered, and has its
links with that reticence or displacement of expression that needs the words
of others to be exposed. Moreover, the scenes in which poems are read or
quoted, themselves filmed in darkness, contribute to this effect. The audience for the film, like the spectator of Wright's painting of the Borgese gladiator, regards a work of art in which a previous, antecedent work of art is
contemplated, or brought to life. Sculpture is akin to oil painting, but not

the same. The gladiator is dynamic, the men are composed, the successor art form is a tribute to the earlier, but quite distinct. The cinema is likewise beholden to the written word, figured explicitly in such scenes. The staging of this regression, forming an enfilade of artistic forms, brings the past into the present, at the same time as it reminds the spectator of that past's unreachable remoteness.

The Flame of a Candle

This chapter has been an essay in the intersections of scientific advance, material culture and artistic experience. It turns on the paradox that Jane Austen, a novelist whose formal attention to lighting is minimal, is now represented in a medium of which light is the essence, and it seeks to address the question of what results this has on the aesthetic status as well as the style of the various films. Austen's novels were always set in the contemporary world, and paid on the whole little attention to its physical appearance. The films, on the other hand, are period or costume, "heritage" cinema. They are inheritors, in a different medium, of the genre pioneered by Ann Radcliffe's Gothic tales, which mutated into the historical novel, precisely set in an earlier time, with Walter Scott's *Waverley, or 'Tis Sixty Years Since* in 1814. This genre, whether in the novel or the film, has many affinities with the Romantic Movement. With Radcliffe's pre–Reformation settings in mind, one might think of these films, then, as inevitably romanticizing (or Gothicizing) a novelist whose initial and continuing impulse was always to render the ordinary "anxieties of common life" and to deflate "the alarms of romance" (NA, 10, 206).

But this is not the end of the story. "Heritage" implies at least vestigial (or imaginative) continuity between the past and the present. Dinners are still held by candlelight. Lights are still bought with shades that spill light in pools. Even when real fires are banned, elaborate electrical simulations of flaming coals are available for purchase. What are we doing when we return to these forms of warmth and light? Surely these impulses cannot be merely dismissed as romantic, or nostalgic, or conservative. Wolfgang Schivelbusch's *Disenchanted Night* is in part a phenomenological investigation that proposes answers to such questions. What he suggests is that candle and firelight recall the primordial emotions of safety and community as the family or the tribe gathered around the hearth and the fire that released them from the terrors of the dark. Deep feelings are activated by old lighting. The ever brighter and ever more efficient forms of industrialized light have often met with almost ecstatic welcome, but that too has its psychological origins, and has often been accompanied by an undertow of regret or longing. And it is this, Schivelbusch suggests, in the concluding passage of his book, that explains the magic of the cinema:

> The world of the diorama and the cinema is an illusory dream world that light opens up to the viewer. He can lose himself in it in the same way that he can submerge himself in contemplating the flame of a camp-fire or a candle. In this respect, the film is closer to the fire than to the theatre. An open-air performance in bright daylight is quite feasible, while a camp-fire in the light of day is as senseless, even invisible, as a film projected in daylight. The power of artificial light to create its own reality only reveals itself in darkness. In the dark, light is life. The spectator sitting in the dark and looking at an illuminated image gives it his whole attention—one could almost say his life. The illuminated scene in darkness is like an anchor at sea. This is the root of the power of suggestion exercised by the light-based media since Daguerre's time. The spectator in the dark is alone with himself and the illuminated image, because social connections cease to exist in the dark. Darkness heightens individual perceptions, magnifying them many times. The darkened auditorium gives the illuminated image an intensity that it would not otherwise possess. Every lighted image is experienced as the light at the end of the tunnel—the visual tunnel, in this case—and as a liberation from the dark.[37]

The cinema then is a version of Aladdin's lamp, its pleasures like that "meeting quite in fairy land!" expressed by Miss Bates. Industrial light makes it possible. But it is editing, and the camera, increasingly mobile, that transmits to the spectator the shifting image of light—now bright, now darker, the shapes of darkness and brightness constantly changing—that recalls the light of a fire, or the flame of a candle.

Beyond Words, Beyond Images: Jane Austen and the Art of Mise en Scène

Ariane Hudelet

Jane Austen is often said to be uncinematic, because her novels are not "visual."[1] But this assertion, which generally refers to the scarcity of descriptions or spectacular action in the novels, seems to rely on a very partial definition of the visual, as well as of cinema. Kamilla Elliot has demonstrated how the literature/film divide created by semiologists such as Bluestone often neglects the important role of the visual in the novel, or the aural and verbal in film, and my method will be influenced by her work in this chapter.[2] I will argue that Austen's texts are indeed often visual, but in an indistinct, tenuous way, relying on micro-movements which establish an intimate relationship between the reader and the scene, as if the text were bringing us very close to the characters, as the close-up or high-definition sound may do in the cinema. I will also suggest that the recent film adaptations manage to recreate this kind of subtle, minute expressiveness most successfully through the treatment of sound—I will thus focus on the (often neglected) "audio" part of this audio-visual mode of expression.[3]

In Austen's novels, readers get to know the characters directly, by listening to their voices, more than in descriptions or explanations provided by the narrator.[4] These voices are used not only to convey a message, but also to flesh out the characters. Each particular voice has its own rhythm, and the speaking body is often perceptible in the pace, in the hesitations or occasional breaks when language becomes a physical, more than a rational or intellectual manifestation. Beyond the obvious wit and irony of the dialogue and the complex social decorum they reveal, Austen's novels are indeed extremely "dramatic," but in a sense that seems to me more cinematic than theatrical.[5] Beside verbal language, we indeed find another kind of language that dispenses with words, when the body itself becomes an expressive entity. Inconspicuous remarks about attitude, expression, tone of voice or gestures imperceptibly influence or alter the meaning of the words. The characters' looks or smiles allow them to express what they cannot communicate with words, the text then suggesting, rather than stating, the characters' intimate feelings or concealed intentions.

In film, of course, the interaction between verbal and non verbal expression is constant, since dialogue is necessarily embodied. Our perception of film is an "audio-vision"[6] in which what we hear is projected onto what we see and vice-versa, and in which the two types of perception constantly interact and influence each other. Besides, the words themselves are only one part of the sound universe which guides our reception of the images. The lines are conditioned by the image they accompany, but also by the texture of the voice which speaks them, by the rhythm, breathing or noises linked with every movement of the body. They are a result of the creativity of several artists—screenwriter, director, actor, sound engineer or editor—but in the case of adaptations, they also feed on the imagined voices which contribute to character building in the novels. Because it is often taken for granted, and so less "obvious" than a visual effect might be, the treatment of sound sometimes manages to reveal these feelings or thoughts that were not supposed to be voiced or shown according to the rules of early nineteenth-century society, to transpose into film the secret and more intimate expressiveness that, in the texts, filters through the proper language and communication regulated by sociability.

Austen Beyond Words

Austen's talent in writing dialogue has already been thoroughly studied[7]; my focus here—the specific kind of mise en scène she resorts to—may seem minor in the overall economy of the novels, yet I will suggest that it is also largely responsible for the appeal of her novels today, notably for the cinema. Let us first tackle an apparent paradox: Jane Austen is not famous for her extraordinary situations or dramatic mises en scène, in the very broad sense that is generally used for cinema, which is the spatial and temporal organization of the visual elements (human or non human) in an image. Several dialogues in her novels do not seem to be "staged" at all, meaning there are few indications as to time or place, and conversation seems to be self-sufficient. The opening chapter of *Pride and Prejudice* is for instance devoid of contextualization: the exact place, time or circumstances of the dialogue between Mr. and Mrs. Bennet, as well as their respective expressions or movements, remains unknown. But this kind of scene is actually quite rare in the novels. Most of the time, the dialogue or scenes are inter-spersed with elements related to an alternate kind of language made of very simple signs: a gesture, a movement, a smile or a particular tone of voice. This "secondary" language, although largely inconspicuous, is never-theless constantly present in the text and influences the words sometimes so radically that it changes their meanings, or substitutes itself for them entirely.

Even within the lines of the characters, we can distinguish passages in which the phonic quality of language seems to overcome its semantic value, when the "feel" of the lines becomes more important than their actual mean-ing. Although the style of Austen's dialogues never ventures to absolute oral-ity, where spelling, syntax or grammar would undergo major transgressions, yet for a certain type of character, and in some passages when emotion over-comes an otherwise rational speaker, discourse is characterized more by its form than by its meaning.

Emma offers two landmark examples of characters whose voices seem to be associated more with the body than with the mind. This kind of lan-guage, made of stylistic stigmata, concerns secondary characters that are intellectually or morally deficient, such as Miss Bates or Mrs. Elton.[8] Miss Bates is a character who speaks a lot, but the reader retains more what feels like an empty logorrhoea rather than any precise message. The accumula-tion of commas, dashes, embedded clauses, asides, syntactic breaks or non sequiturs,[9] creates discursive congestion, a busy and frantic language that lacks structure but overflows with good intentions, foolishness, and exces-sive solicitude:

> Oh! Here it is. I was sure it could not be far off; but I had put my huswife upon it, you see, without being aware, and so it was quite hid, but I had it in my hand so very lately that I was almost sure it must be on the table. I was reading it to Mrs. Cole, and since she went away, I was reading it again to my mother, for it is such a pleasure to her—a letter from Jane— that she can never hear it often enough; so I knew it could not be far off, and here it is, only just under my huswife—and since you are so kind as to wish to hear what she says;—but, first of all, I really must, in justice to Jane, apologise for her writing so short a letter [*E* II, 1, 167–8].

In the novel, this monologue continues for another page. Most of Miss Bates's speeches are very long and the writing manages to convey a sense of nerv-ous urgency; when she arrives at the Crown Inn ball her speech then fills one and a half pages without interruption (*E* III, 2, 348–50); the rapidity of the flow of words is mentioned by the narrator, but is also perceptible through the accumulation of dashes, self-referential remarks, precisions, rhetorical questions, and, most importantly, through the fact that the interlocutors do not answer. Also because, quite naturally, we tend to read faster when Miss Bates speaks—we are as eager to reach the end of this litany as Emma herself—the meaning of the sentences becomes irrelevant, and thus discourse seems to become a physiological, more than a psychological, process.[10] The frantic, broken rhythm, the flow itself, evoke her panting breathing, her constant hurry, and through these long monologues, we feel the corporeal presence of this character, her mannerisms and nervousness. When the narrator interrupts the monologue quoted earlier, the sentence insists on this language as a prolongation of the breath, as a physical performance: "All this spoken extremely fast obliged Miss Bates to stop for breath" (E, II, 1, 168).

Mrs. Elton offers a less touching and more pedantic example of a discourse dominated, not by solicitude or naivety, but by pretension and vanity, as we see when she is gathering strawberries at Donwell Abbey:

> Mrs. Elton ... was very ready to lead the way in gathering, accepting, or talking—strawberries, and only strawberries, could now be thought or spoken of.—"The best fruit in England—every body's favourite—and always wholesome.—These the finest beds and finest sorts.—Delightful to gather for one's self—The only way of really enjoying them.—Morning decidedly the best time—never tired—every sort of good—hautboy infinitely superior—no comparison..." [E III, 6, 389].

Austen uses another technique here: while we are forced to go through Miss Bates's long speeches, in this instance, we are provided with only bits of sentences connected by dashes—snatches of discourse, fragments of direct style,[11] which make the reader just another one of those absent-minded listeners, bored with a pretentious monologue to which they only half listen. What is now perceived is a discourse which is more physical than intellectual—what matters is not what Mrs. Elton says, but the impression it makes on others. Jane Austen uses here what we could call a technique of "point of hearing,"[12] which is not associated with any single character but rather with a fictitious, abstract ear, painfully submitted to Mrs. Elton's discourse. As in the case with Miss Bates, this "physicality," or "bodily" dimension, of the passage contributes to involve the reader more closely in the scene, to bring us in unmediated contact with the characters, a type of closeness which cinema relies on as well.

The intrusion of the body into language is not only associated with deficient characters. The disturbances in the speech of rational characters do not necessarily make them ridiculous or tedious, but on the contrary manage to reveal the emotion underlying a situation. This confusion is all the more striking when it concerns otherwise calm, moderate characters, whose expression is generally concise and well-structured. When Colonel Brandon comes to reveal Eliza's story to Elinor, his conflicting feelings become embodied in his broken, hesitating speech:

> "My object—my wish—my sole wish in desiring it—I hope, I believe it is—
> is to be a means of giving comfort;—no, I must not say comfort—not present comfort—but conviction, lasting conviction to your sister's mind. My regard for her, for yourself, for your mother—will you allow me to prove it, by relating some circumstances, which nothing but a *very* sincere regard—nothing but an earnest desire of being useful—I think I am justified—though where so many hours have been spent in convincing myself that I am right, is there not some reason to fear I may be wrong?"
> He stopped [*SS* II, 9, 231–2].

No real information about what Brandon is about to reveal is given for the moment, but his words reflect his inner turmoil, as he is torn between his desire to help the Dashwoods, his concern at intruding into their privacy, and the sufferings linked with the recollection of a tragic past. The colonel on the whole speaks very little; we can therefore interpret this passage as the striving efforts of a man who is not used to talking about such intimate topics: everything is contained in these incomplete, jerky sentences, in these repetitions and syntactic breaks, in these discursive cracks where emotion lies. We feel the influence of sentimental literature in these passages, notably that of Richardson or Sterne. Even if Austen makes a less intensive use of dashes, exclamation marks, parentheses or italics, yet the same impediments come to disturb the flow of the sentence. As Janet Todd explains, these elements thus also materialize the deficiencies of the written word to represent extreme emotion. Typography here becomes the substitute for gesture, for physical reaction.[13]

Therefore, when emotion is too acute, language seems to yield, to admit its own inadequacy. In some cases, no coherent discourse even seems possible. This often manifests itself through silences, absences or interruptions to which Austen brings our attention. This silence can have different causes and effects in the novels. It becomes comic when it affects otherwise talkative, insensitive characters such as Mrs. Bennet, who remains thunderstruck for the first time in the novel after she hears about Elizabeth's engagement to Mr. Darcy.[14] More generally it takes a dramatic value, enhancing a movement or any other form of mise en scène (here in the sense of visual indications about the characters such as expression). In *Persuasion* for example, Wentworth's silence when he releases Anne Elliot from the grip of the Musgrove boy endows his gesture with particular significance: "His kindness in stepping forward to her relief—the manner—the silence in which it had passed" (*P* I, 9, 87).

But silence is also a sign to interpret, a clue to reveal agitation, as in the relationship between Mr. Darcy and Elizabeth. At the beginning of the novel, Mr. Darcy's characteristic silence, at the Lucas's for instance, is interpreted as a sign of contempt, or distance. When he dances with Elizabeth at Netherfield, it becomes a topic of conversation—it is an anomaly in a world where social relationships are conducted in a codified language:

> "It is *your* turn to say something now, Mr. Darcy.—*I* talked about the dance, and *you* ought to make some kind of remark on the size of the room, or the number of couples."
> ... "Do you talk by rule then, while you are dancing?'"
> "Sometimes. One must speak a little, you know. It would look odd to be entirely silent for half an hour together, and yet for the advantage of *some*, conversation ought to be so arranged as that they may have the trouble of saying as little as possible" [*PP* I, 18, 102].

Paradoxically, conversation becomes a way to avoid talking to each other, a matter of pure form. Mr. Darcy's silence then progressively becomes an illustration of his inexpressible love for Elizabeth, as when they suddenly find themselves alone for the first time at Hunsford or when he proposes to her. Silence can therefore become a dramatic instrument when it stresses what language cannot or should not express. If silence in the novels is above all an absence of words, it is not, however, an absence of communication. It can on the contrary symbolize a form of expression; it even becomes an activity when Emma calls Harriet's attention onto Mr. Martin's inferiority to "real gentlemen":

> "Mr. Knightley's air is so remarkably good, that it is not fair to compare Mr. Martin with *him*. You might not see one in a hundred, with *gentleman* so plainly written as in Mr. Knightley. But he is not the only gentleman you have been lately used to. What say you to Mr. Weston and Mr. Elton? Compare Mr. Martin with either of *them*. Compare their manner of carrying themselves; of walking; of speaking; of being silent. You must see the difference" [*E* I, 4, 33].

There is thus a "manner of being silent," and silence becomes a way to enhance manners, attitude, looks, movements. These can be left to the reader's imagination, but they are also present in the novels, in a great number of indications which set the tone, the intention of the speaker, the expression, and sometimes the movements of characters. Characters and readers also need to decipher and interpret this physical language which can work as a complement, as a counterpoint, or even as a substitute for the spoken word.

The most common movements in Jane Austen are micro-movements— a flicker of the eyes, mouth, limbs—which convey messages to be deciphered. Just as sounds combine into words and sentences to construct a meaningful system of communication, looks, smiles and all other movements constitute a discreet but omnipresent grammar of the relationships between the characters.

Jane Austen uses this bodily grammar in a very precise manner, and makes it resonate with verbal language. The two main elements are the look and the smile, both associated with diverse expressions. They are often associated with adjectives, adverbs or complements which compose a wide range of expressions or intentions. Thus, the term *look* can be associated with epithets referring to a general expression, or on the contrary to a very precise intention: *meaningful, earnest, sharp, shrewish, embarrassed, sour, agitated, impenetrable, eager, grave, frightened, brightened, dictatorial, black,* etc. Complements follow the same logic; we find *a look of meaning, disappointment, doubt, curiosity, haughty composure, anxious entreaty, consciousness,* etc. The frequency and diversity of qualifiers is even more varied for the term *smile: gracious, triumphant, significant, very expressive, good-humoured, arch, serious, relenting, saucy, playful, approving, sweet, affectionate, broad, faint, artificial, courteous, comprehensive,* etc. We can also find the phrases *with half a look* or *with half a smile,* or references to *repressed* or *hidden smiles,* in which expression can seem so subtle that it becomes almost imperceptible, and is supposed above all to signal intention, sentiment. A look or smile can also appear on its own, without qualifiers, and the reader then needs to decode it according to the situation between the characters. Color changes (*blush, flush, glow, blanch*), head or hand gestures, or simply an overall expression, unrelated to a specific part of the body, complement our list of the main elements of this bodily, expressive grammar.

So, a great proportion of what is expressed by the characters does not lie just in the words, but also in these bodily signs which are inconspicuously disseminated in the text so that the reader hardly notices them. We read them as quickly and unconsciously as stage directions in a play.[15] They are simple, concise, deprived of any noticeable stylistic effect, but their precise and recurrent use contributes to the quality of the "scenes" in the novels. They mostly rely on very subtle nuances, on variations and intentions that seem to be perceived from up close, and this element of proximity, of intimacy, today evokes a cinematic point of view rather than theatrical staging.

The face is the main source of bodily expression in the texts, the eyes being the most frequently mentioned, but also the movements of the mouth—the smile, or the more diffuse movements linked with a repressed sigh or a modulation of voice. Expressions such as "with an expressive smile," "with an expressive look," "her eyes full of meaning,"[16] thus often punctuate the characters' lines, supporting what has already been said or confirming an implicit understanding with the interlocutor. Sometimes the meaning of this body language remains vague and serves above all to make feelings concrete, to represent the power of charm, that inexplicable dimension which endows bodies and words with a power of seduction quite distinct from the beauty of features or the quality of the mind, but often related to the expressiveness of the face or voice. For a long time associated essentially with women,[17] body language and expressiveness are, in Jane Austen's novels, associated with both men and women alike.

It is precisely what Sir Thomas lacks at the beginning of *Mansfield Park*: he is never described as more or less benevolent towards Fanny than his wife, yet the heroine fears him, essentially because of his attitude. Whereas Lady Bertram generally smiles, Sir Thomas remains grave: "he had to work against a most untoward gravity of deportment—and Lady Bertram, without taking half so much trouble, or speaking one word where he spoke ten, by the mere aid of a good-humoured smile, became immediately the less awful character of the two" (*MP* I, 2, 13). A smile is still missing to make his departure for Antigua a source of regret for Fanny: "would he only have smiled upon her" (*MP* I, 3, 37).

The reverse is also true: empty words can captivate an audience because of the charm, tone of voice, or implicit appearance of the speaker. Wickham's person is for instance sufficiently attractive to prompt even an astute critic such as Elizabeth Bennet to perceive in his words more than their actual meaning:

> Mr. Wickham was the happy man towards whom almost every female eye was turned, and Elizabeth was the happy woman by whom he finally seated himself; and the agreeable manner in which he immediately fell into conversation, though it was only on its being a wet night, and on the probability of a rainy season, made her feel that the commonest, dullest, most threadbare topic might be rendered interesting by the skill of the speaker [*PP* I, 16, 85].

Body language thus addresses the feelings of the addressee more directly than any verbal language. In *Persuasion*, Anne is convinced that Wentworth still loves her because of this secondary language: "His choice of subjects, his expressions, and still more his manner and look, had been such as she could see in only one light ... —his half averted eyes and more than half expressive glance,—all, all declared that he had a heart returning to her at last" (*P* II, 8, 201–2). Here, body language is the absolute proof.[18]

Sometimes body language completely replaces verbal language, and the same vocabulary is used for both: simple verbs such as "to say," "to speak," "to ask." This often occurs within the context of love relationships, where body language can express sensuality and desire without defying decorum or propriety. Long before Emma understands her own feelings for Mr.

Knightley, the exchange of looks between the two characters at the Crown Inn ball points to her admiration of his figure and air, and to Knightley's jealous feelings (*E* III, 2, 352–3). The communication between the two characters at the ball, where it takes place at a distance, is essentially non-verbal: "her countenance said much, as soon as she could catch his eye again"; "her eyes invited him irresistibly to come to her and be thanked" (*E* III, 2, 355, 357). At the end of the novel, it is no longer physical distance, but overwhelming emotion which requires the final proposal to be expressed by a look and not by words: "He stopped in his earnestness to look the question, and the expression of his eyes overpowered her" (*E* III, 13, 468).[19]

Words can remain trivial, but the look and the tone can make the addressee receptive to the implicit message, and therefore materialize an unspoken understanding. When Elizabeth sees Mr. Bingley again for the first time since he quit Netherfield, the young man cannot explicitly ask about Jane, but Elizabeth is on the lookout for signs of love in Bingley's attitude and words: "There was not much in the question ... but a look and a manner which gave them meaning" (*PP* III, 2, 290). Sometimes, this tacit understanding leads to interpretative errors. In the chapel at Sotherton, Henry Crawford uses his look to pursue his seduction of Maria Bertram:

> "I do not like to see Miss Bertram so near the altar."
> Starting, the lady instinctively moved a step or two, but recovering herself in a moment, affected to laugh, and asked him, in a tone not much louder, "if he would give her away?"
> "I am afraid I should do it very awkwardly," was his reply, with a look of meaning [*MP* I, 9, 103].

Henry's only intention is to flirt with Maria, that is why he pretends to resent her marrying another man, but we can ascertain that Maria endows this look with an additional meaning—she actually expects an explicit proposal. Henry, however, never intends to marry her. This "look of meaning" is therefore highly ambiguous, and illustrates the complexity of a body language which impregnates the most simple sentences with multiple, even opposed, meanings. Maria, like Elizabeth Bennet and Marianne Dashwood before her, will eventually learn that charm can successfully conceal an absence of moral value or honest intentions.

A disjunction between body language and actual meaning or intention can also be seen as another manifestation of Jane Austen's irony. Even when body language and verbal language go together, they do not necessarily work in unison. Divergence may alter the meaning of the spoken words and create a specific type of irony. Such a discrepancy between words and body language often takes a negative connotation, and is used for hypocritical or distant characters. This defect will be mended in the case of Darcy, whose attitude belies his words when he proposes to Elizabeth: "He *spoke* of apprehension and anxiety but his countenance expressed real security" (*PP* II, 11, 212). But there will be no improvement in Mr. Collins (whose excessive and incongruous gestures try to materialize non-existent feelings: "words were insufficient for the elevation of his feelings; and he was obliged to walk about the room" [*PP* II, 15, 239]) or for Lucy Steele, an expert in duplicity. She uses a polite verbal language to preserve appearances, but also displays an aggressive and cruel body language when she reveals her secret engagement to Elinor. From their second conversation onwards, her looks ("her little sharp eyes full of meaning" [*SS* II, 2, 167]) never cease to attack Elinor and leave no doubt as to her real intentions. Their conversation is punctuated by many insistent looks which illustrate how malignantly happy Lucy is to witness her rival's reaction: "eyeing Elinor attentively...; she looked down as she said this, amiably bashful, with only one side glance at her companion to observe its effects on her...; fixing her eyes upon Elinor" (*SS* I, 22, 147–54).

Instead of having the narrator reveal Lucy's true intentions, Austen makes us directly see these motivations in her look, in the tone of her voice. We do not know the color of the women's eyes or the design of their dresses, nor the exact place where they are walking, and yet we feel we are direct, physical witnesses to the scene thanks to this interplay of looks and to these perfidious nuances in Lucy's voice. The tone she uses, the way she stresses certain words in particular (as when she refers to Elinor's "indifference" [*SS* II, 2, 172]) also gives a dual meaning to her words. She pretends to confide in Elinor because she is a neutral party, but her tone and look demonstrate the contrary: she talks only to humiliate and dominate her. Her eyes confirm this discrepancy: when she learns that Miss Dashwood will not be in London for the winter, the two languages simultaneously express perfectly contradictory messages: "'I am sorry for that,' returned the other, while her eyes brightened at the information" (*SS* II, 2, 172).

In previous studies of Austen adaptations, her irony has been considered as one of the most difficult features to translate on screen. Indeed, even though irony is plural in Austen's novels—situational, dramatic, verbal—the latter often gets most attention, and is thus considered uncinematic, since it is endorsed by the narrator, who does not exist as such in film. It generally appears as a discrepancy between the words expected by the reader and those which are effectively used, a paradox expressed in a very condensed manner, which generally displays a refusal of pathos and sentimentality. It manages to establish an implicit connection between author and reader which creates pleasure and surprise. But this Austenian irony can also take a corporeal dimension, whether visual or aural, thanks to the discrepancy between the physical and the linguistic languages, between body and verbal expression.

We do not know to what extent Elinor Dashwood perceives this double language, but the reader is made to adopt a privileged point of view, in which all the meaningful glances and smiles are pointed out. Instead of the narrator telling us about Lucy's intentions, they are displayed through her attitude and actual *performance*. Rather than a general mise en scène which would stress the details of the characters' whereabouts, or broad gestures or movements, Austen prefers to set into relief some gestures which remain discreet on the structural level of the entire scene, but which nevertheless manage to convey an idea, a feeling with a concision and intensity that are closer to cinematic techniques than to theatrical ones. This micro-intensity, this enhancement of details (as in a close-up), reactions (as in shots-reverse shots) or sound nuances through precise voice inflexions or hesitations imply a proximity that cannot but evoke those film techniques to twenty-first century readers.

Jane Austen through the Soundtrack

It may have seemed paradoxical to start this chapter with a study of what lies beyond words in the texts. It will probably sound just as paradoxical to neglect images when analyzing film adaptations. Sound is indeed often perceived almost unconsciously in cinema, as something taken for granted. Studies of sound are a recent phenomenon, and bring very meaningful insights into the questions raised by film adaptations of novels such as Jane Austen's. In these films, sound allows directors to recreate the implicit presence of the body less conspicuously than with gesture or facial expression.

It can be somewhat tricky to concentrate on sound when talking about film adaptations of novels such as Jane Austen's. The danger that seems to be lurking for films ever since they became "talkies" is to rely too much on speech and to forget the essentially visual dimension of the medium, to tell rather than show. When scriptwriters adapt novels with such splendid dialogue as Jane Austen's, the most obvious problem seems to be in the decision of what can be kept, what has to be cut out, and what has to be changed. The real problem is to make the dialogue cinematic, integrated into a lively audio-visual creation, and not just lines pronounced reverently by actors as if they were on a stage, as in the worst kind of "filmed theater."

In film, voices are necessarily embodied by actors. Even if the body from which it emanates does not appear on screen, each new voice has a specific resonance, rhythm and modulation. Yet, voices do not reach the spectator as they might a theater audience. They have been recorded, and then restored, they result from precise choices as to the degree of definition and interaction with the other elements of the soundtrack—noises and music. Just as visual choices of light, costume, framing or editing manage to construct diverse visual ensembles, the treatment of sound and dialogue also reveals diverging approaches. Some films choose to privilege the abundance of dialogue and try to erase the materiality of the body through their handling of voices or sound in general. Others seek to inscribe these voices and words in a realistic, concrete, specific ensemble, to communicate the additional expressiveness the novels achieve through the "stage directions" already studied.

I will focus on the adaptations released between 1995 and 1999 (specifically, the BBC adaptation of *Pride and Prejudice* [1995], Roger Michell's *Persuasion* [1995], Ang Lee's *Sense and Sensibility* [1995], the two 1996 adaptations of *Emma*—the American film directed by Doug McGrath and *Jane Austen's Emma*, the British television film directed by Diarmuid Lawrence—and Patricia Rozema's *Mansfield Park* [1999]) because this period constitutes a turning-point in the history of Austen on film. Previous adaptations, essentially television films, tended to retain a large proportion of the dialogue, and to neglect the properly cinematic treatment of the stories: camera work remained minimal, actors all articulated very precisely, and sound was treated in a very uniform manner, with some resonance due to the direct studio recording, in what resembled more staged versions of the texts than actual films.

But it is not enough to have actors speak passages from the novel's dialogue in order for the emotion, characterization or irony to be instantaneously transferred from novel to film. The best cinematic dialogues are those in which verbal language is not only a code transmitting a message, but also a sound among others, raw material used by the filmmaker to bear on our reception of images, and vice versa. Let us concentrate on these moments when, to use Roland Barthes's terms, "music bursts into language."[20]

Even if, in films made since 1995, dialogue is generally pronounced in an intelligible manner, and diction remains quite homogenous—even American actors (such as Gwyneth Paltrow as Emma or Alessandro Nivola as Henry Crawford) speak with a British accent—the films generally pay more attention to the specificity of voices than previous adaptations.[21] Some, for instance, expand on the association made in the novels between noise and vulgarity. In the BBC *Pride and Prejudice*, Julia Sawalha's Lydia Bennet has a thick voice, she sighs, yawns and laughs loudly, and does not hesitate to shout the name of an officer in the street to catch his attention. In Lee's *Sense and Sensibility*, aural confusion also accompanies the appearances of Elizabeth Spriggs as Mrs. Jennings and Robert Hardy as Sir John Middleton: their peals of voice and laughter mix with the barking of their dogs in boisterous cacophony. Likewise, the high-pitched voice adopted by Imelda Staunton in playing Charlotte Palmer often blends with the ceaseless mewling of her baby. In *Persuasion*, the very high-pitched sound of Phoebe Nicholls/Elizabeth Elliot's voice is opposed to Amanda Root/Anne's rather atonic, sometimes inaudible uttering, while Corin Redgrave/Sir Walter sometimes speaks in so affected a manner that some words become almost incomprehensible.

Because of the time restraints imposed on film,[22] screenwriters, directors and actors need to find alternate techniques to render the speeches of characters such as Miss Bates: it is impossible to keep all or even most of her lines. Yet, the impression of a flow of words needs to be preserved since it is a major comic device and a fundamental element in the characterization. The two adaptations take different options. In Doug McGrath's film, Sophie Thompson chooses to rely on the comic vein above all, notably through exaggeration and caricature. A younger actress than Prunella Scales who plays the part in the television film, she is turned into an old maid thanks to makeup and costume but the character is also made ridiculous by her voice. She moves quickly from a hurried half-whisper to very high-pitched flights punctuated by shrill peals of laughter or repetitions of a word to her deaf mother. She very carefully articulates, insists on some syllables and repeats meaningless words ("lovely, lovely"). To shift from the comic mode to the necessary pathetic key during the Box Hill episode, she introduces pauses and silences in her discourse, where emotion seeps in: "I must make myself very ... disagreeable or she would not have said such a thing to an old ... friend."

With Prunella Scales, we laugh less but we may be more sensitive to the character's pathetic dimension: she suffers from Emma's insult and she is also deeply affected by her niece's situation. Instead of accentuating the modulations of her voice as Sophie Thompson does, Scales speaks in the same tone and rhythm, her words thus disappearing behind the continuous noise of her slightly broken voice—in some scenes, such as the Crown Inn ball and the Box Hill picnic, it functions mainly as a background hum. The editing completes this effect: in the Box Hill episode, Miss Bates starts a sentence in a shot showing the characters beginning to ascend the hill, and she finishes the same sentence in the next shot, which shows the party already settled at the top for the picnic (logically, several minutes later whereas the sound is continuous). The time gap between sound and image thus provides a truly cinematic echo to the ceaseless, uniform flow of Miss Bates's words in the text. We also recognize the "point of hearing" technique previously discussed with respect to Mrs. Elton, since in both text and film, this speech is a familiar buzz that the inhabitants of Highbury (and the readers/spectators) feel physically rather than analyze intellectually.[23]

In moments of intense emotion or distress, the traditional acting stereotypes often imply instability or trembling of voice, but in some passages a subtle diminution of intelligibility is enough, when language as code yields to language as sound, with no precise meaning. Colin Firth is probably the actor who demonstrates this most skillfully. The intensity of his voice can vary greatly in a single sentence, shifting from loud and audible to quick, low and jumbled.[24] This is common in the scenes in which he is alone with Elizabeth and above all when he utters polite formulae that serve nothing but a phatic purpose (for instance: "I hope that your family is in good health," a sentence he repeats at Rosings and at Pemberley in so hurried a manner that we guess the words rather than hear them).[25] These passages make us feel the character's clumsy attempts to establish contact with Elizabeth,[26] as well as his embarrassment when he finds himself in her presence.

Alan Rickman uses a different technique to express Colonel Brandon's emotion. Unlike the textual passage in which his discourse seems broken and hesitant, the film character is inversely characterized by a sort of over-intelligibility, produced by very slow diction and precise articulation. The novel character seems verbally clumsy, whereas Rickman's phrasing, notably during his visit to Elinor in London, illustrates the oratorical talent of the film character and introduces silences and pauses which accentuate the dramatic power of his narrative. His delivery is slow and calm, and his exceptionally deep and low-pitched voice fills the soundtrack completely. This voice contributes to endow the character with an heroic and poetic dimension which does not exist in the novel.[27]

Yet, these voices in film or television only exist through the means used to record and reproduce them. The sound impression produced by the film is above all a question of restitution, or rendering. This is what endows it with significance, just as Jane Austen's mise en scène confers meaning to apparently anodyne gestures.

The choice of direct or post-synchronized sound and variations of intensity among the diverse elements of the soundtrack constitute the sound texture of the film. These choices can call our attention to the material origin of the sound, or on the contrary erase these traces to build a more abstract, disembodied sound. The films of Austen's novels have benefited from considerable budgets, and from elaborate techniques such as Dolby. Whether the characters shout or whisper, the soundtrack can follow the tiniest variation without distortion. Here the question is no longer what the actors express but rather what we are made to hear: when people speak, can we hear their breathing, the noises made by the movements of their lips or their body or, on the contrary, does the film give us clear-cut, neat voices that are devoid of all these bodily traces? The vividness of the characters, the intense physical presence that many viewers feel in front of these films (and which also helps explain their success with a wide audience) is also, I suggest, the result of this specific treatment of sound: it makes us hear these stories as vividly as we see them. Kathryn Sutherland recently pointed out the essential importance of voice in the novels, even considering it as the key to Austen's art:

> what ... has led me on ... has been an interest in sound and voice—a conviction that the voices talking around [Jane Austen] in the private and public scenes of life became the voices talking inside her head that she couldn't stop herself from listening to; and that voices heard and the rhythms of conversation structure her mature novels as audio-experiences.... In Jane Austen's case we miss something vital in her textual transmission if we lose those visual forms which keep her auditory depths alive.[28]

Some passages from the recent film adaptations manage to "keep her auditory depths alive" indeed, thanks to the attention that is brought to voice as an expressive texture, and to the rendition of sound texture and detail around those voices.

All recent adaptations resort both to direct sound and post-synchronization, and aim—as do most narrative films—at a perfect intelligibility of the dialogues. Whether characters speak loud or whisper, the sound remains stable, clear and understandable. Voice, even when it is only a whisper (we have many whispered conversations, between Anne and the different members of the Musgrove family in *Persuasion* (1995), between Fanny Price and Mary Crawford in *Mansfield Park* (1999), and between Emma and Frank in Lawrence's film for instance) is the major element in the soundtrack. Yet, the rendering of the characters' voices can suppress any interfering noise or on the contrary keep breathing or gulping noises and changes of tone resulting from movement or emotion, thus recreating the distinction between the language of the mind (words and meaning), and that of the body (emotion, body language). *Persuasion* (1995) and *Pride and Prejudice* (1995) make a precise use of what Michel Chion calls these "materializing sound clues."[29] We can hear mouth noises, sighs, the breaths that the actors take before speaking, and different types of breathing according to the emotions; we hear Elizabeth's deep breaths of anger after Mr. Collins has proposed to her (his own noisy breath is more supposed to arouse disgust), but the same phenomenon is imbued with a different kind of distress after her unexpected encounter with a drenched Mr. Darcy at Pemberley. In *Persuasion*, characters sometimes speak with their mouths full during meals, and we can hear them chew or swallow and Sir Walter Elliot often clears his throat before speaking. In both films, the characters are presented as material bodies which live, move, exhale, ingest. Doug McGrath's *Emma*, on the other hand, gives us very round, dry voices, with regular, imperceptible breathing, voices that deliver speeches at a rather slow and sedate pace with clear utterances. The materiality of sound seems to be inversely proportional to the visual lushness of the representation: just as *Emma* abounds in luxurious furnishing, cozy upholstering, fashionable costumes and period artefacts, *Persuasion* and *Pride and Prejudice* tend to focus more on the intimacy of the characters, in a logic that is more centrifugal than centripetal.

Many critics resent the excessive visual spectacle that is linked with the heritage aesthetics of most Austen adaptations. John Mosier, for instance, criticizes the filmmakers' tendency to "fill the frames up with characters" or cluttering artefacts, whereas "Austen deliberately strips out all the color, the detail, the minor characters." He then points out that Austen's "highly dramatic scenes ... seem to be played on a minimalist stage, not in the world."[30] Sound manages to conjure up a context, a situation, or a place, without necessarily representing all the details as visual representation would be more likely to do. Sobriety and focus seem to be achieved in these moments when sound is used, rather than image, to make the context implicitly present and felt, and to materialize the characters' feelings or intentions indirectly.

The allusive quality of sound is exploited in *Pride and Prejudice* and *Persuasion*, where materializing sound clues contribute to the building of a specific, physical space in which noises, such as the rustle of clothes, or footsteps on a gravel path or on a hardwood floor, can create effects of intimacy or uneasiness which the spectator will then project on the situation. In *Pride and Prejudice,* for instance, the intimacy between Jane and Elizabeth is enhanced in bedroom scenes by the soft sound of Jane brushing her hair, by the creaking of the bedsprings or the crackling of the fire. Characters are given substantial bodies notably through the specific noises they make: for instance, the sucking noise that accompanies Elizabeth's jump in the mud on her way to Netherfield, the thumps of the bouncing dancers during balls, the creaking of the floorboards when bodies move, sit, or lean on an element of the set.

This materiality of sound manages to translate the expressive silences which are so crucial in the novels, notably during the Netherfield ball and Darcy's first proposal. The long seconds without speech are not strictly speaking "silent," but their quietness is emphasized by the absence of music. Even if the spectator does not consciously notice that the floorboards in the Hunsford drawing room creak under Darcy's footsteps, the sound gives material and emotional value to the long, uneasy silence that precedes his speech. The "several minutes" (*PP* II, 2, 211) of textual silence become a few seconds in the film, yet the choice of background noises instead of music allows for a multiplicity of effects: the materialization of Darcy's uneasiness (felt physically by the spectator thanks to his sonorous breathing), and also the adoption of Elizabeth's point of view or point of hearing. They are alone in a small room and the detailed sound also represents the intimacy that is forced onto Elizabeth when she least wishes it.

McGrath's *Emma* and Rozema's *Mansfield Park* propose a very different sound treatment, especially in the ballroom scenes, where the bodies disappear from the soundtrack and music covers all other sounds, voices excepted. Noises remain always discreet, and are perceived only when absolutely necessary, that is when no other sound is present and it would be strange not to hear anything.[31] McGrath's film almost never shows us characters eating, even in meal scenes. In the only scene where characters do ingest food or liquid, noises typically associated with these actions are absent from the soundtrack, leaving all sound space to dialogue. Since the total absence of noise would feel strange, "atmospheric sounds" have been added, such as the sound of a liquid being poured into a glass, the clinking of cutlery, but they never correspond to any precise element in the frame. In *Mansfield Park*, the treatment of sound is less homogenous. We find some materializing sound clues, such as Mrs. Norris's heavy steps in the gravel walk at the beginning, or Fanny's footsteps when she runs up or down the stairs, the noise here embodying the energy and anti-conformism of the character, in an ideological rather than aesthetic choice.[32] The ball sequence on the other hand is surprisingly disembodied, one never hears footsteps, breathing or clothes rustling.[33] In both adaptations, the bodies seem to have no weight; the scenes are treated essentially for their dream-like dimension and give an impression of lightness and aesthetic excitement. On the contrary, in *Persuasion*, and even more in *Pride and Prejudice*, the music produced by the instruments is less round, less perfect, and the noises made by the dancers' steps occupy a much larger portion of the soundtrack. This dance is not presented only as a show to be watched, as the aesthetic motions of delicate forms; it is also felt—thanks to the sound—as an exercise that implies mass, balance, control. The mixing of these sounds with the conversations also contributes to our feeling that such a balance is not always easily kept, that the harmony, represented here by the association between the movement of the bodies, the rhythm of the music, and the conversation between the dancers, is not something easy and immutable but an unstable ensemble, the preservation of which requires some effort.

Beyond the representation of the relationship between characters, characters' feelings or the immediate physical context, sound can therefore also be used as a medium to represent, symbolically, a society and its codes. In *Jane Austen's Emma*, for instance, distance and restraint can be felt in the particular resonance of voices during scenes such as the first whist party at Hartfield or Emma's exhibition of Harriet's portrait. This resonance gives

the impression of a rather empty, spacious room, which maintains distance
between the characters, as well as between them and us, and establishes contrasts with passages in which the sound treatment suppresses reverberation
and evokes proximity or intimacy. Thus in the first scene at Hartfield, there
is suddenly less echo to Emma's voice when she mentions her complicity
with Mr. Knightley: "we always say what we like to one another."[34]

In other interior scenes, the crackling of the fire or the chime of a clock
is used to punctuate some lines ironically, such as Mr. Bennet's at Longbourn, or Lady Catherine's at Rosings. More recently Joe Wright's version
of *Pride and Prejudice* resorts to a similar technique: the harmonious song
of a blackbird often accompanies Elizabeth, while the squawk of a parrot
comments ironically on the status of Mr. Collins in Lady Catherine's household. This use of noises as punctuation of dialogue or movement is also frequent in *Persuasion*: the sound of a cup put down a little brutally manifests
Anne's emotion when Wentworth's name is mentioned for the first time.
The chimes of a clock (visible on screen) then accompany the Crofts' first
visit at Kellynch, implicitly symbolizing the transfer of power between two
social classes, an historical turning-point. When Elizabeth leaves for Bath,
she makes a list of everything her sister should do and pompously concludes,
"And someone really ought to visit every house in the parish, as a take-leave.
It is the Elliot way," before climbing into her carriage. The unpleasant creaking of the carriage door concludes her tirade, a jarring sound which seems
to point out the discordance between her pompous expression of family pride
and the actual, inappropriate attitude of Sir Walter who is forfeiting his duties
as landowner.

In conclusion, the treatment of sound can, in some films, translate the
expressiveness of body and voice thanks to an effect of proximity, intimacy,
and thus recreate the magnifying of certain minute details that we find in
the novels. This attention to rendering prevents the films from remaining
simplistic interpretations of the novels and saves them from the kind of
stereotyped expressiveness that Virginia Woolf criticized in cinema: "A kiss
is love. A broken cup is jealousy. A grin is happiness."[35] Within the construction of a properly audio-visual recreation of the novels, the treatment of
sound may be one of the most successful ways to capture the specific charm
of the stories and of the characters. Expressiveness is presented unobtru-
sively in the novels, for the imagination fills the gaps that are opened (vol-
untarily) to the reader by the specific rhythm of dialogue, or the subtle
stage-directions. In film, the impression of proximity or intimacy created by
the sound can allow the visual representation to be kept at a distance—sometimes the viewer does not need to stare at a character's face: hearing the tiny
variations of the voice is sufficient. We are still waiting for a masterpiece

among the film adaptations of Jane Austen's novels. Maybe what is missing is a true understanding of Austen's own cinematic quality, a film which relies more on cinematic precision and intimacy than on the broadly dramatic and the spectacular that have been developed in most adaptations. A film which would not rely so extensively on the prettiness of costumes, on lush land-scapes or stately homes as on the subtle interplay between characters, the hid-den feelings or intentions that one can decipher in an intonation of voice, in a gesture of the hand, in a suspension between two lines. A film which, instead of adding movement, widening the scope, multiplying exterior scenes and filling the soundtrack with romantic music, would give body to this Austenian mise en scène. A film which, as Louis Malle's *Vanya on 42nd Street* (1994) manages to achieve with Chekhov's play, would dispense with all para-phernalia or material detail to concentrate on the interior lives of the char-acters, their innermost feelings and thoughts as perceived—that is, seen *and* heard—from up close.

4

Deciphering Appearances in Jane Austen's Novels and Films

ARIANE HUDELET

Most of Jane Austen's novels develop from initial mistakes that the heroines will eventually correct. These mistakes originate in the erroneous interpretation of signs or people: for instance, Elizabeth Bennet draws the wrong conclusions from her observation of Mr. Darcy's and Wickham's attitudes, and Emma Woodhouse is deluded about Frank Churchill's and Mr. Elton's intentions. The questioning of judgment based on first impressions leads to self-questioning, since the knowledge of others also shapes the perception we have of our own actions ("Till this moment I never knew myself," says Elizabeth after reading Darcy's letter [*PP* II, 13, 230]). "First impressions," which gave *Pride and Prejudice* its original title, need to be checked and doubted, but they are not always wrong. Presenting the successive tests that question the reliability, not only of verbal but also of facial or bodily expression, the novels explore the nature of these impressions, and the formation of knowledge, in a manner evocative of Locke's typographical metaphor of the blank page (the human mind) which is gradually "impressed" or covered with characters as experience is formed.[1] The sensations, contacts and exchanges which constitute experience leave their prints on the bodies and souls of the characters who must learn to decipher these impressions, this text in the making.

How can one tell what is real from what is fake, how can one distinguish the true nature of beings through what they allow us to perceive? The difficult progress towards accurate perception and knowledge lies at the heart of both novels and films, in which deciphering appearances is problematic. The definition of "appearance" given by Samuel Johnson insists on the word's ambivalence: both "the thing seen, phaenomenon; anything visible," and "semblance; not reality," indicating the oscillation between reality and illu-

76

sion. The novels explore this ambivalence: can we trust our senses to form a true and just image of reality, and inversely, does the body reveal, in its appearance, movements and expressions, an inner truth about the self, does it reveal the "soul" it shelters? In the past decade, filmmakers seem to have been particularly sensitive to these questions, which allow them to explore also the question of the perception and reception of images, and so the essence of their own medium. Cinema, an art of appearances, also requires the spectators to build their own truth as the film rolls on. The literary questioning therefore seems particularly akin to the audio-visual issue in an age when images can also lie by giving a seemingly irrefutable appearance of truth, while actually tampering with reality or replacing it altogether with virtual images.

This chapter will thus be devoted to the notions of instability and uncertainty in Austen's novels, which can seem paradoxical since many analyses of the recent adaptations tend to show that most films end up diminishing the fundamental ambiguity in Austen's texts, choosing a more univocal interpretation rather than recreating their "openness." Yet, I will argue that her focus on uncertainty and instability contributes to making her texts cinematic to our twenty-first century sensibility. These notions are indeed inscribed in a very modern questioning of identity, appearance and knowledge that seems particularly relevant today, in our society dominated by images and visual modes of expression, a resonance which the film adaptations necessarily take up in their artistic choices.

The Test of Time: Constructing Experience

As we saw in the previous chapter, a substantial part of communication in Austen's novels relies on expressions, attitudes or gestures. But the codes which preside over non-verbal language seem less fixed than those which regulate verbal language, and their interpretation is often problematic. This communication requires a mutual and tacit understanding between the speaker and the addressee, but errors are frequent. It is easy to analyze such mistakes when they come from insensitive, stupid, or immoral characters. This is why Elinor Dashwood never fears that Robert Ferrars might justly interpret her contemptuous look: "[She] could not restrain her eyes from being fixed on him with a look that spoke all the contempt it excited. It was a look, however, very well bestowed, for it relieved her own feelings, and gave no intelligence to him" (*SS* III, 5, 338). Robert Ferrars thinks too highly of himself to imagine he might be despised, especially by someone like Elinor whom he considers to be socially inferior. Body language here is one-sided; its aim is not to be understood, merely to provide Elinor with emotional release (and the reader, the only one to share the communication).

But even the most astute characters can be mistaken. In all of Austen's novels, we find master deceivers, whose pleasant or charming appearance conceals the darker side of their characters. These include Willoughby in *Sense and Sensibility*, Wickham in *Pride and Prejudice*, Henry (and, to some extent, Mary) Crawford in *Mansfield Park*, Frank Churchill in *Emma* and Mr. Elliot in *Persuasion*. In general, they have a pleasing air or address, which seems to guarantee their morality. According to their degree of "talent," they manage to charm few or many: Lucy Steele only fools those who are easily flattered like Lady Middleton or Fanny Dashwood, whereas Willoughby and Wickham more skillfully also beguile the heroines. Willoughby's good faith cannot be doubted, according to Mrs. Dashwood, because his entire person demonstrates his attachment to Marianne, and she is persuaded, unlike Elinor, that this kind of engagement is just as reliable as one expressed in words:

> I have not wanted syllables where actions have spoken so plainly. Has not his behaviour to Marianne and to all of us, for at least the last fortnight, declared that he loved and considered her as his future wife, and that he felt for us the attachment of the nearest relation? Have we not perfectly understood each other? Has not my consent been daily asked by his looks, his manner, his attentive and affectionate respect? [*SS* I, 15, 92][2]

One of the central questions in this novel, as Tony Tanner shows,[3] is the question of the reliability of body language: are expressive looks or pleasant smiles reliable modes of expression, do they reflect true feelings and honorable intentions, or is it necessary to confront them with verbal engagement, with a sort of formal contract? The answer given by the text is never unequivocal. Of course Willoughby ends up abandoning Marianne, but we learn that he did love her and intended to propose. What was at first a superficial flirtation became a sincere attachment, given up for financial reasons rather than lack of feeling. Marianne, who embodies this belief in intuitive cognition, was indeed right in believing in this body language,[4] but she should not have considered it morally sufficient. A similar process occurs in *Mansfield Park* during Henry Crawford's courtship of Fanny Price. Both relationships start as pure libertinage and end with genuine affection, which defects of character come to spoil. These two examples show how much seeming and being are permeable, and influenced by each other.[5]

Even if the theater as such appears only in *Mansfield Park*, performance and play-acting is a recurrent motif in the novels, essentially through the social game to which all characters must submit. The subtle indications of posture and voice studied earlier also illustrate "the rules of the game" of this society, the way it controls and shapes the bodies of its members. Austen shows how difficult it is to know others on the stage of the social comedy (or tragedy) in which we play a part. Society teaches us gestures, attitudes, routines which are codes associated with certain feelings or reactions, signifiers whose signifieds depend on the social and cultural context. Everyone is more or less a performer on this social stage, but some (like Wickham, Henry Crawford, or Willoughby) have acquired a dangerous command of forms, and manage to subvert the codes, to twist them for their own profit. Others, on the contrary, do not master them well enough and cannot make themselves known like Mr. Darcy,[6] or reveal themselves too absolutely and overstep the limits of the code, like Marianne Dashwood.[7] Everyone needs to interpret the characters around them, to seek out the truth through the parts that are being performed. Heroines are both actresses and spectators of the show. The novels, instead of explaining the psychology of the characters, their relations and motivations, let facts and direct experience demonstrate who is finally right or wrong. Thanks to free indirect discourse and to dialogue, the reader watches the story unfold, the characters evolve. If we can guess the characters' mistakes, most of the time we only have proof when they themselves become conscious of them, since the narrative seldom gives us additional clues. Darcy's, Wickham's or Mr. Elliot's first appearances fool the reader as they do the heroines.

The novelist indeed reproduces the process of knowledge as we experience it in reality, without simplification, or systematization. Since the face is not always a reliable index of the soul, since deceit and concealment are possible, sometimes even inevitable or necessary, then how can one ever know someone else? In the novels, this knowledge is generally the outcome of gradual experimentation. Along the narrative, the confrontation between different perceptions, successive experiences, allows the characters to build a fair image of one another. Each perception comes to confirm or contradict the previous ones to build a reliable image of characters as revealed by their attitudes, acts or words. This process seems to be inspired by the empiricist philosophy, or by John Locke's experimentalism, which in *An Essay concerning Human Understanding*, presents the body and the senses as essential elements in the process of knowledge, in the relationship between the I and the outside world, with the image of the Mind as "white Paper" being gradually "furnished" thanks to Experience. As in Locke's philosophy, the journey which separates intuition from knowledge, first impressions from lasting judgments, is closely connected with sensations.[8] The characters must constantly reconsider the agreement, or the disagreement between past and present experiences, and reason must sometimes correct the necessary subjectivity of memory.

This memory, like first impressions, can be reliable as it can be deceptive,[9] as John Wiltshire also shows in his chapter on Mr. Darcy's smile. Acquiring "experience" means being able to confront sensibility and reason, both being essential for a just and true judgment. The novels thus try to demonstrate, not only the variability of people or things, but also the variability of individual perception. It is not so much Darcy who changes in the course of *Pride and Prejudice* as it is Elizabeth's perception of him, as she explains to Wickham: "When I said that he improved on acquaintance, I did not mean that either his mind or manners were in a state of improvement, but that from knowing him better, his disposition was better understood" (*PP* II, 18, 260). The stories end when uncertainties disappear, when a sort of balance or stable knowledge is acquired, as if the real literary matter were this phase of instability, these wanderings in the journey. As Peter Knox-Shaw explains, Jane Austen is typical of what he calls the "sceptical Enlightenment," that is she writes about "doubts, muddles, delusions, mixed motives and feelings," and we should not confuse the "certainty that readers like Marilyn Butler take to be the key feature of her world, [which] is indeed a characteristic of the way she writes," and the realities she represents, based on "the elusiveness of truth," as typified in the famous comment in *Emma*: "'Seldom, very seldom, does complete truth belong to any human disclosure; seldom can it happen that something is not a little disguised or a little mistaken.'"[10]

The fact that in the novels this gradual building of knowledge is conveyed mainly through dialogue or free indirect discourse has been considered uncinematic. John Mosier, for instance, explains that "Austen's main vehicle for character revelation is ... dramatic, but not particularly cinematic. Cluelessness is revealed not through description or action, but through dialogue.... This ... has proven to be an exceedingly tough problem for the current generation of filmmakers."[11] Others, like Roger Sales, regret that the rakish characters' lack of sincerity appears too blatantly in the actors' performances or in the mise en scène: "there is still a sense in which television makes heroes more knowable and understandable earlier on than they are in Austen's novels. It is also usually the case that the villains, through their transparent looks and mannerisms, can be instantly recognized as such." Thus, a large part of the Austenian "suspense" is lost, because of this addition of "signs": in Roger Michell's film, Benwick is too devoid of charm and Mr. Elliot too obviously deceitful to be plausible suitors for Anne. The spectator never really doubts, and wonders how they could fool anyone, let alone Anne Elliot.[12]

Yet, even though some films may fall into these errors, the process itself, and its structural value in the novels, have great cinematic potential. Film indeed seems the perfect medium to render this instability, this uncertainty of identity. Thanks to its duration, to the spectatorial journey it implies, to the simple unrolling of film, characters can reveal themselves, not at once, not as if everything had been given out in advance, but just as they appear in the novels, that is to say in the process of becoming, of gradually discovering (in the sense of understanding and revealing to others) their identity. According to Leo Braudy, this question of identity lies at the core of the actors' performance in film, as opposed to the theater:

> Films add what is impossible in the group situation of the stage...: a sense of the mystery inside character.... A common theme of all drama from the Renaissance on is the problem of honor, fame, and reputation—in short, all the ways in which the individual is known socially. But this theme appears only rarely in films. In its place is the problem of personal identity: who is Charles Foster Kane? who is Charlie Kohler?[13]

Even if this quotation relies on what may seem an obsolete or limiting conception of the theater, it is nevertheless enlightening as to the richness of Austenian characters for film adaptations, since the central question in the novels is precisely the unstable identity of the characters. Leo Braudy's statement sounds familiarly close to some commentaries on Austen's texts, such as Arnold Kettle's:

> Jane Austen ... is fascinated by the complexities of personal relationships. What is a character really like? Is Frank Churchill really a bounder? She conveys the doubt, not in order to trick, but in order to deepen. The more complex characters in *Emma*, like people in life, reveal themselves gradually and not without surprises.[14]

This instability has been a favorite subject of cinema ever since it was born: many film genres have explored the reception of images, the construction of truth from sensorial perceptions—the characters', but also the spectators', since we form an idea of the characters and their relationships from what we hear and see. By confronting the different points of view of a single scene (such as the rape and murder presented in four different points of view in *Rashômon*, or the duel between Ransom Stoddard and Liberty Valance in *The Man who Shot Liberty Valance*), by constructing a character along a series of subjective points of view (such as the journalists trying to find the "key" to the character of Charles Foster Kane in *Citizen Kane*, through different narratives), by showing a character in search of his own identity (such as John Ballantine-Dr Edwards in *Spellbound*), or by raising the question of the narrative status of the image as an icon of truth (as did, more recently, *The Usual Suspects* or *Mulholland Drive*),[15] film is a journey towards truth, or more essentially a questioning of truth and identity.

As Linda Hutcheon shows, the idea that "Interiority is the Terrain of the Telling Mode; Exteriority is Best Handled by Showing ... Modes" is a cliché that cannot resist close examination.[16] Film is perfectly able to find cinematic equivalents to represent what is going on inside a character's mind. This is precisely what some adaptations—essentially those written by Andrew Davies—attempt to do, by stressing these successive, and sometimes contradictory perceptions, these moments when the heroines reconsider the past in the light of new knowledge, and when their vision of others and themselves changes. Both *Pride and Prejudice* (1995) and *Jane Austen's Emma* (1996) develop this idea of a confrontation between different perceptions through the use of subjective flash-backs representing the way a character remembers a past moment, which the spectator also previously saw as part of the linear development of the plot. Film thus also makes the spectator's reception of image and sound problematic. When they see the scene for the second time, spectators are forced to reconsider their initial perception, to doubt what they had directly witnessed and believed as true, to question their own senses. In the light of some new knowledge, the heroine recalls a moment which illustrates her mistakes, and the film shows us this memory by inserting a scene which we have previously seen, but with slight variations. Darcy's letter to Elizabeth is thus filmed to stress Elizabeth's progressive re-judgment. The first half of the letter, which relates facts that only Darcy knows, is performed onscreen while Darcy is reading it. After we see him start writing frantically in his bedroom, he pauses, goes to the window, and a dissolve brings us to the representation of what his voice-over is narrating. These images are directly connected to Darcy's memory while he is writing to enlighten Elizabeth and justify his behavior.

After Darcy has finished the Wickham chapter ("and this, Madam, is a faithful narrative of all my dealings with Mr. Wickham"), the letter is suspended for a while. Darcy had started to write at dusk; it is now dawn. The parallel editing shows Elizabeth going for a walk in the forest, where Darcy finally hands her the letter. Her reading then provides the link with the preceding sequence and Darcy's voice-over takes up the narration, but the flash-backs are now provided by Elizabeth since the contents of the letter belong to her past as well. She first "sees" Wickham's face in the context of conversations they had in Meryton and Longbourn, as well as some scenes from the ball where she had felt ashamed of her own family. These shots are both very similar to, and slightly different from, the shots we saw earlier. Whereas Elizabeth and Wickham appeared in a medium close shot and rarely looked at each other in the garden at Longbourn, the point of view becomes subjective in the heroine's memory, and Wickham now looks at her intently while speaking the same words (explaining why he did not attend the ball at Netherfield). Likewise, in Elizabeth's memory, Mrs. Bennet appears in a close shot unlike the medium long shot used in the original sequence at Netherfield. If her words are the same, her attitude and gestures differ slightly, and the close shot cruelly enhances her red cheeks and the overall impression of vulgarity (she speaks very loudly and with her mouth full). This implicit contrast between two visions of the same scene does capture the flexibility of memory which contributes to the construction of the heroine's identity.[17] Elizabeth's memory is literally modified, thanks to the contrasting point of view that Darcy's letter makes possible. Just as the vision of Mr. Darcy's smile in the portrait at Pemberley reactivates Elizabeth's past, passive perception of his previous smiles (compare John Wiltshire's chapter on the subject), the letter endows her past perceptions with a new quality which the subjective shots transmit to the reader.

Darcy's voiceover continues to narrate while Elizabeth walks quickly back to Hunsford, a journey shown through a series of dissolves between the wood and her bedroom. The movement created by her physical motion also materializes her bodily reaction—a mix of emotion, disbelief and anger—as well as her progressive awareness, her "journey" towards truth (thus closely following the text). Darcy's words, translated into Elizabeth's mental images, are complemented by her physical reactions, which sometimes give in to this new truth, and sometimes resist it. Even when she expresses her anger, the images separated by the dissolves show the evolution in her point of view (such as the image of Jane's too placid countenance, which could denote insensibility to an exterior observer like Darcy). Although spectators cannot directly, simultaneously confront the initial sequences with these shots, yet they do sense something uncanny, and are therefore encouraged to question also their initial perception of the same moments.[18]

Jane Austen's Emma resorts to the same device, only it associates it both with the heroine's illusions and mistakes and with the moments of awakening or reinterpretation. When Emma hears about the engagement between Frank Churchill and Jane Fairfax, she "sees" the key moments again, in which Frank's attitude, his tone or expression, could have betrayed his secret. Here again, the shots differ slightly from the initial sequences, and the sound treatment gives these passages an unreal dimension which befits their status as memories. The camera draws closer, the angle changes to transform the shot into a subjective point of view, in which the slightest tremor, the smallest hesitation become loaded with meaning.

These subjective flash-backs coexist with what we could call phantasmatic flash-forwards, that is to say scenes in which Emma foresees the future, with delight or apprehension. This is how we see Harriet marry fictitiously no less than three times: to Mr. Elton, Frank Churchill (these scenes are shot in slow motion, in a soft light and slight blur, the groom carrying his bride into a carriage or on his horse while rose petals float all around them), then to Mr. Knightley (by contrast, this scene takes place in a gloomy church, the music becomes jarring and Emma bursts into the aisle and violently interrupts the ceremony). None of these three weddings eventually take place, nor does the film show any of the "real" ceremonies. The *outré* style of the sequences illustrates Emma's excessive imaginative skills—she seems amused by them herself, conscious of their ridiculous character. Towards the end, three similar sequences succeed each other in a few minutes, going *crescendo* until the climax when Emma becomes aware of her major mistake—her incapacity to acknowledge her own feelings for Mr. Knightley. The sequence which then takes up moments in Emma and Knightley's relationship uses the exact same shots as the initial sequences—Emma's fantasy no longer distorts these memories, but she sees their relationship as it is, as the spectator also saw it earlier in the film. She recalls Knightley's uncompromising remonstrance at Box Hill, for instance, as well his serious look when he recoiled from the idea of being considered as a "brother" to her at the Crown Inn ball. These accurate memories contribute to her awakening to her own feelings—love comes with clear-sightedness.

Through these successive revisions, time appears—in the novels, as in the films—as the fundamental data of this experimentation. *Pride and Prejudice* (1995 and 2005), *Jane Austen's Emma* (1996), *Persuasion* (1995) and *Sense and Sensibility* (1995) all stress the cycle of the seasons, the weather conditions that give materiality to this evolution of relationships and characters. Just as the wanderer in the eighteenth century landscape garden "discovers different views, different lightings, different fabrics which constitute as many mental observations gathered along his progress, [building], element by element, a concrete knowledge of the premises,"[19] knowledge in novel and film is acquired gradually, at the end of a progress, after the different viewpoints have combined to build a true image. Yet, one could object that the insertion of these brief scenes in Davies's screenplays can also seem a rather heavy-handed, and somewhat stereotypical manner, of representing the heroine's memories, fantasies or, more generally, consciousness. The companion volume to the television film, *The Making of "Jane Austen's Emma,"* devotes two pages to what Andrew Davies call "the detective story" (meaning the discovery of Frank and Jane's secret engagement) and explains that the film had to add clues to the plot.[20] Yet, one may wonder, if the book encourages re-reading, why couldn't the television film do the same? With DVD or VOD today, film is as easily accessible as a printed paperback; one can choose to view it in several sessions, to pause, to move backwards or forwards at leisure, and of course to view it again several times, and it is quicker than re-reading the novel (our students have unfortunately understood that "advantage" of film over literature for a long time). These examples also illustrate an essentially narrative approach to the adaptation of the theme of interpretation and reinterpretation in the novels. Both films rely on an identification between the spectator and the heroine, while eventually providing a reassuring return to the linearity of the plot and to reliable images after the brief distortion linked to subjective memory or proleptic fantasy. Ultimately, the "truth" of the film image is never really questioned, whereas the endings of Austen's novels generally undermine the referential illusion by means of the narrator's self-conscious interventions, or by a subtle reference to the artificiality of fictional endings.[21] The very diverse interpretations of the novels themselves reinforce this horizon of possibilities opened up by the fundamental instability of the novels: all readers find what they wish to find in the texts—those who want to read the stories as fairy tales, to imagine a reassuringly happy continuation for the characters, as well as those who prefer to pursue this interrogation on knowledge and identity. Even if the process of interpretation and judgment is based on successive moments in time in the novels, Austen's irony, an example of which has just been provided, her capacity to convey diverging messages simultaneously, is probably the ultimate tool with which she manages to preserve an openness of meaning, to leave space for diverse interpretations, and calls for an active reading on the part of the reader who also has to decipher the appearances of the text, just as the characters have to decipher the world around them. Some scenes in the recent adaptations manage to recreate this ambiguity, this simultaneity of meaning, thanks to their treatment of film space rather than narrative construction.

Mirrors and Reflections: The Reliability of Images

Although they are said to be "non visual," most of Jane Austen's novels resort, at one point or another, to visual representations or artefacts which epitomize the themes of appearance and essence, perception and interpretation. In *Pride and Prejudice*, the miniatures of Darcy and Wickham, and then the full-length portrait of the owner of Pemberley, lead to Elizabeth's conversion. In *Emma*, the sketch of Harriet works as a way to reveal different characters' perspectives on Emma's friend: according to Mr. Knightley, Emma has made Harriet "too tall," just as she attempts to elevate her unduly in society. Mr. Elton means to flatter the artist by praising her representation of the sitter. And Mr. Woodhouse fears that Harriet may catch cold, because she is portrayed without a shawl. In *Sense and Sensibility*, the lock of hair which Edward Ferrars wears in a ring is falsely interpreted by Elinor as being her own, before Lucy's revelation painfully undeceives her. In *Per-*

suasion, Captain Harville comes to Bath to have Benwick's miniature portrait framed for the upcoming wedding with Louisa Musgrove; since it had been originally painted for his previous fiancée, Fanny Harville, it leads to a confrontation of ideas between Harville's and Anne's different perceptions of female and male constancy in love. Finally, the theatricals in *Mansfield Park* could also be considered, although less clearly, as an example of a visual representation (costumes, setting, mise en scène) which reflects the distorted and mistaken interpretations of the characters. Even if the films take up most of these visual representations, they also add another type of image which the novels strikingly omit: the mirror image. In the novels, the object itself appears only once, in *Persuasion* when Admiral Croft explains the few modifications he brought to Kellynch Hall, implicitly commenting on Sir Walter's vanity:

> I have done very little besides sending away some of the large looking-glasses from my dressing-room, which was your father's. A very good man, and very much the gentleman I am sure—but I should think, Miss Elliot [looking with serious reflection] I should think he must be rather a dressy man for his time of life.—Such a number of looking-glasses! oh Lord! there was no getting away from oneself [*P* II, 1, 138].

The expression "serious reflection" to describe the admiral's attitude, could here be opposed to these other, more frivolous "reflections," in which Sir Walter loves to immerse himself.[22] But the literary author never shows us a heroine absorbed in the contemplation of her own image, whereas all the recent adaptations without exception contain the object, quite logically as part of the interior decoration of the houses, but also as a meaningful, symbolical prop used to structure a shot or a scene. Whether the characters look at themselves or not, whether the reflected image doubles the space of the shot or whether it reveals an additional space, the mirror brings out the characters' relationships with their own bodies and senses, or represents, thanks to optical devices, a space where virtual bodies take on a metaphorical dimension.

The correspondence between mirror and film image has often been used in cinema,[23] and has nourished many reflections on film form: both are very close in their texture, in their photographic precision and in their relationship to light (a mirror in a film is a reflection in a reflection, a frame which reflects light in another frame which keeps the traces of this exposure to light).[24] To look at a heroine looking at herself transforms the character into a self-spectacle, a motif we could link with the emphasis on interiority in Austen's novels. The mirror object can thus stand for the conflicting notions of blindness or introspection, vanity or revelation, according to the films and sequences. Whether it is used as a symbol to reflect the characters' thoughts or nature, or as a metaphor of the relationships between the characters which can sometimes contrast with the contents of the dialogue and reveal ironic distance, the mirror image constitutes a privileged example of the way Austen's very modern questioning of the perception of reality can become a post-modern questioning of the reception and distortion of images. Of course, no adaptation has tackled this question as radically as some post-modern films such as *The Matrix* (1999) or *The Usual Suspects* (1995), but the recurrent insistence on all sorts of reflected images tends to show that this aspect of Jane Austen's novels resonates particularly with our contemporary questioning of visual representation and the iconicity of images.

The presence of a mirror on screen is an ambivalent symbol. On the one hand, it can represent introspection, self-knowledge and the construction of identity. On the other hand, the same object can point to a deceitful absorption in one's own image, and illustrate blindness, an illusory and vain perception of oneself and others, a stagnation on the surface. Thus, the object itself contains the ambivalence of physical appearance as it is treated by Jane Austen, above all the danger of mistakes and errors about oneself and others. Two adaptations stand out in their mise en scène of the relationship between character and reflection, and in their insistence on what this relationship reveals about the character and their morality, expectations or anxieties. Patricia Rozema's *Mansfield Park* and Joe Wright's *Pride and Prejudice* illustrate two opposite treatments of the same ancient motif—the woman at the mirror.[25] The mirror image becomes a double of the female character, an incarnation of her consciousness or unconscious, with which she silently converses. Even though Patricia Rozema decided to turn Fanny Price into a heroine closer to Elizabeth Bennet, full of wit, vivacity, and independent spirit, both films adopt a very different approach, *Mansfield Park* insisting more on the dangers of this narcissistic, potentially deceitful, look, while *Pride and Prejudice* on the contrary develops the revealing nature of this specular introspection.

In these two films, the "mirror scenes" are moments of intimacy, generally in a bedroom or a drawing-room. In *Mansfield Park*, the mirror reflects above all the blindness of the characters who gaze at themselves. The object appears as a trap, a seductive and flattering surface for the characters who are already stigmatized for their selfishness, vanity or lack of discernment. A remarkable sequence is made of parallel scenes all structured around a mirror: in turn, every member of the Bertram household appears in front of a looking-glass, preparing for a meeting with the Crawfords. We do not see the frame of the mirrors, but a small part of the character appears each time, in soft focus on the right hand side of the screen, while the reflection (a close-up of the character's face) is in focus, thus stressing the fading of the real person in front of this evanescent, flattering image. Julia is the first to appear thus; we see her try on an earring, adjust her hair, bite her lips, and practice her smiling. In the next shot, it is Maria's turn to put on some perfume and pinch her cheekbones. Lady Bertram, Mrs. Norris, Edmund and Fanny follow, each shot conveying a different impression: the laudanum which Lady Bertram drinks makes her insensitive to her surroundings, including the mirror; Edmund and Aunt Norris are simply attentive to their own image, while Fanny throws only a very brief, dismissive look at her reflection before dashing out of the room. Several jump cuts within the passages devoted to Julia, Maria, Edmund or Mrs. Norris reveal ellipses implying the length of this physical preparation. Thus, the seven seconds with Julia seem to be only brief extracts of the real-time duration, which contrasts all the more with the brevity (one second) of the single, unedited shot of Fanny. Her lack of concern for her reflection is in tune with the general thematic line of the film which links appearance with vanity and triviality. Fanny alone seems to resist the charms of self-contemplation, and prefers looking at others rather than at herself. Maria and Julia, as archetypal coquettes, are thrilled by their own beauty and consequent power. The mirror is here only a tool in the preparation of the body for a program of seduction which will turn out to be risky and disastrous.[26] For Rozema, the image of the woman at the mirror is solely associated with enslavement by the patriarchal society which reduces women to their appearance, to their body.

In Joe Wright's *Pride and Prejudice*, the mirror becomes on the contrary a key symbol of the heroine's growth and awareness: whereas Elizabeth's "undeception" in the novel is associated with her physical progress through Rosings Park as she reads Darcy's letter,[27] the 2005 film chooses to rely on stillness and optical devices to reflect the interior journey of the heroine. After the melodramatic proposal scene shot outdoors in the pelting rain, the next sequence, in which we follow Elizabeth's slow progression through the house towards a mirror, takes place indoors, at Hunsford parsonage. Elizabeth appears first in a medium close shot, sitting on her bed, as a still, back-lit figure in a chiaroscuro effect, before standing up and walking away from the camera along a narrow corridor, finally moving towards a window, and then a mirror in front of which she stops. We cut from a medium shot of her profile facing the mirror to a reverse angle taken from "behind the mirror," Elizabeth now looking at us since we are where her reflection should be, which creates an effect of maximum identification ("We are her," says Joe Wright in his DVD commentary). Time seems to accelerate while she remains still and expressionless: the sunlight fades and is quickly replaced by firelight. We see Darcy enter the house in the background, leave his letter on the windowsill and disappear quickly before Elizabeth turns around.

The sequence relies on variations of focus and on degrees of visibility. We do not see Elizabeth's face in the opening shot, then the corridor shot frame gradually becomes blurred, and generally the shallow depth of field leaves a large part of the frame out of focus: Darcy is blurred when he appears in the background, and then Elizabeth's face is also out of focus when she picks up the letter. The sequence ends with a close-up on the letter, the only element in focus, while Charlotte, who has just entered the room, is blurred in the background. The film therefore relies on our physical, sensorial identification with the character: Elizabeth is learning to see things clearly, and above all learning that her vision and understanding are partial, just as the spectator's vision is impaired or biased by variations in focus, light (darkness progressively fills the frame), and camera distance (the first half of the sequence takes us closer and closer to Elizabeth, culminating in an extreme close-up on her eyes before she starts reading the letter, after which the camera pulls out to establish some distance from the character). Elizabeth's textual "agitating reflections" (*PP* II, 11, 216) here become transferred into the symbol of real, optical reflections,[28] and into a concrete process of visual accommodation. The true moment of epiphany is indeed when she looks at herself in the mirror, since it also seems to bring a shift from realistic representation to a more dream-like quality. The acceleration of time, the feeling of uncertainty surrounding Darcy's presence (to which Elizabeth does not react at first), and his sudden disappearance when Elizabeth turns around, all seem to question the nature of perception.

This sequence is complemented by the Pemberley sequence in which Elizabeth walks along the sculpture gallery[29]: she first pauses in front of a statue whose veiled face could again be seen as a reflection of Elizabeth's previous blindness. The heroine is framed in a similar, medium long shot, standing in profile and looking intently at an "alter ego," only this time she is on the right facing left, that is to say in a symmetrically inverted mirror image of the Hunsford shot. From Hunsford to Pemberley, Elizabeth has indeed gone through the looking-glass, and has learned to acknowledge her blindness and partiality, and is now ready to discover Darcy's real face. Quite tellingly, this is also achieved thanks to the mediation of a mirror: after gazing longingly at Darcy's bust, Elizabeth continues the visit alone (the housekeeper and the Gardiners having vanished conveniently), hears piano music coming from another room and peeks into it to discover Georgiana and Darcy, or rather their reflections in a large mirror on the wall opposite the door. Darcy indeed appears different at that moment: it is the first time in the film we have seen him smile (one hour and twenty-two minutes after the beginning). The mirror image is thus used by Wright as a symbol of introspection, clear-sightedness and revelation. Austen's novel implies that we need to confront different perspectives in order to construct a true image of others and of ourselves (and also bases its epiphanic moment on the act of looking at a mediated image of Darcy, the Pemberley portrait); Wright's film resorts to optical and visual metaphors of clarity and accuracy. Whereas *Mansfield Park* is infused with a distrust of appearances, mirror images in *Pride and Prejudice* become the symbol of introspection and knowledge.

In both examples, the mirror is a symbol, used to illustrate or reveal some aspect of the characters' identity, nature or evolution. What matters is the relationship the characters have with their own reflections, and how this relationship characterizes them, but the actual mirror images do not provide additional information for the viewer. Let us now see how more complex scenes manage to exploit the visual potential of the mirror image to actually construct ambiguous passages, based on visual irony, in which several meanings seem to coexist.

Without necessarily raising the question of introspection, the mirror is also used in some films as a visual metaphor of the relationships between several characters. Thanks to its optical qualities, it creates an additional space within the shot, and allows play on perspective, shapes or colors, a configuration of bodies and space which works as a complement or counterpoint to the scene performed by the actors. We have, in a way, two scenes taking place at the same time, and the discrepancy between the two provides ironic distance and complicity on the part of the spectator, in a manner evocative of Austen's irony.

In Ang Lee's *Sense and Sensibility*, three mirrors structure the opening scene between John and Fanny Dashwood in their London house, at the beginning of their conversation about the nature of the "help" John promised his dying father he would give to his stepmother and sisters. The immediate association of these characters with the flat and impenetrable surface of the mirror is reinforced by the cold gray and beige colors of the setting to convey their self-complacency, insensibility and conceit.

The virtual space of the mirror image also represents the balance of power in this couple. After a medium long shot of the exterior of the house in which we hear Fanny Dashwood's first line—"Help them? What do you mean, help them?"—we see John facing us in a close shot, looking at the camera. After his answer—"Dearest, I mean to give them three thousand pounds.... The interest will provide them with a little extra income. Such a gift will probably discharge my promise to my father"—we cut to the reverse angle. In a medium long shot, we now see John from the back, standing on the left hand side, and Fanny, also from the back, sitting in front of her dressing table on the right hand side. Both are looking at their respective reflections: in a small oval mirror in front of Fanny, and in a very large mirror which covers most of the wall in front of John. But John is also reflected in profile in the dressing table mirror, and his back is reflected in a third, swinging mirror, behind him, itself reflected in the large mirror. At this point in the scene, Fanny's reflection appears only in the looking glass in front of her.

We then witness a reversal of this symbolical occupation of space. Fanny stands up and comes to stand next to John, facing the great mirror. She now stands in between John and the dressing-table mirror, and she is also reflected in the mirror behind them. We thus move from an image in which John's body is reflected three times and Fanny's only once, to a similar image (it is the same shot, and the camera does not move), this time dominated by Fanny since she now is reflected three times, against two for John. The movement which gives her this advantage is accompanied by her words, "Without question, more than amply," the first in a series of lines which, as they travel to Norland, will prompt John to reconsider the extent of his generosity.[30] When John tries to justify his intentions, "One had rather, in such occasions, ... do too much, than too little," we move back to the same shot as at the beginning, where the camera is positioned in place of the mirror. We see them facing us in a close shot, John nervously glancing at his wife for approval, while her eyes remain steadily fixed on herself, on the camera, on us, while she adjusts the collar of her dress. The weakness in John's look confirms his withdrawal in front of the domineering figure of his wife, who literally comes to insidiously occupy the virtual space delimited by the frames of the mirrors.

The several mirrors make this opening scene very dynamic in spite of the confined environment and the scarcity of movement.[31] They manage to progressively reveal the power balance between the characters: Fanny dominates the scene and quickly crushes her husband's good intentions. While dialogue is employed in the text to depict Fanny as a wonderful manipulator of language,[32] the use of mirrors allows Ang Lee to transpose this manipulation of codes in a visual and metaphorical register. In the novel, this conversation takes place when the couple is already settled at Norland, but the film places it on the morning of their journey, thus using this virtual occupation of the mirror space as a harbinger of the upcoming occupation of Norland, from which they will soon expel Mrs. Dashwood and her sisters.

In a very brief morning scene at Hartfield from *Jane Austen's Emma*, the mirror becomes expressive thanks to the depth of field. It represents the deception of the characters, a cognitive rather than moral blindness. The mirror becomes an expressive surface which allows the film to represent the mistakes characters make in their interpretation of appearances. Emma and Harriet, sitting in front of a three-panel mirror, are having their hair done by two maids. They have just learnt about Mrs. Churchill's death and are wondering whom Frank will marry now that he is independent. The composition of the frame relies on a sort of visual chiasmus, with Emma from three quarter back on the right hand side, Harriet from the back on the left, the reflection of Harriet's face in the right hand side pane, and Emma's reflection on the left hand side pane. Their conversation is very allusive and full of double-entendres:

> EMMA (zoom in on her, she now shares the frame only with Harriet's reflection which is out of focus): "Who will he marry, now he is free to make his own choice?"
> HARRIET (focus on her, now Emma is out of focus): "Yes, who will he marry, now that he has his choice?"
> EMMA (focus on her, now Harriet's reflection is blurred again): "Harriet, I have reformed. My lips are sealed." (She smiles knowingly. Briefly, focus on the same smile from Harriet, before cutting to the next scene)

At no moment in this brief scene are the two characters in focus at the same time. So, while their dialogue relies on allusions, on implicit understanding, the image and the focus on their reflected images represent their mistakes which will be revealed later on. For Emma, Harriet is in love with Frank, but Harriet is actually set on Mr. Knightley, and imagines that Emma could be the object of Frank's affection. The visual chiasmus could thus represent this imaginary and erroneous criss-cross of love relationships. The blur indeed announces the illusion on which these conjectures are based, since Frank will marry neither of them "now he has his choice," but rather Jane Fairfax, an elusive character who remains in the background of the story, in the dead angle, out of focus.

The theme of perception and interpretation, so central to Austen's novels, thus allows cinema to question also the status of images as icons of reality. The manipulation of images—framing, camera movements, variations of lighting, slow motion, music, close-ups, or shots-reverse shots—encourages the spectator to wonder about the reliability of the reality that is here represented, about the mistakes of the characters, which often become our own mistakes. Austen's texts question our ability to read, and judge, and ultimately leave us in doubt, allowing for this uncertainty, this impression that they are "like a person, not to be comprehended fully and finally by any other person."[33] Recent studies have often stressed this dimension which can also, I feel, account for the multiplication of adaptations since the middle of the 1990s.[34]

In the 1990s and 2000s indeed, this doubt manifests itself also in the reception of manufactured images. The recent films have probably been influenced by the evolution in information technology and digital imaging.

How can we be sure today of the status of a recorded image, in a universe saturated with images, where nearly everything can be recorded and stored, and above all when it has become almost impossible to distinguish between a "true," iconic image, and a "false," virtual image (false, that is in its link with the object represented—it represents a false, altered or non-existent reality—or in its intention—it is given for what it is not, it pretends to be the truth whereas it only leads us astray)?[35] The unreliability of perception and vision no doubt provides an explanation of the relevance of these stories today. Even if we do not find, in Austenian adaptations, a consistent meta-filmic discourse as exists in several recent successful adaptations such as Michael Winterbottom's *A Cock and Bull Story* (2005) or Al Pacino's *Looking for Richard* (1996),[36] and even if a part of the audience on the contrary seems to prefer the image of a steady world, in which the access to stable truth seems possible, nevertheless some of these films do try to capture a fundamental dimension of the pleasure provided by the Austenian texts, which could correspond to what Roland Barthes calls "the science of the becoming." Taking up Nietzsche's words, Barthes explains the difficulty of a discourse which would try to fix impermanence:

> We are not subtle enough to perceive the probably absolute flow of the becoming; the permanent exists only thanks to our coarse organs which sum up and bring things to common levels, whereas nothing exists under that form. The tree is something new every moment; we assert the form because we do not understand the subtlety of absolute movement.[37]

The film adaptations are visions of the texts that are inscribed in this movement, in this becoming. They are discourses on the novel and on cinema at the same time as they are representations of a text, integrated in a fixed and immutable temporal process, and so each adaptation is more interesting if we consider, not that they try to impose an absolute truth on the Austenian text, but rather to convey the evolution of this text, the variability of this reading, of this imaginary vision produced by the novels. They have in turn nourished so many interpretations and reactions (the beginning of the cinematic Austenmania in 1995 was followed by a plethora of essays, sequels, prequels, recreations, and adaptations of all kinds) that they should indeed be considered as part of a conversation with Austen's work, which seems particularly vivid at the turn of the twenty-first century, and in which cinema and television occupy a crucial place.

Mr. Darcy's Smile

JOHN WILTSHIRE

Most readers of *Pride and Prejudice* would agree that the scenes at Pemberley are the turning point of the novel's romance. It's here that Elizabeth Bennet, already impressed by the grandeur and good taste of the house in its grounds, listens intently as the housekeeper praises her master in terms that go against everything that she has assumed about Mr. Darcy. "That he was not a good tempered man had been her firmest opinion. Her keenest attention was awakened" (III, 1, 275). Elizabeth longs to hear more, and she does: the housekeeper goes on to amplify her praise, contradicting the idea that "some people call him proud" by relating his consideration for his servants and tenants, and proceeding to praise his kindness to his sister. This leads to one of those moments in the novel when the reader must guess emotions from actions, not from speech. "'He is certainly a good brother,' said Elizabeth, as she walked towards one of the windows." It is a moment to sort out her impressions, to reconcile what she is experiencing now, with her previous knowledge of Darcy. Certainly, as soon as she finds herself in the family picture gallery she goes in search of his portrait:

> In the gallery there were many family portraits, but they could have little to fix the attention of a stranger. Elizabeth walked on in quest of the only face whose features would be known to her. At last it arrested her—and she beheld a striking resemblance of Mr. Darcy, with such a smile over the face, as she remembered to have sometimes seen, when he looked at her. She stood several minutes before the picture in earnest contemplation, and returned to it again before they quitted the gallery. Mrs. Reynolds informed them, that it had been taken in his father's life time.
>
> There was certainly at this moment, in Elizabeth's mind, a more gentle sensation towards the original, than she had ever felt in the height of their acquaintance. The commendation bestowed on him by Mrs. Reynolds was of no trifling nature. What praise is more valuable than the praise of an intelligent servant? As a brother, a landlord, a master, she considered how many people's happiness were in his guardianship!—How much of

pleasure or pain it was in his power to bestow!—How much of good or evil must be done by him! Every idea that had been brought forward by the housekeeper was favourable to his character, and as she stood before the canvas, on which he was represented, and fixed his eyes upon herself, she thought of his regard with a deeper sentiment of gratitude than it had ever raised before; she remembered its warmth, and softened its impropriety of expression [III, 1, 277].

The picture gallery at Pemberley has been introduced into the novel well before this occasion. Miss Bingley, unable to resist teasing Darcy about marriage to Elizabeth, has brought it up: "Do let the portraits of your uncle and aunt Philips be placed in the gallery at Pemberley. Put them next to your great uncle the judge. They are in the same profession, you know; only in different lines. As for Elizabeth's picture, you must not attempt to have it taken, for what painter could do justice to those beautiful eyes?" (I, 10, 57). The splendors of Pemberley have already been the subject of a conversation at Netherfield overheard by a fascinated Elizabeth herself (I, 8, 41–2). And the topic of portrait painting, or "taking" a likeness, is kept afloat in the dialogue between Elizabeth and Darcy, whilst they are dancing at Netherfield. "May I ask to what these questions tend?" says Darcy, and Elizabeth replies, "Merely to the illustration of *your* character." "Illustration" here may mean just explanation, but Darcy picks up its visual implications in his reply: "I could wish, Miss Bennet, that you were not to sketch my character at the present moment." Elizabeth returns his serve with the skill of a professional player: "But if I do not take your likeness now, I may never have another opportunity" (I, 18, 105).

The novel therefore prepares the reader for its moment in the picture gallery, alerting him or her to think about portraits and their relationship to the subject's character and status. But perhaps "alert" and "think" are misleading verbs: these are little sedimentary suggestions, hardly prompts or even indicators, and it's probable that a reader, even one who has gone through the novel several times, hardly records them consciously. It's only the critic or scholar, the reader intent on something other than pleasure, who might note these moments. He or she is performing a reflective or rational function, going back over the text to see what helps to make the Pemberley scene so telling, and resisting immersion in the drama of the moment. The sparkling quality of the novel's dialogue offers an engagement that compensates and distracts us from attention to such underlying metaphors. The narrative's gaps or elisions invite us to fill them with our own assumptions and imagination. And this interplay or tension between present engagement and retrospective or reflective knowledge, is, I shall argue, deeply typical of the novel.

But the moment before the portrait is surprising in more than one way. That smile which Elizabeth remembers to have seen on his face, do readers recall it too? Has it been registered, in the novel? Janet Todd's response in her recent book on Jane Austen can probably stand for many readers' reactions. She writes that "in Pemberley before Darcy's portrait Elizabeth trusts a likeness even over her own experience, or rather she invests this likeness with reordered memory. She had earlier had difficult making her own portrait of Darcy; now she helps an external work by giving it Darcy's now known feeling for herself—its smile becomes one 'she remembered to have sometimes seen when he looked at her,' *a memory rather at odds with what the reader has heard.*"[1] In other words, the reader has never heard of this smile before, and its sudden appearance on the portrait creates a different Darcy from the person Elizabeth and the reader has previously known.

Do readers at this moment recall a different Darcy? Has the reader been wondering why Elizabeth hasn't noticed Darcy's smile before? My thesis here is that the reader has certainly "never heard of" this smile before, and that this curious aspect of his or her response, once recognized, reveals some key secrets of the novel. But to guard against making so many assumptions about "the reader" as I have already made (hiding my own responses behind this figure), I shall use the films adapted from *Pride and Prejudice* as controls on my argument. To do this is to adopt the common-sense view that a film is a kind of "reading" of the novel. All the multiple decisions made during the filming—from the script to the final cut—amount to an interpretation of the novel from which a film is derived. There is a particular pertinence in this case: film-makers, working in a visual medium, have to make decisions about Darcy's appearance, and thus have to decide about Darcy's smile—or nonsmile.

There have been many filmic versions of *Pride and Prejudice*. The 1940 Hollywood adaptation, directed by Robert Z. Leonard, with Greer Garson and Laurence Olivier, was followed by no less than four BBC serials (1952, '58, '67, and '80). Only the last, with script by Fay Weldon, is currently available. It was succeeded by the now-famous BBC 1995 version, directed by Simon Langton, with script by Andrew Davies. This in turn was followed by the commercially successful film of 2005, directed by Joe Wright. One can disregard the Mormon update, *Pride and Prejudice: A Latter-Day Comedy* (2003) and the Bollywood influenced *Bride and Prejudice* (2004) as well as other spin-offs from the plot, such as *You've Got Mail* (1999), since these, though interesting, do not offer to be close versions or interpretations of the source novel. There are, then, four "readings" or interpretations of the novel to be drawn on.

The 1940 film is certainly a challenge to this approach, because the Pemberley sequence does not appear in it at all.[2] Elizabeth doesn't travel to Derbyshire, she doesn't admire the grounds and house, she doesn't listen to the housekeeper's praises—all essential stepping stones in Austen's careful preparation for the climactic and revelatory moment before the portrait. The script was based on a stage play by Helen Jerome, and this may be the explanation; another is possibly the director's desire to present a more democratic, a more American vision of England, which diminishes the novel's stress on class distinctions. Darcy's objection to asking Elizabeth to dance lasts no more than a moment, he soon asks for her hand, and it is she who refuses him. And, as Ellen Belton reports, "While the novel concerns itself with the complex psychological processes by which first the hero and then the heroine fall in love with one another, the film visually suggests a mutual attraction that is almost instantaneous."[3] And, as she adds, "It is obvious from the outset that he is drawn to Elizabeth and makes very little effort to resist succumbing to her charms."[4] So there is in fact no need for a turning point in the couple's relationship.

There is no need for a smiling portrait either. Instead of Mr. Darcy's smile, the film offers Laurence Olivier's smile. In the interpolated garden party scene, the two central characters are already close to a rapprochement. "You're very puzzling, Mr. Darcy," says Elizabeth, smiling. "At this moment, it's difficult to believe that you're so proud." To which Darcy replies, returning her smile, "At this moment it's difficult to believe you're so prejudiced. Shall we not call it quits and start again?" But Olivier's smile, here and in other scenes, is not completely interpretable. It might be one of mere politeness, a smile of grace and charm that is a social mannerism. Or is this smile (more a half-smile in many instances) really a sneer? Olivier's acting was always able to suggest secret recesses of feeling behind a character's face. If Elizabeth finds in the portrait something that she now remembers to have seen, this invests both that portrait and her memory with a certain mystique: was the smile latent in her memory or wasn't it? Was it hardly a smile at all? But if Olivier's smile duplicates or replaces the mysterious aspect of the smile on the portrait, it has no dynamic force, and contributes little to the story's unfolding.

Later films or television versions of the novel keep much closer to its plot, at least. In all of them, Elizabeth's encounter with an image of Darcy at Pemberley is recreated as a key moment. But evidence that a reader does not usually remember or conceive of Darcy as a smiling figure is amply provided in the most recent film. In absolute contrast to Olivier's Darcy, with his graceful, elegant movements and polite if enigmatic smile, Matthew MacFayden's Darcy is not only unsmiling, embarrassed, uncomfortable, he is plainly distressed, and to present him in this guise is clearly the director's intention. Elizabeth twice derides Darcy as "miserable." Just after Charlotte in the Assembly scene has advised her to be cautious, she retorts, laughingly, "I wouldn't have danced with him for the whole of Derbyshire, let alone the miserable half." But in fact Darcy's smile is scarcely discernible in any of the later visual interpretations of the novel.

This 2005 film directed by Joe Wright is inevitably aware of the very successful BBC serial of 1995. Much of the film in fact can be understood as reacting to that earlier success: its choice of settings, its subdued Mrs. Bennet, its unnerving and uncomic Mr. Collins are only some examples. But in this matter of Mr. Darcy's appearance, the film reproduces, with even more emphasis, the conception of the 1995 version. In other words, it produces a reading of Mr. Darcy which concentrates, as did that earlier adaptation, on Darcy's compelling sexual attraction to Elizabeth. The early scenes of the BBC version constantly revert to Darcy's looking at Elizabeth, but he looks at her not with a smile but with a smolder. Overwhelming desire, troubling him because it is in conflict with social position and self-image, seems to be conveyed in his look. In the 2005 version this conflict has intensified. Miserable awkwardness at the Assembly escalates, as the film continues, into looks in which compulsion is fused with distress.

Pride and Prejudice is certainly the text of Jane Austen in which looking is most important. In the first few chapters Darcy's frequent, near-obsessive, staring at Elizabeth catches her attention, and her own appearance is continually referred to. The whole question of reading character from looks is introduced early with Mr. Darcy himself:

> Mr. Darcy soon drew the attention of the room by his fine, tall person, handsome features, noble mien; and the report which was in general circulation within five minutes after his entrance, of his having ten thousand a year. The gentlemen pronounced him to be a fine figure of a man, the ladies declared he was much handsomer than Mr. Bingley, and he was looked at in great admiration for about half the evening, till his manners gave a disgust which turned the tide of his popularity; for he was discovered to be proud, to be above his company, and above being pleased; and not all his large estate in Derbyshire could then save him from having a most forbidding, disagreeable countenance, and being unworthy to be compared with his friend [I, 1, 10–11].

Whatever the warning implied here, Jane Austen does induce one to imagine Darcy's appearance—not from his contrast with Bingley, though, but with Wickham. When Elizabeth first observes Darcy and Wickham encountering each other, "Both changed colour, one looked white, the other red"—and the reader may experience a momentary hesitation as to which is which (I, 15, 81). Wickham is established as having a "very pleasing address" (I, 15,

81) a man, as Elizabeth thinks, whose "very countenance may vouch for [his] being amiable and good natured." On the other hand, despite the playfulness with which the narrator stresses how unreliable conclusions about character can be when drawn from appearances, it is probable that a reader's conception of a "striking resemblance" of Mr. Darcy would be of a stiff, proud, austerely detached man, perhaps not unlike his great uncle, the judge. Whatever else the novel has trained the reader to think of him, it is not as gallant or sweet tempered or amiable.

Darcy's smile is an instance of what Ariane Hudelet calls the "body language" of Austen's novels, in Chapter 3. Jane Austen is usually very sparing of physical description. But by "body language" Hudelet suggests the signals that Jane Austen, in an abbreviated and telegraphic way, inserts into her novels to communicate meanings that supplement, or sometimes are at odds with, the verbal exchanges. It's actually facial language, however, that counts in *Pride and Prejudice*. Important examples occur, for example, when Elizabeth is embarrassed by her mother's impertinence and rudeness. She "blushes for her mother" when Mrs. Bennet misunderstands Darcy's comments about life in the country (1, 9, 47). When Mrs. Bennet at the Netherfield ball rattles on about the prospect of Jane marrying Mr. Bingley and indirectly insults Mr. Darcy, Elizabeth tries repeatedly to stop her, but without success: "Her mother would talk of her views [meaning her schemes] in the same intelligible tone. Elizabeth blushed and blushed again with shame and vexation." Well she might, as she notices the expression on Darcy's face "change gradually from indignant contempt to a composed and steady gravity"(1, 19, 111–12). This deep, visceral response is not merely caused by her mother's interference in Jane's life.

Perhaps as interesting is the novel's suggestion of an affinity between Mrs. Bennet and her least dear daughter. *Pride and Prejudice* continually shows Mrs. Bennet pushing herself into her daughters' affairs, as when Jane receives a note from Netherfield. "Mrs. Bennet's eyes sparkled with pleasure" because she assumes, wrongly, that it comes from Bingley, Jane's marriage prospect. Soon, Mr. Bennet, relishing the mystery he is creating, tells the family to expect a visitor and once again, "Mrs. Bennet's eyes sparkled." No other indication of her physical being is given except her "sparkling" eyes. Is there then a connection between Mrs. Bennet's eyes and those "fine eyes" of her daughter which are noticed by Mr. Darcy and kept before the reader in Miss Bingley's jealous taunts? One might suspect that Elizabeth's acute feelings in her mother's presence are the result of their consanguinity, their affinity—perhaps of the fact that in her forwardness, her baffled energies, Mrs. Bennet is an embodied caricature of her daughter's own transgressive high spirits.[5]

No doubt that is taking it too far. I introduce the idea here because it may suggest that this novel, which the author herself described as "rather too light & bright & sparkling,"[6] may actually have hidden recesses or depths which bear on the question of Mr. Darcy's smile. "Such a smile as [Elizabeth] remembered to have sometimes seen." What kind of smile was that? Condescending? Grateful? Enigmatic? Shy? Perhaps. Ironic? Mocking, more likely: "He has a very satirical eye," says Elizabeth to Charlotte, but then again, she may be teasing, or she may be projecting her own embarrassment (I, 6, 26). The narrative contains nothing but the dialogue. And the fact that Darcy smiles several times in the text does not in fact actually resolve the issue I am intent on pursuing.

The first occurs in the midst of the awkward conversation already referred to, in which Mrs. Bennet dominates the floor—all the more difficult for Elizabeth because her mother has initially stepped in to support her daughter against Darcy's apparent disparagement of country life. "I wonder," says Elizabeth, hastening to divert the conversation from her mother, "who first discovered the efficacy of poetry in driving away love!"

> "I have been used to consider poetry as the *food* of love," said Darcy.
> "Of a fine, stout, healthy love it may. Every thing nourishes what is strong already. But if it be only a slight, thin sort of inclination, I am convinced that one good sonnet will starve it entirely away."
> Darcy only smiled: and the general pause which ensued made Elizabeth tremble lest her mother should be exposing herself again [I, 9, 49].

Does the last quoted sentence mean "Only Darcy smiled—alone among the group it was Darcy who smiled?" This is quite plausible, given that the rest of the sentence apparently separates him from the other people present. Or does it mean, in effect, "Darcy might have laughed, but he smiled and that was all"? It is safe to say that the second alternative is the one assumed by almost all readers. The reader will scarcely notice, or not reckon with, this smile. Why?

The exchange is arranged so that the reader's sympathies are all with Elizabeth. She needs to distinguish herself from her mother, and she does this by the exercise of her wit—a wit which presumes an alliance with Darcy as a cultivated man who will recognize this and respond to her—as he does in his allusion to the first line of *Twelfth Night*. If the reader "sees" (or fleetingly imagines) his smile, it will be as merely polite or cold—hence the ensuing pause. This is because he or she has been conditioned by Mrs. Bennet's presence to share Elizabeth's apprehensions that the conversation is likely to embarrass her still further, and is thus ready to find Mr. Darcy non-responsive. Elizabeth's nervousness is captured in a rather stridently witty response, and Darcy's reaction is also perhaps keyed into the awkwardness of the situation. Darcy thus is presented here as giving minimal encouragement to Elizabeth's wit, maintaining a distant, controlled interest, but no more. The dominant feeling in the scene which stops Elizabeth (and the reader) from registering Darcy's smile is her fear that her mother will "expose" herself again.

I am tracing two distinct psychological processes here—the imagined inner life of a fictional character, and the actual trajectory or history of the reader's responses. But these two phenomena engage, like gears, to increase each other's power in passages like this. Theoretically (and as it turns out, correctly) it would be possible to read Mr. Darcy's smile as a signal that only he, of all the group, recognizes and appreciates Elizabeth's wit. It is certainly possible for a (re)reader to step back from the imagined situation, to note and remember Mr. Darcy's smile. But that would be to disengage, to pull against the drive of the text.

In Joe Wright's film, this exchange takes place at the Assembly. Darcy has already rejected Elizabeth, but there are indications amid the rowdy mêlée that he is seeking her, and when the camera tracks Mrs. Bennet hurrying through the crowd towards Jane and her sister, it discovers Darcy standing at left within the group. The dialogue at first follows the novel quite closely. Darcy says, "I thought that poetry was the food of love." Elizabeth replies with her joke about sonnets scaring away lovers. Darcy does not smile, but asks instead, "So what do you recommend to encourage affection?" To which Elizabeth replies "Dancing. Even if one's partner is hardly tolerable." The camera rests on Darcy's reaction to this impertinence. It is difficult to interpret, but one thing is certain—there is no smile on his face.

In this very conversation, Elizabeth declares, "People themselves alter so much, that there is something new to be observed in them forever" (I , 9, 47). One of the reasons, in fact, why *Pride and Prejudice* is such an engaging novel is that the conversations between Elizabeth and Darcy constantly challenge the reader's powers of interpretation. This was pointed out long ago in a famous essay, Reuben Brower's "Light and Bright and Sparkling." He wrote of "Austen's keen sense of the variability of character ..., her awareness of the possibility that the same remark or action has very different meanings in different relations. What most satisfies us in reading the dialogue in *Pride and Prejudice* is Jane Austen's awareness that it is difficult to know any complex person, that knowledge of a man like Darcy is an interpretation and a construction, not a simple absolute."[7] Sometimes, that is to say, we read these conversations one way, sometimes another: coming back to the book, there is something new to be observed, or construed, forever.

Jane Austen famously "lopt and cropt"[8] her text before sending it for publication, and it may be that some of the ambiguity or, to use a more exact term, undecideability of the dialogue is due to the stripping away of a narrator's interpretive comments. In the next chapter of *Pride and Prejudice* there is another example. During the evening at Netherfield, Darcy is teased not by Elizabeth but by Bingley, which could lead to very different conclusions about his character from those which Elizabeth in fact seems to draw:

> "I declare I do not know a more aweful object than Darcy, on particular occasions, and in particular places; at his own house especially, and of a Sunday evening when he has nothing to do."
> Mr. Darcy smiled; but Elizabeth thought she could perceive he was rather offended; and therefore checked her laugh [I, 10, 55].

Was he offended or not? Should this be read with the emphasis on "*thought*" (so that "thought she could perceive" becomes a clear hint that she is not as good an interpreter of Darcy as she thinks)? But the author lets Elizabeth get away with it. Is Darcy really "offended"? One assumes that he is. But the fact that his close friend teases him before a comparative stranger ought at least to qualify the assumption which Elizabeth makes here, and expresses in the next dialogue, that Darcy is "not to be laughed at," or that he is unable to take a joke. He certainly smiles, but somehow that smile is erased in the shift to Elizabeth's interpretation.[9]

What I'm interested in is how the novel excludes the reader from perception of what they are reading. The next occasion in which Darcy smiles occurs in the exchange which follows:

> "Mr. Darcy is not to be laughed at!" cried Elizabeth. "That is an uncommon advantage, and uncommon I hope it will continue, for it would be a great loss to me, to have many such acquaintance. I dearly love a laugh."
> "Miss Bingley," said he, "has given me credit for more than can be. The wisest and best of men, nay, the wisest and best of their actions, may be rendered ridiculous by a person whose first object in life is a joke" [1, 11, 62].

The conversation continues in this pattern: Elizabeth vivaciously exaggerating and provoking, Darcy correcting her with sober, thoughtful comments—responses which in their apparent humorlessness amuse her still more. At its center is Darcy's account of his own nature: "My feelings are not puffed about with every attempt to move them. My good opinion once lost is lost for ever." Elizabeth, of course, jumps on this: "*That* is a failing indeed!" "Implacable resentment *is* a shade in a character." Warming to the attack, she goes on,

> "And *your* defect is a propensity to hate every body."
> "And yours," he replied with a smile, "Is wilfully to misunderstand them" [I, 11, 63].

Because of the contrast between the severity of Darcy's remark and the smile, this might be the occasion when Elizabeth takes most notice of his facial expression. But what in fact does Darcy's smile mean here? It might be a way of putting an end to the conversation, politely recognizing that she has gone a bit far. It could also be that smiling qualifies the severity of his remark—turning it, in fact, into a kindly gesture, matching Elizabeth's bold speech by an equivalent exaggeration. In the 1980 BBC version, which reproduces this dialogue accurately, Mr. Darcy does smile, slightly, and the camera cuts to dwell for a moment on Elizabeth's reaction to his rebuke. This interprets the moment quite differently from the novel, where the dialogue is broken into by the comically jealous Miss Bingley, crying, "Do let us have a little music." The exchange is left hanging in the air, unexplained and enigmatic. The absence of any account of Elizabeth's emotions is intrinsic to the effect: it allows readers to forget what has just been read.

Elizabeth, five chapters time later, all ears, listens to Wickham's account of Darcy:

> "I had not thought Mr. Darcy so bad as this—though I have never liked him, I had not thought so very ill of him—I had supposed him to be despising his fellow-creatures in general, but did not suspect him of descending to such malicious revenge, such injustice, such inhumanity as this!"
>
> After a few minutes reflection, however, she continued, "I *do* remember his boasting one day, at Netherfield, of the implacability of his resentments, of his having an unforgiving temper. His disposition must be dreadful" [1, 16, 90].

"There seems something more speakingly incomprehensible in the powers, the failures, the inequalities of memory, than in any other of our intelligences," Fanny Price is to suggest in Austen's next novel, *Mansfield Park* (II, 4, 243). Memory is indeed as volatile, unpredictable and complex as eighteenth-century psychologists since Locke have contended. Few people recall the exact words spoken in a conversation, and most remember much more exactly what they themselves have said, than what another person has said to them. Elizabeth here may be no exception to the rule. Darcy has in fact said, "My temper would perhaps be called resentful," but this, in context, is far from a boast. "Implacable resentment" is her phrase, her on the spot and boldly teasing exaggeration of his much more hesitant, nuanced account of his temperament. "Boasting" is a tendentious description, to say the least, of the tone and intention of that speech. Elizabeth, infatuated with the handsome and insinuating Wickham, entirely forgets that Darcy has corrected her misconstruction the moment she has made it. Is it a memory or, more properly, a mental revision, a "false memory" stimulated by the presence of Wickham?[10] Elizabeth "remembers" what is pertinent to, or called up by, the present moment. "Memory" and "imagination" are words which designate separate "intelligences," in Fanny Price's words; but in fact memory and imagination infuse and constantly recreate each other. With this conversation, *Pride and Prejudice* has introduced an instance of the layering of memory that is to play such a key role in the portrait scene at Pemberley.

Elizabeth's exchange with Wickham, however, effectively blankets, or erases, the earlier dialogue from the reader's own memory. It represses the precedent reality, as recorded in the text. This is engineered through the reference to "one day," which seems to date the occasion some time in the past. In the novel's time scheme it is less than a week, but because Jane Austen has introduced Mr. Collins's letter, his arrival, and the family's reactions to him in the subsequent five chapters, she has made a much longer interval appear to intervene. It is plausible that Elizabeth's recollection of an exchange that happened "one day," or quite some time ago, is reliable. A reader might just recognize the discrepancy between Elizabeth's statement here and the conversation read earlier, but because the exact tone or manner in which Darcy speaks of his nature is not recorded, it is likely that Elizabeth's revision or reconstitution will stand, at least for the time being. Is Elizabeth's recollection colored, and in effect produced, by the emotion of the moment, and Wickham's presence? Would she have somewhere or other a memory of the "true" (textually presented) conversation? These are complex psychological questions, which the novel does not answer.

During the exchange over the piano, much later in the novel, when Elizabeth and Darcy are both at Rosings, he smiles twice (II, 8, 196, 197). Elizabeth is more challenging to Darcy than ever. Wickham's story has confirmed her prejudices, and when Darcy comes towards the piano, and stations himself "so as to command a full view of the fair performer's countenance," she responds with polite aggression. She tells Darcy, in Fitzwilliam's company, that she could tell things about him that would "shock your relations to hear." His response is unperturbed: "'I am not afraid of you,' said he, smilingly." Then Elizabeth gives him a little lesson in good manners, suggesting that he could overcome the shyness which forbids him making himself pleasant to strangers:

> "My fingers," said Elizabeth, "do not move over this instrument in the masterly manner which I see so many women's do.... But then I have always supposed it to be my own fault—because I would not take the trouble of practising. It is not because I do not believe *my* fingers as capable as any other woman's of superior execution."
>
> Darcy smiled and said, "You are perfectly right. You have employed your time much better. No one admitted to the privilege of hearing you, can think any thing wanting. We neither of us perform to strangers" [II, 8, 197].

Once again Austen preserves the enigmatic quality of the conversation by having it cut off at this point by a rude interruption—here by Lady Catherine's calling out "to know what they were talking of." In this instance, the 1995 television version does allow Darcy a faint smile.

The evidence is clear. When Elizabeth, in front of the portrait, beholds "Mr. Darcy with such a smile over the face, as she remembered to have sometimes seen when he looked at her," Jane Austen has not necessarily cheated. Mr. Darcy's smiles have been hiding there all along in the text, though—as I have been assuming—neither Elizabeth nor the reader has taken note of them. The question arises though as to what noticing them would mean. For something to be recovered in memory, it must first have been recognized in consciousness. Elizabeth, the fictional figure, must have registered Mr. Darcy's smiles, even though the novel has not allowed the reader, in turn, to register this fact. This is because the text normally gives no sign that Elizabeth has noticed, no indication of a reaction for the reader to identify with.

But the last occasion when Darcy smiles is rather different. It occurs during the proposal scene. Elizabeth angrily informs him that she knows he interfered in Jane's romance with Bingley. "She paused, and saw with no slight indignation that he was listening with an air which proved him wholly unmoved by any feeling of remorse. He even looked at her with a smile of affected incredulity" (11, I, 213). This scene is written completely from Elizabeth's point of view—so much so that Darcy's proposal is merely reported, and its actual words obliterated, keeping the focus on Elizabeth's responses. Given what we know (or think we know) the reader is right behind her. She does react this time to his smile, and entirely accurate as her reading seems, she is probably mistaken. Darcy's is a smile, not of "affected" but of real incredulity. He is sure, as he later says in his letter (II, 12, 220) that Jane's feelings were not deeply involved. And is even possible that his smile, like some earlier, is a signal of his pleasure at her spiritedness. Perhaps this is the smile she recalls in front of the portrait?

If it is plain then not only that Darcy smiles, but that Jane Austen uses his smile as a recurrent motif or trope, what is the significance of this small discovery? What does Darcy's smile reveal about the relationship depicted in the novel? And what does the omission or elision of his smile in the recent film versions—and in much criticism—imply? And why do readers miss it?

Reading backwards from the novel's final chapters, some answers can be given. Darcy's smile means that he appreciates Elizabeth's wit. His smile means that he appreciates her courage and boldness. His smile means that he accepts her rebukes. It implies that he feels kindly towards her. All this in turn means that the relationship is not exclusively based on sexual attraction. "No sooner had he made it clear to himself and his friends that she had hardly a good feature in her face, than he began to find it was rendered uncommonly intelligent by the beautiful expression of her dark eyes" (I, 6, 25–6). This momentary excursion into Darcy's consciousness is important: in his attraction to Elizabeth physical beauty and intelligence are intertwined. The medium of the genteel prose novel represents that attraction as reciprocity of styles—style in its verbal sense, working metonymically to implicate embodiment. Darcy's smile represents an attraction to the "easy playfulness" of Elizabeth's manners, so different from those of every other woman he has known. It is conversation, banter, the exchange of wit and wisdom, vigorous verbal exchange that encourages Darcy's feelings for Elizabeth. Both of them enjoy it. And is it too obvious to say that the reader (this figure to whom I am continually resorting) enjoys it too?

In the 2005 film, the relation is depicted in a radically different way. Elizabeth and Darcy's sparring at the Netherfield ball leads to a sequence in which they appear to dance alone in the room. The camera swings around the lovers, first in one direction, then in the other, as they move towards the camera and back, to the accompaniment of high strings on the sound-track.[11] This creates a disorienting and troubling effect, but it makes a clear point. Before one condemns this depiction as a surreal departure from realism, it is worth noticing that *Pride and Prejudice*'s most vigorous conversational exchange between the two at Netherfield in Chapter 11 also appears to take place in a space occupied by them alone. Jane and Bingley, as well as Miss Bingley and the Hursts are actually supposed to be in the same room, but they vanish from the text, as the novel's attention focuses exclusively on Elizabeth and Darcy. The film sequence also picks up on the "gravity" (I, 18, 105) which ultimately characterizes the feelings of both participants in this dialogue (though Darcy opens it by smiling, once again, at Elizabeth's wit) and builds on the mutual silence which follows their conversational confrontation. It is indicating that there is, even at this early stage, a passionate, magnetic attraction that holds the two together. Dangerous and inconvenient, not necessarily productive of pleasure—that is why the camera moves so differently from that joyous kinship with the dance which is conveyed in so many other Austen ball scenes, for here the dance is a metaphor for a willless, disorienting linkage. The sequence is a kind of apotheosis of film, since (in complete contrast to the novel) an attraction represented in the text largely through verbal exchanges is here rendered completely wordless.

In its stress on overpowering sexual attraction the sequence copies the 1995 version. But the suggestion of mutuality in the magnetism is a difference. Darcy's stares at Elizabeth in 1995 are the stares of a man drawn by compulsive desire, and carefully, as in the novel, kept distinct from Elizabeth's responses to him. There is little hint of gracious amusement: instead there is a steady, unsmiling seriousness that registers the man's interest in Elizabeth, and at the same time his need to keep his feelings for her under control. And this does, of course, reflect a main emphasis of the novel: "In vain have I struggled. It will not do. My feelings will not be repressed" (II, I, 211), Darcy declares in opening his proposal. As I have been suggesting, *Pride and Prejudice* has contrived it so that many readers do not notice Mr. Darcy's smiles, with the result that this presentation of a Darcy who does not smile is a perfectly plausible reading of the text. But that means that Elizabeth has nothing to remember when she sees his picture.

The 1995 television version reproduces the sequencing of the visit to Pemberley almost meticulously. As in the novel, Elizabeth and the Gardiners see the house from the grounds; the housekeeper shows them the miniatures of Wickham and Darcy, and then praises Darcy as a kind master and a good brother; they climb stairs to the upper gallery; and finally Elizabeth is brought before the portrait. In the 1980 version, Elizabeth's précis of her thoughts in the novel is given in voice-over.[12] But in this film, the sequence concludes with Elizabeth standing, looking up at the portrait, perhaps half-smiling herself, and that is all. As she stands, the film cuts to show the gentleman riding towards Pemberley, and the now-notorious scene follows in which, sitting beside a pond, evidently troubled, he hesitates briefly and then, untying his cravat and taking off his jacket, dives in. In this sequence the film is certainly referencing the portrait, but its meaning is the converse of Austen's tracing of Elizabeth's thought processes. Instead, focusing on Darcy as rider and swimmer, filmed underwater, it underlines gendered status and privileges. Some feminist critics have appreciated this filmic intervention, praising it because, in a reversal of cultural commonplace, it offers the male body to the female gaze.[13] But it could be argued that by implicitly contrasting Darcy's free athleticism (and unappeased passions) with Elizabeth's transfixed, stationary admiration of the portrait, it re-enforces masculinist prerogatives. Bonneted, Elizabeth gazes at the picture. Because there is no anterior memory to be revived, her own moment is empty.

Other feminist critics have found the passage about the portrait troubling. Focusing on the later occasion when Elizabeth, returning to the portrait, "fixed his eyes upon herself," they have read this as a rendering of her capitulation to male dominance. "When she visits Pemberley and understands Darcy's power," Maaja Stewart writes, "she looks at his portrait and directs his gaze—which she had earlier avoided—upon herself, thus subjecting not only their shared experience but also herself to his interpretation."[14] Susan Fraiman similarly understands this moment as a key stage in what she defines as "the humiliation of Elizabeth Bennet." "Now her gaze sees only how she looks to him," she writes, which, "as with Darcy's letter ... seizes the

female reader and turns her into the object of its force and her own hatred"—
a "self-consciously strange" description which underlines the cost of female
reconciliation with patriarchal power.[15]

Comparing the 1995 episode with the novel, Erica Sheen, on the other
hand, reads Elizabeth as seizing power, and suggests that the film's transfer
of attention to Darcy "reproduces the curious episode of reversed spectator-
ship that occurs before the portrait of Darcy at Pemberley, where Elizabeth
'fixed his eyes upon herself ..., thought of his regard with a deeper sentiment
of gratitude ... and softened its impropriety of expression.' Note the force-
ful way Elizabeth takes Darcy's look, *and* its improprieties. Adequate grounds,
I think, for suggesting that making Darcy take his clothes off and dive into
the pond *at exactly the same moment* is faithful, passionately so, to the text's
concealed pleasure in its own promiscuity."[16] In other words, Elizabeth's taking possession of the portrait in fixing Darcy's eyes upon her licenses the
film to take possession of the novel and do what it likes with it. This suggestion only works because Sheen herself elides part of the text. "She thought
of his regard with a deeper sentiment of gratitude than it had ever raised
before; she remembered its warmth and softened its impropriety of expression." The idea that she is responding to "improprieties" in Darcy's look, in
the modern sense, is misleading; the "impropriety" is what she commented
on in the proposal scene by calling his manner "ungentlemanly." Darcy's
"regard" is predicated on his smile, but like the other critics I have mentioned,
Sheen ignores it.

This moment before the painting is the climactic visual encounter in
the novel and at first blush one would think a gift to a filmmaker. If Mr.
Darcy had been shown smiling in the previous encounters, it might have
been possible to treat it as the portrait of Frank Churchill is treated in the
1996 telefilm of *Emma*, for which Andrew Davies also wrote the script. Here
the image not only smiles, it steps out of the frame to greet the heroine.
Something needed to be done to bring the portrait to life, for Austen's rendering of Elizabeth's thoughts in her two visits to it is complex and intriguing. The smile on the portrait is the trigger: like the house itself and the
housekeeper's praises, it is external evidence which Elizabeth now feels she
needs to reconcile with her previous assumptions about Darcy. In this context, she understands that when he smiles at her from the portrait, a likeness
painted for his father, and for the family, he is showing his true personality
as it is known to them. So that when he smiled at her he was expressing the
genuine, if perhaps shy, amiability of his nature. When she fixes his eyes
upon herself, momentarily endowing the portrait with a kind of magical life,
she becomes not less, but more, fully a person. And this is because, adven-
turing into the past, recovering memories, is to deepen the self, to experi-

ence the self as existing in time. This still, internal moment in which memories secreted in the past flower into meaning in the present is not only a discovery for her, it is a discovery for her author, a precursor of the more complex sense of personality and memory in the later novels.

But in 2005, Wright's handling of the portrait scene takes quite a different route. Like Austen's novel, it crowns a structure built in the past narrative. Using the term suggested by Jan Fergus, one might call his film a "neopurist"[17] adaptation. Wright does not jettison the internal passage but instead reworks, rethinks and recreates it, so that some of the essential drama that Austen embeds in her prose account of Elizabeth's thoughts and feelings can be communicated through cinematic techniques. So there is no painting at Pemberley; instead there is a portrait bust in white stone among the other figures in what has now become the sculpture, rather than picture, gallery. Elizabeth is shown bemusedly wandering through it, statues disposed around her, some of them priceless Canovas, in polished white marble. In this beautifully conceived, filmed and edited sequence, takes merge and fade into each other, and render a visual equivalent of absorbed, dreamlike, contemplation. A bust of a veiled woman captures Elizabeth's attention: she moves on to a figure of a fallen gladiator, the camera showing the statue from the back, and allowing the viewer to imagine her glance as it passes over the nakedly exposed male body. Without over-emphasis, the sequence underscores the erotic aspect of Elizabeth's feelings about Darcy. The camera moves up the polished torso of another white figure, drawn into a kind of visual caress by its lustrous beauty. Elizabeth then sees a bust of Mr. Darcy. The camera, positioned behind, allows the viewer to see in her face the mixture of desire and regret that the film has already suggested must be present in her feelings during this visit.

The bust itself carries little suggestion of the smile that, in the novel, Elizabeth detects on the face in the portrait. She is still facing this image in this white, brightly lit salon, when the housekeeper and the Gardiners come upon her; and with the housekeeper's words, "This is he," the music that has accompanied this sequence reaches a climax, and suggests that an emotional turning point has been reached.[18] Elizabeth cannot, as in the novel, "fix his eyes upon her" since this is a marble bust where the eyes are empty globes, but the aesthetic pleasure communicated to the viewer by the graceful and almost sensuous movement of the camera, the romantic music and the statues, substitutes for, and almost turns into, that feeling of affinity which is Elizabeth's awakening love.

What Wright does with Mr. Darcy's smile is even more interesting. Darcy has been played as a proud, but shy and embarrassed man, made miserable by his unconventional passion. He has never once smiled. But in the next sequence, this pays off. As she drifts through grand salons, Elizabeth's hands touch and caress various *objets d'art*. "In the alchemy of love," Robert Polhemus writes of the Pemberley chapters, "the material and the immaterial can be transmuted."[19] She hears sounds of piano music and is lured to a room where, as she perceives in a mirror through a half-open door, Georgiana Darcy is playing. Suddenly, Darcy is present in the reflected glass. (Why a mirror? Because a mirror, like a portrait, is a mediation of reality). The image she has seen in the gallery, white and immobile, is instantly animated as Darcy teases and romps with his sister. He is not only smiling, he is laughing. Elizabeth sees him now (as she had imagined him in front of the portrait) at home, kind, loving, happy in his family. As Darcy laughs with his sister, the mirror discloses the Darcy of the portrait commissioned by his father. Thus the delayed notice of Mr. Darcy's smile which contributes to the portrait scene's importance as turning point in the novel is transformed, now not into a recovered memory, but a glad, postponed recognition.

Why then doesn't a reader "see" Darcy smiling in the novel? An important signifier is continually repeated in the text, but somehow not taken into consciousness. The obvious answer must be because *Pride and Prejudice* seduces the reader into taking Elizabeth's point of view. Though the novels have much in common, this one works quite differently from *Emma*, where only readers dumber than Harriet Smith will fail, for instance, to read the signs that the heroine is mistaken about Mr. Elton's designs. The truth is that almost everything in the novel's first volume, at least, contrives to make the reader adopt Elizabeth's attitudes. This "everything" includes her vivacity, her wit, her cheekiness, and her attractive difference from the standard accomplished young lady. But most of all, as I have hinted earlier, it's because of the presence of her mother. Mrs. Bennet activates every adolescent's fear of being identified with his or her parent of the same sex, every adolescent's need to separate themselves from their family.[20] Such intense feelings do not disappear in adulthood, but—like Elizabeth's before Darcy's picture—lie in wait to be activated, to be revived by the work of art, in the portrait that is the novel. This "light & bright & sparkling" comedy, then, draws on deep and instinctive human sources. Magicked into Elizabeth's family romance, in which everything makes this vibrant, intelligent young woman fight to establish her own style, her independence, her freedom, the reader has no energy or time to spare on the other side of her confrontations. Because we are all young at heart whilst we read *Pride and Prejudice*, we miss the significance of Mr. Darcy's smile.

This chapter is dedicated with love to Jo Barnes.

6

Reinventing Fanny Price: Patricia Rozema's Thoroughly Modern *Mansfield Park*

DAVID MONAGHAN

Academic criticism of Jane Austen's novels has taken a radical turn during the last twenty-five years as scholars have constructed an Austen who is our contemporary in her treatment of gender, sexuality, including incest and lesbianism, ideology and colonialism.[1] Recent film and television adaptations of Austen's novels intermittently demonstrate a similar revisionist spirit, as is evidenced by the overt sexuality in *Pride and Prejudice* (1995), explicit ideological conflicts in *Jane Austen's "Emma"* (1996), and feminist elements in *Sense and Sensibility* (1995) and *Persuasion* (1995). By and large, though, as White argues,[2] filmmakers have remained stubbornly traditional in their approach to Austen, with the result that her complex texts have been reduced to amusing and romantic stories played out within a mise en scène made up largely of nostalgic images of Regency England.[3]

Apart from *Clueless* (1995), Amy Heckerling's postmodern appropriation of *Emma*, the only film to have been significantly shaped by contemporary critical thought is *Mansfield Park* (1999), written and directed by Patricia Rozema. The influence of recent scholarship, most notably Claudia Johnson's *Jane Austen*, is particularly conspicuous in Rozema's presentation of Sir Thomas Bertram as a domineering patriarch and cruel, sexually-abusive slave owner; Mary Crawford as a bi-sexual; and Fanny Price as a committed feminist/abolitionist who suffers the incestuous attentions of both her father and her uncle. Ultimately, though, Rozema, who is, after all, an artist rather than a scholar, takes liberties with *Mansfield Park* that no critic would contemplate. There is, for instance, not even the most tenuous textual evidence to support her decision to offer drug addiction as the cause of Lady Bertram's apathy—clearly identified by Austen as a genetic trait that she shares with

111

her sister, Mrs. Price, whose "disposition [is also] naturally easy and indolent" (*MP* III, 8, 451)—or, more important, for her transformation of
Austen's "inhibited, and frail" Fanny Price into the film's "sturdy, self possessed ..., plucky, and physically energetic"[4] heroine.

In adapting *Mansfield Park* for the screen, Rozema rejected the model
provided by the Fanny Price of the novel because she considered her "annoy-
ing," "not fully drawn,"[5] and altogether "too slight and retiring and internal
and perhaps judgmental to shoulder a film."[6] In her place she creates a character intended to express the "anarchic spirit"[7] of the Jane Austen who wrote
scurrilously satirical juvenilia and chose the life of an artist in preference to
the safe option of marriage. The inspiration for Rozema's radical interpretation of Fanny Price is to be found not just in her dissatisfaction with the
character as she appears in the novel, but also in her determination to demonstrate Austen's compatibility with modern liberal attitudes. However, there
is something rather questionable about an approach that privileges a portrait of the author over her fictional creation, especially when that portrait
both conflates the teenage Austen with the mature woman who wrote
Mansfield Park and makes highly selective use of biographical evidence.[8] It
is not surprising, therefore, that if we remove the obstructing figure of
Rozema's "Jane Austen" from our field of vision, a relationship between film
and source text emerges that is rooted in difference rather than in similar-
ity. The fundamental nature of this difference emerges with particular clarity from a comparison of the movement motifs that play an important part
in the structure of both novel and film.

Regardless of the subversive tendencies that critics have uncovered in
her novels, Austen, owes a great deal ideologically to the kind of eighteenth-
century conservatism that is most effectively expressed in the works of the
philosopher-politician, Edmund Burke, particularly *Reflections on the Revolution in France*.[9] As a Burkeian conservative, she is committed to an organi-
cist model of individual and social growth in which innovation and rapid
change are rejected in favor of principles of "conservation and correction."[10]
In *Mansfield Park*, Austen is therefore equally critical of the physical and
intellectual immobility of Lady Bertram and the restless energy of the Crawfords, Tom and Maria Bertram, and Mrs. Norris.[11] The middle ground
between these two extremes is occupied by the person who is mobile but
who moves in such a way as to foster group harmony rather than to satisfy
personal desires. This ideal was given ritual expression in the longways country dance, the most popular of all the dance forms during Austen's adult
years.[12] Thus, when performed in the "sedate"[13] manner with which Austen
would have been familiar from her attendance at formal balls held in the
Bath Assembly Rooms, the country dance required its individual participants

to execute precisely choreographed movements that combined with those of their fellow dancers to create intricate and aesthetically pleasing patterns. As Alison Thompson reminds us, dancing was taken so seriously as a mirror of individual and social excellence that "in Regency as in former times, it was felt that the skill of a person's dancing expressed the quality of his or her soul or spirit ..., and one measure of determining whether a man was truly a gentleman was by his ability to dance with confidence."[14] The specific Burkeian values expressed by the measured motion of the gentleman's dance performance include a respect for custom and tradition, adherence to a code based on duty and obligation to others, the maintenance of clear distinctions between ranks and of a complex system of manners, an awareness of the country estate's centrality in the community's life, and the cultivation of reflective and rational patterns of thought.

Although balls and informal private dances play a part in all of her novels, Austen never describes the structure of country dancing in detail. Nevertheless, she was clearly aware of its social significance. This awareness is evident both in Austen's tendency to mirror her conservative themes in novelistic structures that derive from aspects of the country dance and to judge her characters according to either their grasp of ballroom etiquette or their performance on the dance floor.[15] In this context, it is significant that Fanny Price, the only character in *Mansfield Park* who consistently models Austen's Burkeian conception of the socially responsible individual, wins general approval at the Mansfield ball for the "modest[y]" and "gentle[ness]" (II, 10, 321) of her dancing, which presumably lives up to Henry Crawford's image of her "gliding about with quiet, light elegance, and in admirable time" (II, 7, 291). An exploration of the complex process by means of which Austen's heroine moves from a passive and hence morally impotent position on the fringes of Mansfield society to one in which she stands at the very top of the great social dance, thereby fully embodying the macrocosmic implications of her accomplished ballroom performance, provides a solid foundation for a reasoned response to Rozema's view that Fanny Price is "not fully drawn."

Far from valuing measured movement, let alone the periods of quiet reflection and reading that serve as necessary precursors to responsible social involvement in Austen's world, our age is obsessed with speed and efficiency. Fast food chains compete to shave a few seconds off the time it takes to serve a hamburger, new fashions appear monthly, and personal computers operate at ever-faster speeds. As social commentators have observed, nowadays "the fast eat the slow." "Speed is increasingly equated with efficiency," and thus, "haste, once a vice, is a virtue."[16] Given her determination to demonstrate Austen's contemporary credentials, it is not surprising, then, that Rozema chose to displace a heroine who is easily worn out by moderate walking and never moves faster or more spontaneously than is permitted by the rhythms and patterns of a country dance, with one who is hasty and impulsive, and who cherishes the feeling of freedom offered by reckless horse-back riding. In Rozema's *Mansfield Park,* stillness and limited movement have no positive connotations and are usually equated with entrapment.

People who take the view that adaptations, particularly of canonical works, should remain faithful to the originating text dislike Rozema's *Mansfield Park* because of its revisionist approach to Austen's main character. Others, who are perhaps more aware of the considerable literature challenging the demand for fidelity,[17] admire Rozema for the forthright manner in which she modernizes the novel. Such judgments are, of course, largely dependent on the expectations that viewers bring to bear on the film. Whether or not the film actually succeeds has far more to do, I will be arguing in the rest of this chapter, with the extent to which Rozema can make a plot and a conclusion lifted fairly directly from the novel function as vehicles for the expression of a world view quite alien in some important respects to Austen's. In order to answer this question, it is necessary to look more closely at the significance attributed to movement in the novel and film versions of *Mansfield Park.*

Movement in Jane Austen's Mansfield Park

In *Mansfield Park,* Jane Austen demonstrates a complex and sophisticated understanding of the social and moral significance of a wide range of ways—physical, intellectual, and emotional—in which human beings either remain still or move. There are, for example, at least three types of stillness in the novel: Lady Bertram's self-indulgent lethargy, Fanny's passive response to behavior that her active moral faculties identify as objectionable, and Fanny's later stubborn persistence in refusing to compromise her emotional and moral integrity by accepting Henry Crawford's marriage proposal. Whereas Lady Bertram is little more than an allegorical figure for the lack of female agency fostered by a patriarchal society, Fanny's stillness is sufficiently complex in both of its phases to merit detailed examination.

Tom Bertram has little patience with his young cousin's timidity and describes Fanny as a "creepmouse" (I, 15, 171). A more perceptive observer might have taken note of the importance of environment in shaping Fanny's behavior. The active role Fanny played at home in Portsmouth—where she served as "play-fellow, instructress, and nurse" (I, 2, 16) to her siblings— demonstrates that she is not by nature passive. Fanny's failure to be "useful" (I, 4, 40) to the Bertrams must therefore be attributed to the circumstances she encounters after moving to Mansfield Park, most significantly to the ambiguous position, somewhere between the family and the servants, into which she is forced by the malign Mrs. Norris.[18]

Although relegated to the role of passive bystander by her uncertain status amongst the Bertrams, Fanny never allows herself to become intellectually inert. On the contrary, she uses her periods of enforced solitude to pursue a program of reading designed to cultivate the sound principles and good judgment needed to balance her lively imagination. However, such qualities are of limited value unless they can be put to practical use. For this to happen, periods of quiet reflection must be followed by opportunities for social engagement. No one is more aware than Fanny of the limitations of her isolated and frozen position on the fringe of the Bertrams' family circle. In her imagination, she is always mobile and sometimes travels vast distances—to China (I, 16, 183) and even to the stars (II, 9, 304). In real life, however, while she takes every opportunity to cater to the whims of her pampered aunt, Fanny never achieves the degree of acceptance required to exercise a moral influence on Mansfield society. The feelings of impotence created by her isolation become particularly intense during the rehearsals for *Lovers' Vows*. Thus, although she disapproves of the whole enterprise, Fanny feels envious of the "consequence" that accrues to Mrs. Grant for taking on the part of Cottager's wife: "She alone was sad and insignificant; she had no share in any thing" (I, 17, 187).

The larger social implications of Fanny's lack of a meaningful role within her social milieu are made particularly obvious by the trip to Sotherton. Fanny owes her inclusion in the touring party entirely to Edmund's intervention, and once he abandons her in the wilderness, she is "left to her solitude" (I, 10, 116), powerless to intervene as Edmund sets off on a "serpentine course" (I, 9, 110) with Mary, and Maria breaks the bounds of her fiancé's estate in order to be alone with Henry: "Her cousin was safe on the other side [of the ha-ha], while [Fanny's] words were spoken" (I, 10, 116).

A period of active social participation with a concomitant increase in consequence, which I discuss below, ends, somewhat ironically, with Fanny once again immobilized as a result of her refusal to become engaged to Henry Crawford. This time, though, in contrast to the situation she experienced at Sotherton when she was ignored and left to sit alone on a bench, Fanny is now the focus of everyone's attention. As far as the Bertram family and Mary Crawford are concerned, Fanny has been presented with an opportunity to secure her future through marriage to a most eligible young man, and they repeatedly press her to move in the direction opened up by Henry. Fanny Price's response to Henry is, of course, complicated by her secret love for Edmund Bertram. However, we should never lose sight of the fact that, far from being a screen designed to conceal the real target of her affections,

Fanny's statement that "I cannot approve his character" is the product of a clear-sighted judgment based primarily but not exclusively on Henry's "behaving ... improperly and unfeelingly" (III, 4, 404) towards Rushworth and Maria during the theatricals. So far as Fanny is concerned, Henry Crawford is so deficient in "feeling and humanity where his own pleasure [is] concerned" that "had her own affections been as free—as perhaps they ought to have been—he never could engaged them" (III, 2, 379). Clearly, then, the source of Fanny's unwillingness to respond to Henry's romantic overtures is to be found in neither a debilitating passivity nor an already engaged heart, but in her firm moral commitment to preserve the traditional values associated with Mansfield Park from further erosion by the Crawfords. As Tanner puts it, "in her stillness [Fanny] is not inactive," and "her resolute immobility ... is a last gesture of resistance against the corrosions of unfettered impulse and change."[19]

By holding firm, even during a period of difficult exile in Portsmouth, Fanny eventually sets in motion a sequence of events that culminates in the salvation of Mansfield Park. Henry tires of Fanny's resistance and elopes with Maria; Mary's complaisant attitude to her brother's behavior breaks the spell she has cast over Edmund; both Lady Bertram, who meets her on her return to Mansfield with "no indolent step" and the words, "Dear Fanny! now I shall be comfortable" (III, 15, 517), and Sir Thomas, for whom she has become "the daughter that he wanted" (III, 17, 546), at last acknowledge Fanny's worth and accept her as a full member of the Bertram family; Maria and Mrs. Norris are exiled from Mansfield; and Edmund finally proposes marriage, thus allowing Fanny to complete her personal journey by acquiring a social status that is her due in terms of both personal worth and birth.[20]

Just as she is careful to discriminate between different types of stillness, Austen also draws distinctions between the more active role Fanny plays in the period following Maria's wedding and the behavior of the novel's other energetic characters. It requires the absence of Maria, Julia, and Henry Crawford to open up space for Fanny within the Bertrams' social circle. However, once she is given a chance to become socially involved, Fanny quickly learns to mount a lively, appealing and occasionally assertive performance that wins her the admiring notice of Sir Thomas Bertram and the romantic attentions of Henry Crawford. Even more important, Fanny is generally successful in maintaining an appropriate balance between fulfilling her own desires—as expressed by her "audacious[ly] independent[t]" (I, 4, 251) acceptance (admittedly dependent on Edmund's mediation) of an invitation to dine at the parsonage—and the need to maintain group harmony. Given that Fanny proves herself to be such a skillful social dancer, it is particularly appropriate that her official entry into the world should take the form of a coming-out ball organized in her honor by Sir Thomas. "Young, pretty, and gentle" (III, 10, 321), and in a state of "high spirits" (II, 10, 317), Fanny conducts herself at the ball in such a way as to win "general favour" (II, 10, 321).

Mary and Henry Crawford's movements are not only quicker but qualitatively different from Fanny's. Whereas she conforms to prescribed patterns of socially responsible behavior, they are motivated almost entirely by self-interest. Mary and Henry move not because they wish to be part of a social dance but because they are seeking fresh sources of stimulation for minds and bodies grown jaded by too much self-indulgence. Henry, despite owning an estate at Everingham, neither has nor desires "permanence of abode"—the "limitation of society" (I, 4, 47) that would result from a fixed residence could only be tedious for a man uninterested in buckling down to the duties of the responsible landowner. Instead, he "loves to be doing" (I, 6, 67) and is always seeking "change" (I, 12, 136) and "bustle" (II, 5, 262). Henry is never happier than when his "hands [are] full of business" (II, 7, 279), even if the business amounts to nothing more important than managing Lady Bertram's and Fanny's cards as well as his own during a game of Speculation. However, none of Henry's schemes—which range from the improvement of Everingham to the seduction of Maria Bertram and the courtship of Fanny Price—nor the succession of brilliant roles he assumes can sustain him for very long. Indeed, the more active and inventive his imagination becomes, and the quicker he executes his plans, the more rapidly Henry is "a devourer of [his] own" "happiness" (I, 6, 72). Henry's fate, it would seem, is to go faster and faster in order to gain less and less satisfaction until he is finally left to confront the void at the centre of his existence.

Mary Crawford is not given to such erratic changes of personality and direction as her brother, but she is almost as restless. Like Henry, Mary gets great satisfaction from "bustle" (I, 11, 128), and she considers "tranquillity" to be "tediousness" and "vexation" (II, 2, 331). In marked contrast to Fanny, Mary is unable to remain still for more than the briefest time in the wilderness at Sotherton, even when there is no advantage to be gained by altering her position: "'I must move,' said she, 'resting fatigues me.—I have looked across the ha-ha till I am weary. I must go and look through that iron gate at the same view, without being able to do it so well'" (I, 9, 112).

Whereas the Crawfords move freely because they lack an anchor, Maria's longing for "independence..., liberty..., [and] bustle," is rooted in a need to "escape" from the "restraint" (II, 3, 236) imposed first by her father and then by her husband, Rushworth. For her, Mansfield Park and Sotherton are "prison[s]" (I, 6, 62), and she compares herself to the caged bird in Laurence Sterne's *A Sentimental Journey* that "cannot get out" (I, 10, 116). Because she is almost entirely motivated by a desire to flee unwelcome confinement, Maria rarely gives sufficient thought to the direction in which her movement might take her. An ill-judged marriage to a fool is followed by an elopement with the untrustworthy Henry Crawford, as a result of which, far from achieving personal liberation, Maria is finally condemned to be "shut up together" with Mrs. Norris in a "remote and private" "establishment" (III, 17, 538).

Unlike the Crawfords and Maria, Mrs. Norris, *Mansfield Park*'s final "busy" (I, 12, 141) character, intends her "bustle" to express an "anxiety for every body's comfort" (II, 1, 211). The Bertram sisters in particular and Mansfield Park in general are the constant objects of Mrs. Norris's attention, and she proclaims herself ready at any moment to make "sacrifices" in the form of "hurried walks and sudden removals from her own fire-side" to ensure the "interest and comfort of [the Bertram] family" (II, 2, 220). Taken at her own estimate, Mrs. Norris shares Fanny's commitment to socially useful action. In reality, though, it matters far more to this solipsistic woman that she convey an appearance of importance than that she be of genuine service to others. Her bustling has a momentum of its own and is rarely motivated by the Bertrams' real needs. Rather than achieving productive ends, Mrs. Norris's pointless bouts of activity frequently upset what was previously stable, as is the case with her "fresh arranging and injuring the noble fire which the butler had prepared" (II, 10, 317). When Maria elopes and a real crisis arises, Mrs. Norris deflates like a balloon and is of no use to anyone.

Because the object of this book is to examine Austen's cinematic dimensions, my analysis of *Mansfield Park* has focused on ways in which the novel exploits what is, by the very nature of a medium that relies so heavily on moving images, one of the most powerful tools available to the filmmaker: the metonymic potential of actual movement (in Austen's case, of course, mental as well as physical) and its opposite, stillness. However, my analysis would be incomplete if I did not draw attention to the part played in Austen's development of her movement motif in *Mansfield Park* by tropes of motion that are more literary than cinematic. The word "bewildered" is, for example, used both metonymically and metaphorically to convey Austen's disapproval of uncontrolled movement. When Henry Crawford says of the day at Sotherton, "we were all walking after each other and bewildered" (II, 7, 285), he is trying to come up with an innocuous explanation for his mysterious disappearance with Maria Bertram and obviously intends the word to carry the literal meaning of "to stray" or "be lost." However, the structure of Henry's sentence also allows "bewildered" to be taken in the more common metaphorical sense of "to confuse in mental perception." Used in this way, "bewildered" accentuates rather than diverts attention from Henry's lack of firm moral principles and convinces the reader that neither his intentions, nor perhaps his actual behavior with regards to Maria during their clandestine outing beyond the boundaries of her fiancé's estate were in the least innocent. Later, when Edmund says that Mary Crawford's mind has been "led astray and bewildered" (III, 6, 423), his use of the term is entirely metaphorical. However, by juxtaposing "bewildered" with the more obvious metaphor of movement contained in the phrase "led astray," Austen is reminding readers of the literal meaning of bewildered, and is thus once again establishing a connection between uncontrolled motion and moral or mental confusion.

The experience of bewilderment is not limited to characters who indulge in uncontrolled motion but also extends to anyone who is caught up in its tumultuous wake. Sir Thomas, for example, is described as "bewildered" (II, 1, 214) when he returns home from Antigua, anxious for "quietness" and "the repose of his own family-circle" (II, 3, 230), only to be confronted by the "general air of confusion" (II, 1, 213) created by the theatricals, a project originating in the restless energy of the Crawfords and the younger Bertrams. In the course of a quickly moving sequence that perfectly matches physical disorientation and mental confusion, thereby blending the two meanings of bewildered, Sir Thomas is first "astonished" by "the removal of the book-case from before the billiard room door," then "rejoice[s]" at "having the means of immediate communication" required to investigate the strange "hallooing" emanating from the room, and, finally, in a moment of total disorientation, "finds himself on the stage of a [completely unfamiliar] theatre" where he is confronted by "a ranting young man, who appeared likely to knock him down backwards" (II, 1, 213). The word "bewildered" is also used in reference to Fanny Price immediately following her arrival in Portsmouth: "she sat in bewildered, broken, sorrowful contemplation" (III, 7, 442). The reader thus becomes aware that Fanny has escaped the turbulence whirling around Mansfield Park only to come up against new threats to her moral firmness and emotional stability deriving from the oppressive busyness of her parents' noisy and chaotic household.

Austen makes considerable use of movement tropes during the theatricals episode in *Mansfield Park*, beginning with Edmund's explanation of how he has been "driven" (I, 16, 180) to take a part in *Lovers' Vows* in order to "restrain" Tom from "riding about the country in quest of any body who can be persuaded to act" (I, 16, 182). Edmund is clearly struggling here to establish a moral distinction between his own metaphorical and Tom's literal movement. Fanny, however, is uneasy with a decision she suspects is motivated as much by a desire to take a part opposite Mary Crawford as it is by a concern to avoid the involvement of outsiders in the affairs of Mansfield Park. Consequently, she employs yet another image involving motion while reflecting on Edmund's "unsteadiness" (I, 17, 187). The movement trope resurfaces shortly after rehearsals have been brought to a close by Sir Thomas's return from Antigua. Faced with his father's disapproval of the theatricals, Tom employs successive metaphors of motion in a desperate attempt to justify his behavior. Initially, he tries to make Yates responsible for the "spread" of the "infection" (II, 1, 216) of the theatricals. But then he employs a much more benign image of movement in order to pass off amateur acting as an established Mansfield practice: "It was like treading old ground again" (II, 1, 216). The contradictory nature of these metaphors serves to underline Tom's moral instability.

Movement in Patricia Rozema's Mansfield Park

Patricia Rozema is an intelligent and insightful filmmaker, and it must be presumed that her inability to see Fanny Price as "fully drawn" is the result of a culturally conditioned blindness to the temperamental and moral register within which Austen is working. Whatever the reason, in her version of *Mansfield Park*, Rozema substitutes a much less complex Fanny for Austen's richly nuanced original. This Fanny feels little attachment to a Mansfield Park transformed by Rozema from a modern building into an oppressive and menacing semi-ruin. In addition to being tormented by Mrs. Norris, as in the novel, Rozema's Fanny has strong objections to Sir Thomas's sexist view of women and to the family's dependence on an income derived from slave labor. Thus, rather than struggle to find a place within the Bertram family, the film's Fanny is determined to liberate herself from the confines of her adopted home. Fanny's later entanglement in the Crawfords' erotic games and in Sir Thomas's marital plans adds a second strand to this imprisonment/escape motif.[21]

The escape strategies employed by Fanny are both physical and intellectual, and she is frequently seen either riding wildly away from Mansfield on horseback or immersed in various kinds of subversive writing. Rozema would appear, then, to be endorsing precisely the spontaneous, reckless, antisocial type of movement that Austen critiques in *Mansfield Park*. As a result, it is sometimes difficult to draw clear moral distinctions between Fanny and restless characters such as the Crawfords and Maria Bertram. Rozema exacerbates this problem by putting words spoken by Mary in the novel into Fanny's mouth. Thus, in the film it is Fanny and not Mary who employs the cynical movement metaphor, "a manoeuvring business" (*MP* I, 5), to describe marriage.[22] Similarly, whereas it is Maria alone who is identified with Sterne's caged bird in Austen's *Mansfield Park* (I, 10, 116), in Rozema's version, this metaphor of frustrated flight is used to express both women's longing for escape from patriarchal control (Fanny, 66–7; Maria, 131).

The philosophical gap between Austen and Rozema is particularly evident in the filmmaker's use of Austen's juvenilia. These childhood stories are primarily satires aimed at the sentimental fiction so popular in the latter part of the eighteenth century and, as such, repeatedly highlight the flaws inherent in the premise that immediate emotional responses provide an infallible guide to correct conduct. From Austen's conservative perspective, following one's feelings usually means giving license to selfishness and fosters a disregard for the needs of family and community.[23] However, under the supposed authorship of Fanny Price, stories such as "Love and Freindship," "Henry and Eliza," and "Frederic and Elfrida" function not just as literary satires but as revenge and escape fantasies in which Fanny identifies herself with the wild and sometimes savage heroines roundly mocked by Austen.

While it could be argued that she missed a great opportunity by failing to take her cue from Austen's cinematic exploitation of the metonymic potential of stillness and movement, Rozema must be granted the freedom to shape her source material according to her own artistic imperatives. As she puts it herself, "interpretation is impossible to avoid."[24] The real question at issue, then, is whether Rozema goes far enough in re-imagining *Mansfield Park*. Whereas marriage to Edmund and integration into the Bertram family is the logical conclusion of Fanny's quest in the novel, the film's similar ending does not seem such a good fit with the plot that precedes it, in that Fanny has consistently demonstrated scant regard for any of the Bertrams apart from Edmund.

The analysis of *Mansfield Park* that follows—in which I will be discussing Rozema's presentation of Fanny Price as a mobile, independent, and modern young woman—will conclude with a consideration of the problems posed by the apparently conventional conclusion to this otherwise transgressive film. While remaining somewhat skeptical about Rozema's achievement—unlike Claudia Johnson, I do not consider *Mansfield Park* to be "an audacious and perceptive cinematic evocation of Austen's distinctively sharp yet forgiving vision"—I will be arguing against John Wiltshire's claim that "what the film represents is the marketing of a new 'Jane Austen' to a post-feminist audience now receptive to its reinvention of the novel."[25]

The rapid sequence of scenes with which *Mansfield Park* opens is structured around a number of images of entrapment and escape that almost immediately distinguish Rozema's Fanny Price from Austen's. Even before the main action gets underway, Rozema creates a lyrical montage of close-up tracking shots that transforms candle-lit pages of manuscript into an expansive and golden landscape. Then, in a scene set in the Prices' dingy and cramped Portsmouth house, the feelings of confinement created as the camera tracks down from a bird's-eye position onto the bed occupied by Fanny and her sister, Susan, are quickly dissipated by the voice of the young Fanny Price narrating a story of rebellion, frantic movement, and flight. Taken together, the two scenes are highly suggestive of the almost magical ability of art—be it Rozema's filmmaking or Fanny's fiction—to alter reality and liberate the individual.

The soaring helicopter shots of the carriage that carries Fanny away from the poverty of Portsmouth and towards the supposed grandeur of Mansfield Park echo the film's opening sequence and establish that Fanny responds with a similar exuberance to both real and imagined escapes. In the event, Mansfield Park, described in Rozema's script as "vaguely sinister" (16), and its intimidating owner, Sir Thomas Bertram, prove to be no less oppressive than Fanny's former home. Nevertheless, even as Fanny stands alone in the cold, sparsely furnished hall while Sir Thomas decides what is to be done with her, the camera cuts and pans restlessly in order to demonstrate how little this free-spirited young girl is disheartened by the unpromising circumstances in which she finds herself.

Fanny is sustained throughout her adolescence by imaginative and actual gestures of escape. Unlike Austen's original character who spends most of her time in the East Room reading, quietly reflecting, and receiving Edmund's moral tutelage, Rozema's Fanny composes outrageous stories about rebellious children who serve as surrogates for her own desire to flout Sir Thomas's patriarchal authority. In one example, taken from Austen's "Henry and Eliza," the heroine defies her parents by eloping to Paris, getting into debt, suffering imprisonment, and planning murder. The pattern of disrespect for parents is extended into the next generation when Eliza's starving children partially eat their mother.

Fanny's lack of regard for Sir Thomas and the "solemnity" (Rozema, 59) of his role as family patriarch is expressed more directly when she disobeys her guardian by racing noisily through the hallowed halls of Mansfield Park and across a courtyard before riding off into open country on horseback. Hand-held camera shots, blurred images, and frequent changes of distance are all employed during this sequence as ways of communicating Rozema's admiration for Fanny's disruptive energy. The connection established here between Fanny and the heroines of her stories, who "run mad as often as [they] choose" (Rozema, 80), is reinforced towards the end of the scene when she describes herself as "a wild beast" (Rozema, 32).[26]

In contrast to Austen's heroine, the Fanny Price of Rozema's film clearly has little trouble asserting her independence during the period leading up to early adulthood. However, with the arrival of the Crawfords and the return of Sir Thomas from Antigua, Fanny's life enters a new phase during which she is defined, in both liberating and restricting ways, by her sexuality. Prior to Mary Crawford's visit to Mansfield, Fanny's relationship with her cousin, Edmund, is unproblematical. She has not yet come to think of him as a lover, but he is her confidant, an audience for her stories, and a collaborator in her gestures of escape. However, once Mary arrives on the scene, their relationship is altered dramatically. Suddenly Edmund is too distracted by thoughts of his entrancing new friend to pay attention when Fanny regales him with her latest story. Later, he deprives Fanny of her most cherished form of physical escape by allowing Mary the use of her horse. Successive shots, which establish a sharp contrast between the Fanny who bounds eagerly down the stairs while slashing her riding crop and the plaintive figure who peers through the bars of a mullioned window at the horse-riding party, clearly demonstrate the threat Mary poses to Fanny's cherished sense of freedom.

A finely-balanced relationship between two equals that offered Fanny ample opportunities to express and act out her rebellious urges has been suddenly transformed into a tight triangle from which she is powerless to extricate herself without first relinquishing Edmund to Mary. Twice during an impromptu rehearsal in Fanny's room and once in front of Mansfield Park immediately prior to Fanny's departure for Portsmouth, Rozema gives visual expression to the situation in which Fanny has become entangled by creating triangular tableaux out of Edmund, Fanny, and Mary's bodies. The sense of oppression Fanny experiences as a result of Mary Crawford's intrusion into her life is powerfully communicated in this last scene by a downward tilt shot that seems to bring the full weight of the Mansfield Park gatehouse crashing down onto her head.

Fanny's scope for movement becomes further constricted as Mary Crawford, Sir Thomas, and Henry Crawford become aware of her as a sexual being. Not content with seeking Edmund's affections, Mary also seizes two opportunities for erotic interaction with Fanny. First, during a private rehearsal for *Lovers' Vows,* Mary exploits her male role by openly caressing Fanny's body. Second, after Fanny has taken refuge from the rain at the parsonage, Mary engages in a quasi-seduction routine during which she slowly strips off her visitor's wet clothes while expressing admiration for her physical beauty. Fanny is paralyzed by these unprecedented experiences of the polymorphous possibilities inherent in human sexuality. The tracking camera that slowly inscribes a circle around Fanny while she is held in Mary's arms during the rehearsal scene serves as a visual metaphor for her feelings of entrapment. A less titillating but more serious threat to Fanny's autonomy is posed by Sir Thomas's realization that his niece has grown into a sexually attractive and hence marriageable young woman. His plan to hold a ball, where "surely some young man of good standing will sit up and take notice" (Rozema, 62), makes Fanny, who has just been speaking out against slavery, feel as if she is to be "sold off like one of [Sir Thomas's] slaves" (Rozema, 63).

With the emergence of Henry Crawford as a potential lover, Fanny becomes further entangled in the snares of sexuality. By now, Fanny is well aware that her feelings for Edmund are more than sisterly and that she prefers him to Crawford. Henry is, however, a cunning manipulator of female affections. On one occasion, he enters the library where Fanny is reading and moves around her seated figure with a menacing, feline grace. Fanny tries to ignore him, but Henry soon grabs her attention by brilliantly reading aloud from her book. During the reading, the camera, in an echo of the rehearsal scene, marks Henry's success in trapping his prey by tracking in close up around their heads. Ironically, the passage that captivates Fanny—the encounter between Yorick and the caged starling in Sterne's *A Sentimental Journey*—is one that expresses her own longings for freedom.

Fanny's reaction to these various forms of sexual entrapment is twofold. On the one hand, she employs some familiar escape strategies. Her immediate response to Sir Thomas's plan to transform her into a commodity in the marriage market is, for example, to mount her horse and ride off angrily into the stormy night.[27] Later, in order to break the romantic spell Henry Crawford has cast over her at the Mansfield ball, Fanny picks up one of her stories and reads aloud a comic warning about the dangers of "fainting fits and ... swoons" (Rozema, 80). Freed from enchantment, Fanny is able to respond to Henry's appearance beneath her bedroom window by snuffing out her candle, a gesture that symbolically denies his phallic power and literally removes her from his gaze. On the other hand, Fanny realizes that, despite the dangers inherent in the erotic sphere, she must accept and even foster her sexuality if she is to continue to develop along her chosen path towards maturity. Unlike Austen's Fanny Price, who seeks social engagement rather than erotic fulfillment, the Fanny of Rozema's film is more concerned with heart than head, and her morality is the instinctive kind cultivated by the heroines of sentimental fiction. Henry Crawford, for instance, praises Fanny for "the moral taste and the steadfastness of her heart" (Rozema, 61). Rather than reject sexuality outright, then, Fanny's task is to distinguish between sexuality as a social construct; sexuality as an expression of perverse and selfish desire; and sexuality as an outlet for intense and sincere passion.

Rozema provides a clear visual marker of the significant shift that takes place in Fanny's sexual attitudes by juxtaposing two scenes in which her eroticized body functions very differently. In the first, Fanny is the passive and unwilling object of Mary Crawford's attentions, and she stands almost hypnotized while Mary, who is clearly treating sex as a perverse power game, slowly undresses her. In the second, the Mansfield ball scene, Fanny wears a low-cut dress, thus for the first time making a voluntary sexual display of her body. Plunging necklines are a feature of Fanny's wardrobe from this point on in the film.

Given the evidence of sexual awakening provided by her dress—and by an earlier deleted masturbation scene (Rozema, 76)—it is not surprising that the ball proves to be the first occasion on which Fanny has a positive and powerful experience of the liberating potential of erotic interaction. In contrast to the rigid triangles and enforced couplings that have constituted her previous sexual experience, Fanny is now more than happy to participate in the "circulation of erotic interest" that flows freely "between and among" Henry, Mary, Edmund, and herself during the episode's central and "semi-private"[28] dance scene. The intensely sexual nature of the dance is communicated by Rozema's use of slow-motion, tracking, and close shots of heads, hands, and other body parts. By demonstrating that women can exercise power in the erotic sphere, the ball makes a major contribution to Fanny's search for personal freedom. This newfound confidence in her ability to control the direction of a sexual relationship is particularly evident in her reaction to Henry Crawford's first open declaration of love. Fanny, who has paused while climbing the stairs to her room, remains several steps above Henry throughout the encounter; engages in skillful verbal fencing; and finally continues her journey upwards, leaving him to descend the stairs, defeated but more sexually entranced than ever. The female dominance suggested by the mise en scène is emphasized by a sequence of alternating shots in which Henry is consistently viewed from a high angle and Fanny from either a low angle or eye level.

However, because sexuality has a social as well as a personal dimension, especially in a patriarchal society, Henry need only make his marital ambitions public for Fanny to find herself under attack by Sir Thomas, Edmund and Mary, all of whom are determined to control her erotic destiny. As a result, Fanny, like her novelistic counterpart, becomes immobilized and is uncharacteristically restricted to sitting or standing throughout several successive scenes. In Rozema's world, unlike Austen's, there is nothing to be gained from such a lack of mobility. It is therefore not surprising that the film's Fanny views the visit to Portsmouth proposed by Sir Thomas not as a punishment for intransigence but as a golden opportunity to once again become mobile.

In the event, Portsmouth proves to be another potential prison. Rozema demonstrates this by introducing several scenes in which the camera closes in tight on Fanny seated in a cramped and dark window alcove, where she endures the torments of the younger Prices or listens to her mother's warnings about the dangers of poverty. Nevertheless, in spite of the obstacles she faces, nothing can prevent Fanny from setting off in directions of her own choosing. She continues to write stories full of young ladies who have "frenzy fit[s]" and "run mad" (Rozema, 101) and maintains her physical mobility in frequent escapes from the house. Most important of all, Fanny proves to be too nimble for Henry Crawford, who follows her to Portsmouth in order to press home his suit. Henry does his best to convince Fanny that a union with him will help rather than hinder her pursuit of personal autonomy. He even organizes a display of fireworks, climaxed by the release of a flock of white doves, as a symbolic representation of his respect for her love of liberty. Under the alarming influence of her mother's warnings about the constricting effects of poverty, Fanny allows herself to be convinced by Henry's assurances and agrees to become his wife. However, the way in which Henry takes hold of Fanny and swings her around in celebration of his successful proposal provides the viewer with a strong hint of the loss of personal power marriage will actually entail. Almost inevitably, Fanny, mirroring an incident from Austen's own life,[29] reevaluates her decision during the night. Thus, when Henry next tries to control her movements by leading her in an impromptu dance in the Prices' kitchen, Fanny breaks free and announces that she cannot marry him.

What happens subsequently comes as no surprise to readers of *Mansfield Park*. A crisis occurs at Mansfield (created in this case by Tom's illness rather than Maria's elopement), and Fanny is summoned home. In the weeks that follow, Tom is cured and reformed; the Crawfords, Maria, and Mrs. Norris are exiled; Susan becomes part of the household; and Edmund finally gets over Mary Crawford, leaving him free to redirect his erotic attention towards Fanny. In the novel, this ending serves as the fulfillment of Fanny's deepest desires because, despite some outrageous mistreatment, she has always remained committed to Mansfield Park and the values it represents. However, when Rozema's Fanny, in an almost direct echo of her counterpart's thoughts in the novel, says, "Portsmouth is Portsmouth and Mansfield is home" (*MP* III, 14, 499; Rozema,115), we wonder why she should suddenly claim an attachment to a place she has always found oppressive and about which she continues to speak sardonically. Has Rozema simply run out of ideas or does she lack the nerve to come up with an ending different from Austen's? Clearly the last few minutes of the film version of *Mansfield Park* require careful consideration.

It could be argued that Mansfield Park finally becomes acceptable to Rozema's Fanny because it has experienced some important changes. In addition to those taken directly from the novel, Sir Thomas has come to see the error of his ways not just as a patriarch but also as a slave owner, and Lady Bertram has risen from her couch and begun to take walks. However, the tone in which Fanny narrates these changes and improvements is extremely facetious. She implies, for instance, by speaking of the reader's ability to guess "exactly" the appropriate time for the event to occur, that the "whole delightful and astonishing truth" (Rozema, 142) that Edmund has finally fallen in love with her is more a matter of romantic literary convention than it is psychologically plausible. Furthermore, any credit accruing to Sir Thomas for giving up his plantations in Antigua is offset by Fanny's blatantly anachronistic joke about his switching to the modern sin crop of tobacco. The narrator of *Mansfield Park* is equally flippant in her account of the novel's almost-too-perfect conclusion: "Let other pens dwell on guilt and misery. I quit such odious subjects as soon as I can, impatient to restore every body, not greatly in fault themselves, to tolerable comfort, and to have done with all the rest" (III, 17, 533). However, there are significant differences between a narrator speaking from outside a fictional world and a character speaking about her own and other characters' situations. The narrator may not take *Mansfield Park*'s ending entirely seriously but Austen's Fanny certainly does. Rozema's Fanny, on the other hand, despite her earlier assertion of attachment to Mansfield, seems almost as disaffected with the Bertram family and their home as ever.

The contradictions that appear to bedevil the conclusion of the film version of *Mansfield Park* can be at least partially resolved, I would argue, once we recognize that, far from suggesting that her character has been integrated into Mansfield society, Rozema is presenting us with a Fanny who, like the flock of starlings that soar into the air between each section of her summarizing narrative, now occupies a position high above it. In effect, Fanny has become more an omniscient than a first-person-participant narrator. From her new position of lofty detachment, Fanny no longer feels the need to escape from the despised Bertram family but rather values its members for the crucial roles they can play as the subject matter of her art. The Bertrams have in effect become her puppets, and the power that Fanny now exercises over them is clearly expressed on the several occasions when groups of characters are frozen, not to be released until she gives permission with the comment, "It could have turned out differently, I suppose ... but it didn't" (Rozema, 141). She might just as well have said, "because I chose that it didn't." Fanny's unexpected attachment to Mansfield Park is, then, entirely a function of its ability to provide her with raw material for the fictional work entitled *Mansfield Park* that, as a surrogate for Jane Austen, she is about to write.

In the last few moments of her film, Rozema creates a final sequence of motion images designed to sum up Fanny's achievement. The camera tracks away from the Bertram family, made redundant by the completion of their story; cranes up the wall of Mansfield's ruined west wing; and then cuts to Fanny and Edmund, who have turned their backs on the company and are walking towards their private retreat in the parsonage, all the time flirting and discussing Edmund's success in finding a publisher for his fiancée's stories. Camera and character movement thus combine with dialogue in this scene to confirm that Fanny has succeeded in her ambition to be free of the Bertrams—with the exception of Edmund who serves her need for a sexual partner and a literary agent—and has found roles for herself outside of Mansfield society as an independent woman, an artist, and a lover.[30]

Although technically very proficient, Rozema's treatment of movement in her film *Mansfield Park* is less subtle than Austen's. Neither does her implicit argument that Austen, thinly fictionalized as Fanny Price, shares her own admiration for assertive individualism, the moral power of feeling, and speed of thought and action stand up to a serious consideration of the ideological perspective adopted by her novelistic predecessor. Nevertheless, Rozema's version of *Mansfield Park* is a far more substantial work of art than adaptations that are simply parasitical on their source texts. Throughout the film Rozema follows her own agenda rather than Austen's, and her final move, in which she makes Fanny the author of her own narrative, should not be dismissed as a fashionable gesture towards postmodernism. On the contrary, Rozema is creating a powerful symbol of her heroine's ultimate triumph over a society that has tried to force her into a mould rather than respecting her urge for autonomy. By so doing, Rozema confirms that, for all its limitations, the film version of *Mansfield Park* is genuinely hers and not a pale imitation of the novel of the same name.

7

"A Cheerful Confidence in Futurity": The Movement Motif in Austen's Novel and Dear/Michell's Film Adaptation of *Persuasion*

DAVID MONAGHAN

My purpose in this chapter is to examine how images of stillness and movement function in Austen's *Persuasion* and the 1995 film adaptation written by Nick Dear and directed by Roger Michell. In this novel Austen employs the movement motif to create distinctions between three groups: a socially and morally paralyzed landed gentry; the Musgroves, a family thrown into disorder by a generational shift from "the old English style ... [to] the new" (I, 5, 43); and the navy, a dynamic but flawed professional class that is challenging the hegemony of the old order.[1] Images of movement also serve to establish the subtle modulations of pace forced on Anne Elliot as she seeks to adapt her traditional orientation towards graceful and controlled motion to the erratic tempo of the new worlds that she encounters after leaving Kellynch Hall. The relatively radical vision of Austen's last novel is clearly attractive to Dear and Michell and, to a large extent, they make similar although rather less subtle use of images of stillness and movement in order to portray a society in transition.[2] However, the film version of *Persuasion* deviates significantly from its source text in its treatment of Anne Elliot and Captain Wentworth, both of whom become more single-mindedly oriented to the future and hence closer to the sensibility of a twentieth-century audience. The effect of these changes is to give plausibility to a revised ending in which Anne, having demonstrated that she possesses the mobility and energy required of a career woman, accompanies her new husband on his next sea voyage in a capacity close to that of professional partner.

Persuasion: *Movement Motifs in a New Social Order*

Austen's treatment of Louisa Musgrove's fall from the Cobb establishes a degree of continuity between *Persuasion* and Austen's earlier works. Louisa herself stands in a line of "wild" (I, 6, 51; I, 11, 101) young women traceable back as far as the juvenilia and the qualities that cause her to leap heedlessly into space—youthful high spirits, sexual arousal, and an unwillingness to listen to advice—are similar to those by which Laura in *Love and Freindship*, Marianne Dashwood in *Sense and Sensibility*, and Maria Bertram in *Mansfield Park* are motivated. Louisa's companions are far too shocked by the sight of her prostrate and apparently lifeless body to think of passing judgment on her behavior. However, Austen's narrator introduces a more detached and implicitly unsympathetic perspective by recording the reactions of the "workmen and boatmen" who "collected near them ... to enjoy the sight of the dead young lady" (I, 12, 120). Later, Anne Elliot and Lady Russell, "a couple of steady, sensible women," agree that "the sad catastrophe ... had been the consequence of much thoughtlessness and much imprudence" (II, 1, 137).

However, the same Anne Elliot responds very differently to her first-hand experience of Admiral and Mrs. Croft's dangerous style of carriage driving which, as Wentworth reports earlier, often results in them being "tossed out" (I, 10, 91). In this instance, Anne judges an incident in which only his wife's timely intervention prevents the Admiral from running into a post to be more significant as an indicator of the Crofts' ability to work cooperatively in negotiating life's challenges than it is of their foolhardiness. Although she clearly continues to value the Burkeian social ideal of measured motion, as evidenced by her condemnation of the reckless Louisa Musgrove, Anne has obviously come to accept that it is possible to be a virtuous person while failing to meet such a standard. The flexibility that characterizes Anne's moral code constitutes a pragmatic but still principled response to her disillusioning experience of the old social order as represented by Sir Walter Elliot, a self-indulgent man who consistently resists his daughter's efforts to persuade him to put his responsibilities as the baronet owner of the Kellynch estate ahead of personal pleasure. Rather than despair at the disintegration of a way of life that she learnt to value under her mother's tutelage, Anne demonstrates a healthy openness to any new style of behavior that seems likely to assist in the revitalization of English society. One model for this new style is provided by the Crofts, who may be impulsive, brash and unsophisticated but are also warm-hearted in their social relations, able to improvise in the face of crisis, and, as they have demonstrated in the recent war with Napoleon, strongly committed to the preservation of the nation.

Like her heroine, Austen seems to view Sir Walter Elliot's shortcomings as symptomatic of some serious problems with England's ruling class. Responsible landed gentlemen in Austen's earlier novels, such as Darcy and Mr. Knightley, recognize that high rank confers a complex set of obligations to family, tenants, neighbors, and the nation. Sir Walter, on the other hand, considers the title of baronet as sufficient in itself to give him all the "consequence" (I, 2, 12, 15) a person could ever aspire to achieve. "Vanity," or self-conceit, as opposed to the justifiable pride that a gentleman derives from the responsible performance of the duties that go along with rank, is, as the narrator notes, "the beginning and the end of Sir Walter Elliot's character" (I, 1, 4).[3] Performance of one's duty is not simply irrelevant so far as Sir Walter is concerned but is a positive evil to be avoided because the effort involved "cuts up a man's youth and vigour most horribly" (I, 3, 21). Encouraged by the flattery of his sycophantic female associates, who convince him that he is immune to the ravages of time, Sir Walter cultivates a frozen mode of existence rather than involve himself in the workings of an organically evolving society.

Austen offers two defining images of Sir Walter Elliot, and hence of the class that he represents. In the first, he reads "his own history" (I, 1, 3) in the *Baronetage*—a publication that, as Deidre Lynch points out, "aspires to bring time to a standstill" by "celebrating" the "continuity" of "bloodlines"[4]—and, in the second, he poses in front of one of his many mirrors. Whether gazing into an actual or, what Tanner terms, "a textual mirror,"[5] Sir Walter demonstrates a fundamental immobility born of a view of the world that is limited to a solipsistic regard for reflections of his "person and ... situation" (I, 1, 4). As Admiral Croft notes, in Sir Walter's world of "looking-glasses," there is "no getting away from oneself" (II, 1, 138).

The two "little social commonwealth[s]" (I, 6, 46) encountered by Anne Elliot in her search for an alternative to the abandoned country estate are both much more vital and energetic than the Elliot family's. However, neither the Musgroves nor the naval characters are adequate substitutes for the old order at its functioning best because they lack the rootedness in firmly established practices and forms of social interchange, most notably a complex system of manners, required to give shape to the present and a degree of predictability to the future. The Musgroves, a family of country squires and long-time occupiers of a manor house at Uppercross, have experienced a generational fracture, "the father and mother [being] in the old English style, and the young people in the new" (I, 5, 43). As a result, the now functionless Mrs. Musgrove is stranded on her couch, wallowing in fabricated memories of her worthless son, Dick, while her daughters, Henrietta and Louisa—whose innovations have caused an "overthrow of all order and neatness" and given the Great House an "air of confusion" (I, 5, 43)—rush heedlessly into the future. Both are "wild" (I, 6, 51; I, 11, 101) for new and stimulating experiences in the form of impromptu dances, a hastily arranged walk to Winthrop, and a visit to Lyme that takes place at a day's notice despite their parents' preference "for putting it off till summer" (I, 11, 101).

Unreflective people who act on the impulse of the moment can expect at best to "trifle away" (I, 6, 47) their lives, as Charles Musgrove does. At worst, their lack of foresight will plunge them into disaster. Thus, while the defining image of movement associated with the younger Musgroves is imbued with energy, mobility and "a cheerful confidence in futurity" (I, 4, 32), qualities quite lacking in Sir Walter Elliot, it does not constitute a viable alternative to his state of immobilization. I am referring, of course, to the episode discussed above when Louisa leaps from the Cobb, full of hope and self confidence but "too precipitate by half a second," as a result of which she misses Wentworth's outstretched hands and ends up "lifeless" (I, 12, 118) on the pavement below.

Whereas the younger Musgroves have cut themselves loose from their roots, rootlessness is intrinsic to the naval characters' profession. As depicted by Austen, in wartime, sailors cover large portions of the globe on a variety of ships; during periods of peace, they occupy temporary lodgings in different parts of England. Wentworth, for example, has been the commander of both the Asp and the Laconia, on which he voyaged to the Azores (I, 8, 70–2), and while on leave divides his time between visiting the Crofts at Uppercross, the Harvilles at Lyme, and his brother, Edward, in Shropshire before following the Musgroves and the Crofts to Bath. Similarly, Admiral and Mrs. Croft have "crossed the Atlantic four times, and have been once to the East Indies, and back again" (I, 8, 76), and report having rented accommodations in North Yarmouth and Deal prior to becoming Sir Walter Elliott's tenants at Kellynch (II, 6, 185). It is not surprising, then, that sailors sometimes behave in a manner reminiscent of the Musgrove sisters. The Crofts, as noted earlier, like to drive their carriage recklessly about the countryside and Wentworth, who is in more danger than he realizes of rushing into the "foolish match" (I, 7, 66) about which he jokes, gives little thought to the consequences of his romantic entanglements with Henrietta and Louisa.

However, the instability inherent in wartime life on board ship, with any day as likely to bring death as glory and fortune, was mitigated during the extended war that forms the backdrop to the main action of *Persuasion* by a policy of professionalization that encouraged officers and men to develop specialized skills and habits of command and obedience. An awareness of the important part played by the navy in ensuring that the nation survived the threat posed by Napoleon was even more crucial in giving structure and meaning to sailors' lives.[6] Austen's naval characters therefore prove ultimately to be much more substantial and purposeful people than the Musgrove sisters. For example, Wentworth's rapid actions are only occasionally impulsive in origin. More often, they take the form of well-judged interventions on behalf of people in distress. In the course of his visits to Uppercross, Wentworth moves "instantly" (I, 8, 73) to comfort the grieving Mrs. Musgrove, needs only a "moment" (I, 9, 86) before stepping forward to release Anne Elliot from the grip of the child Walter, and "clear[s] the hedge in a moment" (I, 10, 97) in order to secure a place in the Crofts' carriage for the weary Anne.[7]

Furthermore, although in one sense living from moment to moment throughout their time at sea, always subject to the vicissitudes of the weather and attacks by the enemy, sailors, unlike the Musgrove sisters, also have a keen understanding of their experiential origins and of the ways in which the past has shaped the present and potentially the future. This becomes particularly obvious if we look beyond the immediate purpose of Wentworth's dinner-table tales of naval derring-do—which is to provide some cheap thrills for Henrietta and Louisa—and take note of an underlying structure that demonstrates the teller's sophisticated understanding of his life as a coherent narrative woven out of the interplay between personal initiative, luck and divine providence (I, 8, 71).

Finally, the skills acquired while coping with the cramped quarters available on board ship enable sailors such as Admiral Croft and Captain Harville to transform short-term, rented accommodations into "snug" (II, 6, 185) quarters that possess an "order and neatness" (I, 5, 43) quite lacking at Uppercross. Anne is particularly impressed with the "ingenious contrivances and nice arrangements" employed by Captain Harville to create a "picture of repose and domestic happiness" out of the raw materials provided by a deficient "lodging-house" (I, 11, 106).

In contrast to the single episode that is sufficient to define the Musgrove sisters' hasty and impulsive natures, several images of motion, each with a different tempo, are required to reflect the greater complexity of the naval approach to experience. Wentworth's account of the Crofts tipping from their carriage is the most dramatic but it must be supplemented, first by Anne's observation of how Mrs. Croft, working cooperatively with her husband, "coolly giv[es] the reins a better direction," thereby averting the "danger" posed by "a post" (I, 10, 99) and second by the peaceful image of sailors at rest in other people's homes which, with a "few alterations" (II, 1, 138), they have made their own.

Because of the inability of the three major social groups in *Persuasion* to live up to the Burkeian ideal of measured motion, the situation facing Anne Elliot is very different from that of any of Austen's earlier heroines. At twenty-seven years of age, Anne, who has been well educated by her mother, possesses "good principles" (I, 1, 5), "warm affections and domestic habits" (I, 4, 31), and "an elegance of mind and sweetness of character, which must have placed her high with any people of real understanding" (I, 1, 6). In other words, she is the complete gentlewoman who, in an earlier novel, would already have married and taken a well-defined position within the upper echelons of a morally sound and socially vibrant rural community. However, as we have already seen, no such community exists in *Persuasion*. The choices facing Anne are, then, to either remain within a milieu of such moral vacuity that it judges her to be "nobody" (I, 1, 6) or to seek fresh social horizons. Anne's decision, once Sir Walter Elliot has abandoned Kellynch for Bath, a place unlikely to yield many opportunities for a woman who longs to be "of some use" (I, 5, 36), is to strike out on her own in the hope of finding a position as "a not unworthy member" of a new "social commonwealth" (I, 6, 46).

Three forces combine to hinder Anne as she attempts to develop a degree and style of mobility unique amongst Austen's heroines. First, her emotional energy has been severely drained by the loss of two loved ones: her mother, who died when she was fourteen, and a suitor, the penniless but ambitious sailor, Frederick Wentworth, whom she was persuaded it would be prudent to reject. As a result, and in spite of the value she has learnt to give to "a cheerful confidence in futurity" (I, 4, 32), Anne, whose "bloom" (I, 4, 30) has long faded, believes that her own "prospects [are] blighted for ever" (I, 11, 105) and that she has transcended the emotional expressiveness of youth: "Anne hoped she had outlived the age of blushing" (I, 6, 52).[8] Second, because they lack a sophisticated understanding of the broader moral significance of good manners, neither the Musgroves nor the naval characters are able to adequately value Anne's elegant and refined social performance. As a result, she is blocked from gaining entry into two social circles that possess qualities—personal warmth and, in the case of the navy at least, a commitment to service—lacking in her own family. Third, the frequent presence of her former lover, Wentworth, at Uppercross seriously hampers Anne's efforts to find practical ways of proving her worth to the Musgroves. Instead of engaging as fully as possible in the affairs of the family, as she intended, Anne either absents herself from gatherings attended by Wentworth or remains on the fringe of the group. Anne's behavior during the walk to Winthrop is typical: "Anne's object was, not to be in the way of any body" (I, 10, 90).

Despite the barriers that confront her, in the course of *Persuasion* Anne

Elliot moves decisively away from a debilitating state of mourning and entrapment within a decaying old order and towards a situation that promises emotional rebirth and social liberation. However, unlike Austen's earlier initiate heroines, who are guided towards their almost pre-destined places within orderly and ideologically coherent societies by a well-established system of manners and heavily ritualized forms of interpersonal communication, an already mature Anne, aided only by her own considerable stock of personal resources and occasional good luck, must improvise a route through the pitfalls and perils of an almost chartless social landscape.

Fortuitous circumstances first come into play in creating the situation in which Anne is most likely to experience the emotional thawing crucial to her personal rebirth. The unexpected reappearance of Wentworth after an absence of eight years causes Anne a good deal of discomfort and, as already noted, hinders the development of her relationship with the Musgroves. However, it also serves a valuable function at this stage in Anne's life by giving lie to her conviction that she no longer has a young woman's capacity to feel. "A thousand feelings rush on Anne" at her first sight of Wentworth and, although she considers it "absurd to be resuming the agitation which such an interval had banished into distance and indistinctness!" (I, 7, 64), each of their subsequent meetings generates a complex of emotions. These range from despair at "his cold politeness" (I, 8, 78) during a brief private encounter to the "emotions so compounded of pleasure and pain, that she knew not which prevailed" (I, 10, 98) stirred up by Wentworth's kind gesture of securing her a place in the Crofts' carriage.

Luck and contingency continue to be important factors even when Anne is working with great deliberation to create a place for herself within the Musgrove and naval communities.[9] Generously accepting the elder Musgroves' partiality for their own daughters and their consequent inability to make an objective assessment of the quality of her manners and accomplishments, Anne takes full advantage of any opportunity to win their regard by proving herself useful. For example, Mr. and Mrs. Musgrove, who generally have little appreciation of her considerable "musical powers," value her playing country dances "by the hour together" (I, 6, 51) during Henrietta and Louisa's impromptu balls. However, given Anne's peripheral position within the Musgrove family and amongst the naval characters, such occasions do not occur very often in the normal course of events. It therefore requires a pair of fortunate falls, in which Mary Musgrove's son breaks his collarbone and Louisa Musgrove is left unconscious beneath the Cobb at Lyme, to carry her from the periphery to the centre of her new worlds.

Neither the Musgroves nor the sailors are able to cope with the demands created by these two incidents despite the generally chaotic nature of life at

Uppercross and the familiarity of naval officers such as Wentworth and Benwick with moments of crisis requiring an immediate and decisive response. Instead, it is Anne, drawing on her rich resources of reason, self-control, and commitment to service, qualities acquired as part of her training for a position within a landed gentleman's household, who takes charge on each occasion. Throughout "an afternoon of distress" at Uppercross, Anne rather than the hysterical Mary or the "frightened" (I, 7, 58) elder Musgroves has "every thing to do at once" (I, 7, 57). Similarly, while the two sailors present prove to be useless in dealing with a crisis that falls beyond their area of professional expertise, Anne, "attending with all the strength and zeal, and thought, which instinct supplied," responds to Louisa's accident by orchestrating a series of "rapid moments" (I, 12, 119) until order emerges out of chaos.

The Cobb incident in particular is critical in opening up a future for Anne Elliot and in guaranteeing that her apparently blighted life will "have spring again" (I, 10, 91). Faced with the imminent departure of a woman who until recently played only a peripheral role in their family circle, the Musgroves now ask, "'What should they do without [Anne]?'" (II, 1, 132). Wentworth's proposal that "Anne will stay [at Captain Harville's to nurse Louisa], no one is so proper, so capable as Anne!" (I, 12, 123) demonstrates that he too has come to depend on her good sense and nurturing qualities. Even more important, his ready assumption that Anne belongs within a household made up of members of his extended naval family suggests that Wentworth is once again contemplating a close personal connection with his former fiancée.

However, the courtship process that follows is extremely complex because it takes place within the fragmented and highly flawed context created when the novel's three major social groups—the stupidly elegant and chilly Elliots, the warm but chaotic Musgroves, and the companionable and mobile sailors—congregate in Bath. Austen's main goal in the concluding section of her novel is to underline the remarkable level of nimbleness and adaptability required of Anne if she is to negotiate her way through social milieus that function at varied and dissonant tempos, while simultaneously continuing to struggle with the turbulent emotions aroused by Wentworth.

A comparison of three meetings between Anne and Wentworth, the first during a concert held in the Assembly Rooms and the other two in the Musgroves' lodgings at the White Hart, highlights the very different types of problems posed by a decadent old order and an unsophisticated new one. The Elliots, demonstrating their typical disdain for broader social obligations, attend the concert only because it provides an opportunity to enhance their own prestige by cultivating an acquaintance with Sir Walter's socially superior relative, Lady Dalrymple. As a result, Anne, who has a polite obligation to remain with her father's party, is denied any socially sanctioned space within which to communicate with Wentworth. Taking advantage of a brief pause while the Elliots wait for the arrival of Lady Dalrymple, Anne tries to remedy this lack by improvising "a little advance" that encourages the passing Wentworth to deviate from "the straight line to stand near her" (II, 8, 197). However, the promising conversation that ensues is soon interrupted when she finds herself "necessarily included" in the group that forms to greet Lady Dalrymple and is thus "divided" (II, 8, 200) from Wentworth.

As the concert begins, Anne is compelled to take her "properly arranged" (II, 8, 202) place. Once "surrounded and shut in" by the Elliot-Dalrymple party, Anne can only try in vain to catch the eye of an unresponsive Wentworth as he stands "among a cluster of men at a little distance" (II, 8, 205). The situation improves during the interval when "a little scheming" (II, 8, 206) on Anne's part brings her to the end of the bench and creates an opportunity for Wentworth to approach and renew their conversation. Once again, though, the demands of good manners ensure that their time together is brief. After "a few minutes" (II, 8, 207), William Walter Elliot asks Anne to translate an Italian song for Miss Carteret and she is forced to direct her attention away from Wentworth. Angered at his rival's success in garnering Anne's attention, a jealous Wentworth makes an early exit from the concert. In the end, then, despite Anne's attempts to maneuver within the tight space provided by her polite social obligations, the evening at the Assembly Rooms creates rather more confusion than communication between the two lovers, and she is left wondering how "the truth [of her affection is] to reach [Wentworth]" (II, 8, 207).[10]

The next encounters between Anne and Wentworth take place in the Musgroves' lodgings at the White Hart. Anne feels much more at home in the company of Henrietta and Mrs. Musgrove, from whom she receives "the kindest welcome" (II, 10, 239), than she does with her own uncaring family. Nevertheless, bridging the gap that separates her from Wentworth proves scarcely easier amidst the "thorough confusion" (II, 10, 240) that continues to characterize social interactions involving the Musgroves than it was in the situation created by the sterile formality of the concert. As a result, Anne becomes concerned that being "in company with each other" in such a "quick-changing, unsettled scene" will create a barrier to communication, by "exposing them to inadvertencies and misconstructions of the most mischievous kind" (II, 10, 240). Despite her anticipatory anxiety, Anne once again, and with rather more success than before, rises to the challenge posed by flawed social circumstances and, on the first occasion, uses her improvisional skills to open up channels of communication with Wentworth. Denied the opportunity for extended private dialogue, Anne delivers an important coded message to Wentworth that he is positioned to overhear. By telling Mrs. Musgrove of her disinclination for the Elliott's private party, she is able to convince Wentworth that familial loyalties will no longer stand in the way of their union. However, as John Wiltshire emphasizes in Chapter 2, for her more crucial communication with Wentworth during the second occasion, Anne is, as has been the case several times in the past, dependent on good fortune rather than planning. The pointed comments that she addresses to Captain Harville about female fidelity may serve as a thinly veiled declaration of her continuing love for Wentworth but they are not intended for him, and she is unaware that he is eavesdropping on the conversation. Thus, "Anne was startled at finding him nearer than she had supposed" and suspects that he is "striving to catch sounds, which yet she did not think he could have caught" (II, 11, 254).

Even as they come close to achieving mutual understanding, Anne and Wentworth must cope with the turbulence that swirls around them. The "hardly legible" letter in which Wentworth proposes marriage is written under the pressure of an immediate commitment to Harville and, after being "hastily" folded and concealed beneath "scattered paper," is retrieved and placed before Anne after its author has reentered the room and "instantly cross[ed]" (II, 11, 257) to the writing desk. Then, Anne, overwhelmed by Wentworth's passionate declaration of love and longing for "half an hour's solitude and reflection" in order to settle her agitated emotions, is "interrupted" (II, 11, 258) after only ten minutes by the arrival of Charles, Mary and Henrietta Musgrove. The strain of maintaining her poise in the face of personal and social confusion finally becomes too much for Anne and she is "obliged to plead indisposition and excuse herself" (II, 11, 259).

After one more experience of hasty improvisation—she has only "two moments preparation" (II, 11, 260) before encountering Wentworth in the street—Anne is able to modulate her emotional and physical pace to something approximating the measured motion that has always previously served Austen as a marker of the fully functional society. The unusual degree of detail that characterizes Austen's descriptions in the White Hart and out on the streets of Bath allows us to describe her shifts in rhythm and pace in precise cinematic terms: a tightly shot interior sequence comprising quick cuts and swish pans gives way to a series of lengthy tracks and slow dissolves after the action has moved outdoors. As they "slowly pace the gradual ascent" of a "comparatively quiet and retired gravel-walk" (II, 11, 262), Anne and Wentworth have time at last for calm "retrospections and acknowledgements" (II, 11, 262) regarding their "so many, many years of division and estrangement" (II, 11, 261). The bond that is established between Anne and Wentworth is thus a satisfying blend of the rational and the emotional. However, in this instance, the union of the two lovers is not accompanied by any wholesale social regeneration. This is underscored by Austen's use of a dance metaphor that serves to separate rather than, as is the case in all the earlier novels, to bring together the public and the personal: "There could be only a most proper alacrity, a most obliging compliance for public view; and smiles reined in and spirits dancing in private rapture" (II, 11, 261). Instead of a "landed estate" and the comfortable security of a well-ordered life amongst the gentry, as a sailor's wife Anne will be the "mistress of a very pretty landaulette" (II, 12, 272), a two-person open carriage that symbolizes her continued mobility; will probably live in a series of rented accommodations; and will "pay the tax of quick alarm" at "the dread of a future war" (II, 12, 275).[11]

Movement and a Modern Perspective in Dear and Michell's Persuasion

The film version of *Persuasion*, written by Nick Dear and directed by Roger Michell, is in many respects a fairly close rendering of its source text. The film's subject matter, as defined by Nick Dear in the introduction to his script, is close to the novel's: "The story essentially describes an old order fading away into decadence, and a new tribe, a meritocracy, coming to the fore" (ii).[12] Furthermore, the film makers have clearly recognized the important part played by images of motion and stillness in Austen's *Persuasion* and structure their film around an analogous although by no means identical motif. There are, however, important differences between novel and film, particularly in the film's treatment of Anne Elliot and Captain Wentworth. The analysis that follows will focus on Dear and Michell's use of movement images in creating a film that at once remains close to and both simplifies and deviates in significant ways from the novel upon which it is based.

The opening sequence of the film version of *Persuasion* is largely invented. Nevertheless, in its reliance on images of motion and stillness to define essential differences between the old landed gentry, as represented by the Elliots, and the new men of the navy, the film reveals a clear debt to it source text. Close shots of oars and longer shots of sailors rowing in unison, combined with a low angle shot of Admiral Croft seated in the prow of the tender, a white ensign flying proudly behind him, serve as powerful visual representations of what are, for Austen, three of the navy's most important characteristics: professional expertise, teamwork and patriotism.[13] Also implicit within this sequence is an image of harmony within social hierarchy perhaps intended to suggest, as Austen never does, that traditional styles of authority and deference might survive under the leadership of new men such as Croft.[14] The subsequent introduction of three successive tracking shots in which the point of view switches back and forth between Admiral Croft, now on board a man-of-war, and the sailors lined up for inspection further communicates the reciprocity of the relationship between the commander and his men.

In sharp contrast to the novel, the film's first visual representation of gentry life involves images of rapid motion in the form of close shots of the quickly turning wheels of the carriage that is carrying Mr. Shepherd and his daughter to Kellynch. In fact these shots communicate a much greater sense of urgency than do the rather stately images of the naval tender with which they are intercut. However, as is made evident by the flurry of hand-held tracking shots, quick cuts and a swish pan employed in filming the mob scene that develops as Sir Walter Elliot's creditors crowd around Shepherd on his arrival at Kellynch, swift movement is used on this occasion to communicate a sense of crisis rather than of vitality. Feelings of crisis are intensified by the contrast that is established between the urgency and desperation of both the paid employee, Shepherd, and the creditors, and the elegant inertia cultivated by Sir Walter. The perfectly formed but petrified nature of life at Kellynch is brilliantly communicated by a mise en scène that captures the exaggerated symmetry of the great house's entrance hall. An impressive oak table occupies the foreground of the middle third of the screen; three servants and a window stand in perfect mirror image on each side of the table; and, in the background, Lady Russell's carriage is framed by a grand doorway.

The displacement of objects by people fails to bring Kellynch to life. Characters remain for the most part seated, and hence immobilized, throughout four alternating day and night time drawing room and dining room scenes. In the drawing room they appear as tiny figures stranded in a vast, cold space while, in the dining room, they are crowded uncomfortably around the over-decorated table. Sir Walter either moves to or already occupies a central position in each scene but he fails throughout to establish any but the most nominal authority or to harmonize the group. He is made to look ridiculous by the excessive number of liveried servants standing to attention behind him in the dining room and, during the episode in which he agrees to rent out Kellynch, repeated cuts away from long shots of his dependents scattered about the room to closer shots of individuals and pairs of characters communicate a powerful sense of things falling apart.

The marked differences between gentry and navy are further pointed up by a cross cut to a scene set aboard a British man-of-war. Unlike the drawing and dining rooms at Kellynch, the ship's ward room is small, dark, smoky and filled with animated naval officers whose unity and camaraderie are communicated in two ways: the inclusion of the whole group in a single, tight circling shot and the placement at the center of the mise en scène of a table-top whose surface is almost covered by a scattering of various types of naval headgear, jumbled together to suggest the cohesiveness that exists amongst men of different rank, and by a warmly glinting decanter of the port that fuels the sailors' conviviality. These casual but deeply meaningful table "decorations" are clearly intended to contrast the elegant but literally cold swan-shaped ice sculpture that dominates those seated around the dining table at Kellynch and isolates them from one another. Most significant of all, though, at the very moment when Sir Walter is declaring that he intends to abandon Kellynch, thereby relinquishing responsibility for his estate and, by implication, his country, Croft is announcing that the war against France has ended in a victory won in large part by a navy whole-heartedly committed to the defense of the realm.

Similar explicit contrasts between a sterile, frozen and fragmented old order and a dynamic, purposeful new order are made in the second half of the Dear/Michell *Persuasion*. Scenes set in the Elliots' lodgings in Bath feature individuals marooned on elegant chaises longues. Hand held tracking shots in which the camera moves with a fluid leisureliness around the room emphasize the immobility of characters who, in their fine costumes, have become little more than a part of the stylish decor.[15] The occasionally increased tempo that accompanies Sir Walter's and Elizabeth's expressions of anxiety regarding possible barriers to a renewal of social intercourse with their aristocratic relative, Lady Dalrymple, serves as an ironic comment on the worthlessness of lives dedicated to marks of prestige and displays of self importance. A first shot of the almost inanimate Lady Dalrymple, made wraithlike by the use of backlighting and by the whiteness of her diaphanous clothes and caked-on facial cosmetics, decisively demonstrates the lack of real substance in the Elliots' object of desire.[16] A later shot of a ship's deck bustling with activity and presided over by the towering figure of Captain Wentworth preparing for the challenges of a new voyage stands in sharp contrast to these images of immobility and death. Two final extreme long shots of a man-of-war sailing into a huge sunset complete the motif, built around contrasting images of movement and stillness, used to dramatize the vital and energetic navy's superiority over the decaying landed gentry.[17]

The extreme polarization that characterizes Dear and Michell's comparison of the gentry and naval milieux suggests that the choices facing the film's Anne Elliot will be rather less complex than they are in the novel. Whereas Austen, for instance, makes several references to life at Kellynch under the guidance of Anne's admirable mother in order to remind her readers that the landed gentry once provided the nation with responsible leadership, Dear and Michell scarcely hint that Sir Walter Elliot's class was ever anything but

vain and foolish. Thus, while Lady Elliot is given credit for introducing "mod-
eration and economy" (Dear, 11) into the affairs of Kellynch Hall, no mention is made of her grasp of a range of less pragmatic values or of her role in
Anne's education.

As a result, there is little reason for Anne to feel any sense of loss at quit-
ting Kellynch Hall. So far as she is concerned, Kellynch is a dead place that
is draining her of spiritual and physical energy. This feeling is represented
visually by a shot of a pale Anne, dressed in white and seated amongst furniture covered in white sheets, described as a "shroud" for a "dead house"
(10) in Dear's script.[18] Thus, whereas the novel's Anne struggles right up to
the moment she leaves Kellynch to compensate for her father's failings as a
landed gentleman, in the film it is Elizabeth, albeit in a spirit of sterile conformity, who proposes that "someone really ought to visit every house in the
parish, as a take leave. It is the Elliot way" (Dear, 10).

As she sorts through the detritus of the Elliot family's tenure at Kellynch
Hall in the days prior to her departure, Anne turns up a single item capable
of eliciting an emotional response: "a letter folded up into a paper boat" concealed inside a copy of the "Navy List, 1806" (Dear, 11). Clearly, then, while
mementos of a lost lover, the sailor Frederick Wentworth, still have the power
to create troubling and destabilizing bonds between Anne Elliot and her past,
she has few regrets about the loss of a way of life. In general, the film's Anne
is much freer than her novelistic counterpart to move on to new social are-
nas. The optimistic undercurrent that alleviates the gloom of the Kellynch
scenes is brought to the surface in two invented scenes designed to draw
attention to Anne's mobility and hopeful prospects.

First, rather than simply shift location, as Austen does, Dear and Michell
dramatize the journey that takes Anne from Kellynch to Uppercross. A
sequence that begins as the camera cuts away from Anne looking backwards
to a shot of a receding Kellynch Hall, and concludes with a lengthy pan that
brings a distant Uppercross into view, serves to put Kellynch firmly into the
past and to establish Anne's arrival in the Musgroves' village, where for the
first time the sun lights up her face, as a decisive new beginning. Second, a
scene occurring early in the Uppercross section of the film in which Anne
enthusiastically launches paper boats onto a fast flowing stream, transforms
the significance of what was earlier an image of mourning and loss. Rather
than representing an old love affair buried in an apparently irretrievable past,
the paper boats now offer hope that the relationship between Anne and
Wentworth will be renewed in a swiftly approaching future. By connecting
the second set of boats, which were folded by Admiral Croft, not just to
Wentworth but more broadly to the navy, Dear and Michell remind the audience that marriage to Wentworth will also provide Anne with a point of entry

into the group already established as the one most likely to fill the leadership void left by the failure of the landed gentry.

Because they want to maintain a focus on the end point of Anne's search for a new home, Dear and Michell minimize the barriers that stand in the way of her transitional integration into Uppercross society. Although they display many of the same flaws as their predecessors in the novel, the film's Musgroves are immediately much more appreciative of Anne's good qualities and ready to receive her into their family circle. In the course of a greatly expanded version of Anne's first visit to the Great House, Henrietta displays a genuine appreciation of her piano playing; Mr. Musgrove tells her that she is "most welcome amongst us" (Dear, 19); and Louisa converses with the new arrival rather than listen to her sister's harp playing. The family's ready acceptance of this new member of their community is expressed visually by two long shots in which Anne is located at or near the centre of a cluster of Musgroves.

While Dear and Michell are, to some extent, merely simplifying and speeding up the same journey that Anne takes in the novel, they are also moving her towards a somewhat different future than the one envisaged by Austen. For Austen, the navy is even "more distinguished in its domestic virtues than in its national importance" (II, 12, 275) and it is clear that, peripatetic as their life together is likely to be, Anne and Wentworth will nevertheless make homes for themselves on dry land rather than on board ship.[19] However, Austen's sentence is turned on its head in the film version of *Persuasion*.[20] Whereas the navy's professional role is only summarized in the novel in contrast to its domestic achievements which are described in some detail, Dear and Michell begin and end their film with powerful visual representations of life at sea but pay little attention to the sailors' capacity for making homes out of rented accommodations. Given this change in emphasis, it is not really surprising that, in the film's final scenes, rather than take on a married woman's traditional role, Anne joins Wentworth as he returns to active service. In order for this revised ending to make sense at an individual as well as an institutional level, Dear and Michell create a hero and heroine who differ in some significant ways from Austen's Frederick Wentworth and Anne Elliot. An analysis that again pays attention to images of movement will serve to clarify these differences.

In the novel, Captain Wentworth experiences some difficulties in adapting to the pace of civilian life after a career in the wartime navy. This is particularly evident in his impetuous approach to courtship. Nevertheless, prior to the unsettling experience at Lyme and the emotional confusion caused by his renewed love for Anne, Wentworth, as we saw earlier, often demonstrates a gentlemanly capacity for decisive and appropriate action in the service of people in distress. Apart from the incident in which he steps forward to secure a place for Anne in the Crofts' carriage, the film's Wentworth differs markedly from his novelistic counterpart in that he typically either remains motionless or follows the lead of the Musgrove sisters. A hero at sea, Wentworth lacks agency on dry land and his tall, erect and powerfully masculine figure functions frequently as little more than the object of Henrietta and Louisa's erotic gaze, particularly during his first visit to Uppercross Cottage and a later hunting scene. Whenever he does move—whether dancing wildly with Henrietta, being led along the hedgerow by Louisa, or catching Louisa as she leaps down from stiles during the walk to Winthrop—Wentworth is guided almost entirely by the young women's sexual energy. His ineffectuality in the civilian sphere is expressed most powerfully by the high angle swish pan that records his desperate but unsuccessful attempt to catch Louisa Musgrove as she falls from the Cobb.

Wentworth remains a powerful phallic presence when the action moves to Bath, where an umbrella and pen replace the shotgun he carries at Uppercross. However, he is, if anything, even less successful than the novel's Wentworth in either conveying his feelings to Anne or meeting the romantic challenge presented by William Walter Elliot. When not motionless, Wentworth now tends to withdraw from situations that call for decisive action. In Molland's, he can only stand by impotently as Anne takes Mr. Elliot's umbrella in preference to his. Later, although the concert scene begins with him striding decisively through the Assembly Rooms, it concludes with another victory for his rival, who leads Anne back to her seat while Wentworth moves off in the other direction. Similarly, a brief conversation with Anne at the White Hart is brought to an abrupt end when Mary calls her sister over to the window to observe William Walter Elliot in the street below. The extent of the gap that continues to exist between the potential lovers is conveyed by a deep focus shot in which a table and three seated figures separate Wentworth in the close foreground from Anne at the back of the frame. Rather than bridge that gap, Wentworth once again turns away from Anne and leaves the room.

It is not until the later White Hart scene that Wentworth demonstrates an ability to bring something of the vitality and vigor of his naval role to bear on his relationship with Anne. On this occasion, after once again exiting, Wentworth suddenly reenters the room, his finally aggressive body invading and overflowing the frame, and directs Anne's attention to a letter containing his declaration of love. He is equally decisive in moving to claim and then kiss Anne in the street outside the White Hart and in boldly interrupting the Elliots' card party in order to publicly announce his engagement to Anne. Wentworth's power on this latter occasion is such that, as he declares his marital intentions, he seems to draw the rapidly tracking camera to the rear of the frame where it ends in a close shot of his face. However, these belated positive images of Wentworth do more to prepare the way for the resumption of his naval career than to suggest that he now possesses the domestic capabilities of his counterpart in Austen's novel. Wentworth is not, therefore, completely himself until the last scene in the film when a low-angle long shot reveals his commanding figure standing on the upper deck of his ship, in total charge of all that surrounds him and ready to meet the challenge of whatever it is he is surveying on the horizon. The fully extended telescope that Wentworth holds aloft is the most prominent of the several admittedly not very subtle phallic symbols with which he is associated in the course of the film. No longer the passive object of the erotic attention of others, Wentworth now controls the film's gaze and his own destiny.

Just as they modify Austen's Wentworth so that he becomes unsuited to a life away from his ship, so Dear and Michell create an Anne Elliot who is plausibly destined for direct involvement in her husband's career. Like Austen's character, the heroine of the film version of *Persuasion* is a model of female gentility: quiet, elegant, well-mannered, principled, and always concerned to be of service to others. Additionally, though, and to a much greater extent than the character in the novel, Dear and Michell's Anne exhibits many of the characteristics of a more modern ideal of womanhood in that she is openly emotional, assertive, physically energetic, and displays a capacity for leadership. The revisionist impulse implicit in Dear and Michell's portrayal of Anne Elliot becomes obvious early in the film, first, in her overtly distressed response to Sir Walter's mention of Wentworth's name and, second, in the direct manner of her questions to Lady Russell about the wisdom of her advice to reject Wentworth.

Anne's behavior during the Uppercross and Lyme episodes is closely based on Austen's text. Thus, she alternately strives to become a useful member of her new communities and withdraws from social involvement whenever Wentworth is part of the group. One scene in particular, though, is structured in such a way as to take full advantage of the suggestion made by Austen in her version of the episode that, while circumstances might sometimes defeat her, Anne is fundamentally an energetic woman well suited to a leadership role.[21] In the moments before the child Walter is brought home with a broken collarbone, Anne is shot in dim candlelight sadly contemplating herself in a mirror as she prepares for a first meeting with Wentworth that she is clearly "dreading" (Dear, 24). No sooner do sounds of distress penetrate the gloom that surrounds her, however, than Anne becomes animated and, in a sudden movement, the speed of which is emphasized by a quick pan, goes over to the window. All is chaos below but the calmness of the interior scene that follows demonstrates the speed and efficiency with which Anne has imposed order on the situation. A track left, which follows the doctor as he moves away from the more centrally located Charles and Mary in order to consult with Anne, emphasizes her position of leadership within the group.

Dear and Michell's revisionist tendencies are most pronounced during scenes set in Bath in which Anne displays a level of self assertion that sometimes verges on the aggressive.[22] On two occasions, she directly opposes her family by putting into words what remain as thoughts in the novel. First, she arouses the anxious anger of her father and sister by speaking unenthusiastically about the prospect of meeting Lady Dalrymple and, later, she responds to Sir Walter's cruel mockery of her friend with the sharp comment, directed at the Elliots' protégée Mrs. Clay, that Mrs. Smith "is not the only widow in Bath, with little to live on, and no surname of dignity" (Dear, 67). Anne is equally forthright in expressing herself when, in a moment of spontaneity captured by a fast tracking shot, she ignores propriety and runs across the Pump Room to greet the Crofts. Later, the frustration experienced by Anne as expectations mount that she will marry William Walter Elliot finds an outlet in two angry outbursts, one aimed at Lady Russell and the other at Captain Wentworth.

Some of Anne's most assertive behavior occurs in situations involving her relationship with Wentworth. At the concert, for example, she ignores the rules of decorum that severely restrict her attempts to create opportunities for conversation with Wentworth in Austen's novel. Thus, rather than merely make "a little advance" (II, 8, 197) to attract Wentworth's attention, Anne forces him to halt his rapid progress through the Octagon Room by blocking his path. Later, observing that Wentworth is leaving, she immediately terminates her conversation with William Walter Elliot and rushes down the aisle to intercept him. The mixture of circling camera and character movements used as Anne and Wentworth maneuver around each other communicates a clear sense of her urgency and disregard for formal rules of conduct.

In the novel *Persuasion*, Anne's open display of emotion after reading Wentworth's declaration of love and the lovers' subsequent improvised meeting in the street show that Austen's usually controlled and proper heroine is moving in a direction that somewhat resembles the one she takes in the film. However, although they closely follow the earlier parts of Austen's proposal scene, Dear and Michell clearly do not believe that what happens once the action moves onto the street goes far enough in expressing their conception of Anne Elliot. Thus, they introduce a public kiss, the passion of which is conveyed by the metonymic use of a wildly exuberant circus parade, and replace the novel's lengthy process of retrospection with Wentworth's almost cursory comment that "I tried to forget you. I thought I had" (Dear, 88), in order to ensure that their Anne continues to be more informal and focused on the future than Austen's.

Dear and Michell use the film's last two scenes to complete their revisionist portrayal of Anne Elliot. In the first, the Elliots' card party, Anne displays a supreme confidence and considerable mobility. Now dressed in a rich bronze that sharply contrasts the deathly white that she wore in the early Kellynch scenes and followed almost obsequiously by a hand-held camera, Anne glides amongst the tables, pausing only to smile in secret delight at her sister's misguided attempts to seize control of the newly acceptable Wentworth, to listen with amusement to more advice from Lady Russell, and to casually dismiss William Walter Elliot's declaration of love. In the second, which serves as a brief coda of her progress during the film, Anne leaves a dark, secluded and cramped cabin, climbs up two flights of steps towards the light, and takes her place on the upper deck of a man-of-war, the obvious equal of the commanding figure of Captain Wentworth.[23]

As a result of their skilful handling of Austen's movement motif, sometimes staying close to their source text and sometimes deviating markedly from it, Dear and Michell create a film that is at once deeply rooted in the ideological and social turmoil of early nineteenth-century England and yet reflective of a late twentieth-century view of the role of women. Their approach has a lot in common with Jane Campion's in *The Piano*, a film alluded to several times in the film version of *Persuasion*.[24] Thus, just as Campion's Ada McGrath is both a victim of Victorian patriarchy and colonial oppression and a prototype for the modern, independent woman, quite the equal of any man and capable of pursuing a career of her own, so Dear and Michell's Anne Elliot is simultaneously a product of a specific historical era and a woman of our times. The difficulties inherent in achieving what might be called a stereoscopic viewpoint, one that aims to combine two pictures of the same subject shot from slightly different angles into a single satisfyingly three-dimensional image, are illustrated by Patricia Rozema's sometimes clumsy efforts to overlay Austen's *Mansfield Park* with a patina of contemporary feminist and liberal values. However, Dear and Michell, undoubtedly aided by the strong awareness of approaching modernity present in Austen's novel, are quite successful in realizing their goals. The film version of *Persuasion* manages to encapsulate many of the issues that were preoccupying Austen late in her career while creating a heroine likely to appeal to the sensibilities of a late twentieth-century audience.

The Construction of a Myth:
The "Cinematic Jane Austen"
as a Cross-Cultural Icon

Ariane Hudelet

In the previous chapters, the search for Jane Austen's "cinematic" quality has been conducted in her texts, and in some correspondences between texts and films. But "the cinematic Jane Austen" could also be seen as a cultural phenomenon at the turn of the twenty-first century. The cinematic Austenmania (which started in 1995, and in spite of many prophecies of its demise, has continued to develop until now)[1] has slightly altered the meaning of "Jane Austen" as a public phenomenon, a cultural icon. The relationship between Austen and film has led even her texts (as this book tries to show) to be read differently—today, Jane Austen is cinematic also because film has changed the way we know her.[2] Some could object that her texts remain what they have always been, and what they always will be. Yet, some of the most interesting analyses written recently about Austen pay attention precisely to the instability of the texts themselves: Kathryn Sutherland, for instance, reminds us that a text is subject to variations according to the different editions, to the illustrations that accompany it, and more essentially, to the object through which it is transmitted:

> What is the identity of a literary work of art? ... Can we know it apart from a document or a text that embodies it? ... As editors and critics, we are less and less willing to believe in the singularity of the work, its status as object.... And since with literature, as with music, we are dealing from the outset of its public life with a disseminated and not a uniquely identified art form, can't we simply forget about ideas of authenticity?[3]

Sutherland here raises the question of the diverse modes of existence of a text, in an era which sees an impressive multiplication of these, which necessarily also changes the nature of the text, and thus of the way it is received.

The function of cinema and television in providing access to literary works today cannot be ignored. Jane Austen, in this regard, occupies a very special position, since her works have always called for recreation, interpretation, performance (as Sutherland explains, "her novels' insight appears as decisively settled as our appetite for their reinvention is determinedly unappeased and unsettling"),[4] a phenomenon that has been increased tremendously by the plethora of cinematic adaptations since the 1990s. We may sometimes regret the nature of this evolution, often linked to a reassuring, unproblematic, rather conventional form of romance and wish fulfillment, yet this "Jane Austen" also brings us back to a fundamental aspect that has contributed to her popularity over the ages: the association between the reassuring closure of romance, and the very modern exploration of self-formation.[5]

I will consider now the function the texts seem to serve for very diverse types of audiences,[6] and explain how her works can become more mythical raw material than a textual narrative that demands conformity. The choice of the term "myth" can seem surprising for texts which are at the same time as precisely realistic, and as local and circumscribed, as Austen's.[7] Yet the word seems particularly relevant when one considers that her plots and characters have proven endlessly adaptable to different contexts and cultures (from a Beverly Hills high school to a rural village in Tamil Nadu); that for many adepts, the limit between fiction and reality is often blurred as far as Austen is concerned (Austenian characters are often discussed as if they had an independent life of their own, and Austen herself becomes a fictional character in the many biographies and two bio-pics recently released); and that a real cult has developed around the texts and films (a brief browse on the web demonstrates this). The six novels, the numerous films, the (often fantasized) existence of the author herself, combine into a composite narrative which means something else than itself, and which is felt to provide answers, explanations and moral lessons (about the self, the meaning of life, love and companionship) to readers or viewers, however remote Austen's original world may be from their own existence, setting or era.[8] Thus, these Austenian characters and stories seem to escape from their original context to become appropriated by diverse groups, because they convey what are considered universal truths.

Whole books or articles could be written about the reasons for this "mythical" destiny of the texts, about the elements which give them such a resonance today. I choose, however, to consider how just two recent films, the American production *The Jane Austen Book Club* and the Tamil film *Kandukondain Kandukondain* (English title, *I Have Found It*), reflect the malleability of Austen's texts and the type of function they seem to serve today through their multiple incarnations. Of course these are not the only examples I could have chosen; there are many other modern appropriations, or "makeovers," of Austen. *Clueless, Bridget Jones's Diary, Bride and Prejudice,* and to some extent *Metropolitan* or *Jane Austen in Manhattan,* have already provided modern "seasonings" of Austen's characters, plots or themes. I reduced the selection to these two films because they embody, each in their different manner, the radical way with which the cinematic Jane Austen seems to serve some specific needs among contemporary audiences, from one end of the planet to the other.

A Fable on Tradition and Modernity: Kandukondain Kandukondain

Why would a Tamil director decide to adapt Jane Austen in a mainstream Indian production? Probably thanks to her international cinematic fame—*Kandukondain,* in many ways seems to be more a remake of Ang Lee's film than an actual adaptation of Austen's *Sense and Sensibility.*[9] Yet the film is fascinating for the way it uses the backbone of Austen's story to reflect on the mutations of India at the turn of the twenty-first century. In *Kandukondain,* the story, characters and themes are perfectly assimilated to Indian references, which brings us back to the question of why an author as typically English, local and circumscribed as Austen can seem so appropriate a filter to represent current issues in a context apparently so remote as modern-day Tamil Nadu. For more clarity, it is necessary to sum up the plot briefly. Life in the village of Poongudi is ruled by a rich and powerful family: old and sick Chandrasekhar (the equivalent of Henry Dashwood), his daughter Padma (Mrs. Dashwood), and his three granddaughters, Sowmya (Elinor), Meenakshi (Marianne) and Kamala (Margaret). Meenakshi believes in romantic love and spends her days dreaming about a providential man who will win her heart by declaiming poems by Barathiyar, her favorite poet. Sowmya, a serious, responsible computer engineer, has a reputation for bad luck because of her birth date, and thus cannot find a husband in spite of her mother's efforts. Then Manohar (Edward), an aspiring filmmaker, appears and falls in love with Sowmya but wants to direct his first film before marrying her. Major Bala (Colonel Brandon), a survivor from the Kargil war, falls in love with Meena, but she meets Srikanth (Willoughby), a young golden boy financier who shares her love of Barathiyar's poetry.

When the grandfather dies, his will, which had been drafted while he still resented his daughter for marrying without consent, bequeaths everything to his son who comes to take possession of the estate with his wife. Humiliated, Padma and her daughters are forced to leave the village and live in miserable conditions in Chennai, until Sowmya can find a suitable job. In the meanwhile, Srikanth's company has gone bankrupt and he chooses to marry a rich heiress in order to save his business. Meenakshi, broken-hearted, almost drowns herself in a monsoon flood. Saved by Major Bala, who then encourages her to work on her musical talents, she becomes a successful singer and eventually falls in love with her rescuer. After a series of misunderstandings, Manohar, who has managed to direct his first movie, comes back to Sowmya who agrees to marry him. The film ends with a double wedding.

The duality in Austen's title evokes the mutations of the long eighteenth-century, which is often separated into two movements, the age of reason (the Enlightenment, pragmatic philosophy, scientific discoveries, the notion of progress), and the age of sensibility (characterized by sentimentalism, or the insistence on the power of imagination). As Tony Tanner and Claudia Johnson show, Austen's novel was written at a time when the excesses of sensibility were being called into question (notably because of the horrors caused by the revolution in France), but the novel does not take sides exclusively with one or the other.[10] This evolution cannot be dissociated from the socioeconomic context of the time: as John Wiltshire explains, Austen wrote at a time of "more generally diffused affluence," which meant a "shift from traditional to commercial society, or the modern, [which] has been and is now, much later, replicated in other parts of the globe."[11] India is precisely undergoing a comparable evolution at the turn of the twenty-first century, and Austen's story thus provides an apt metaphor of "the emergence of the modern"[12] which is currently taking place in the subcontinent. *Kandukondain* develops the exchanges and tensions between the two poles of sense and sensibility by applying them to the deep mutations which affect gender roles, the status of women, and the debate over arranged marriages, but also to the political and military situation (here presented through the character of Major Bala), as well as the economic and cultural evolution of the country. The film stresses notably the opposition between traditional economy and capitalist enterprise, and more generally sets the influence of Western models against more traditional values, and ancestral religious and cultural references.

One of the attractions of Austen's story for the filmmaker seems to have been the focus on women. *Kandukondain,* a product of the Chennai film industry,[13] is original within the context of Indian cinema because of its focus on the relationships between two sisters, and between mother and daughters, rather than the more common plot model which represents the relationships between mother and son.[14] The story of the film revolves around marriage, and the two sisters' diverging perceptions of it which reflect the changes in modes of thinking in contemporary India resulting from the modernization of the country and the growing influence of the West. Arranged marriages are indeed more and more questioned, especially in urban areas, just as, in Austen's novels, women have recently acquired "the power of refusal"[15] which leads to crucial individual decisions. The sisters in *Kandukondain* represent two different conceptions of marriage. For romantic Meenakshi, it can only be the result of intense, passionate love, whereas Sowmya trusts her mother's judgment to find a suitable husband for her. In their first scene, she links the chance governing her existence with that which will preside over her marriage: "I did not choose any of this, why should I choose only the husband?"[16] The duality between the two sisters leads to an ironical reversal, since Meenakshi eventually marries Bala, who initially came as a possible suitor for Sowmya, while the latter marries Manohar for love.

But beyond this focus on women and marriage, the crucial appeal of Austen's story for the Indian adapters is its exploration of the question of identity, and the eventual balance it advocates between the personal and the social, between sense and sensibility. Just as in Austen, the love stories in the film are inscribed in a very present socio-economic context. The references to the mutations of modern-day India, in terms of economy, way of life or ideology, are complex and tend to revolve around the poles of modernity and tradition, without systematically preferring one to the other, but instead promoting an enlightened balance. Meenakshi is probably the character who evolves the most during the film; she embodies some aspects of modernity and of the Western influences at first since she rejects arranged marriages, but she is in fact the most traditional in her way of life. She remains idle, even when her family is on the brink of misery (she spends all her time trying to find Srikanth's phone number, while her mother is forced to sell her jewelry and work) until the Major leads her towards an artistic career. All the energy and passion which the young woman devotes to feelings for much of the film are transformed finally into a sort of generous, matronly bluntness, an attitude more generally associated with the stereotype of the wife or mother: she scolds the Major when he refuses her help, and considers, with ironic tenderness, the last fight between Manohar and Sowmya. The latter, on the contrary, is educated and has a "serious" job, and leads an active life which does not prevent her from accepting the logic of arranged marriages.

Next to these characters, the film represents also a whole society in search of its identity. Different economic sectors are represented through the activities of the characters. Major Bala belongs both to the military and rural worlds: his previous military career indeed contrasts with his current occupation, since he owns an horticultural business, "Bala Blooms," a traditional activity associated with the beauty and ritual importance of flowers in Hindu life. His rival, Srikanth, represents the exact opposite of this way of life. His first appearance on screen follows a scene featuring the two sisters praying in a temple. After a sequence in which the young women, dressed in colorful saris are presented in traditional postures of devotion, the viewer encounters, without transition, a very saturated shot in which silhouettes of men in Western suits stand out in a frame where everything is black, grey and white. One understands after a while that this is a television program presenting Srikanth's business as the perfect example of India's dynamism and modernity, a proposition which proves to be an illusion when his business collapses because of speculation, thereby ruining most of his customers. To save his business and thus avoid shame and dishonor, Srikanth marries a rich heiress. But modernity is not only associated with this negatively presented character: Manohar is also at the crossroads between all these mutations and influences, this time in the artistic domain. He wants to direct his own screenplay, but when he realizes the changes the studio wants to impose to him (to transform his action film into a "real Tamil picture," with songs and a mother character), he quits. After finding other financing sources, he then accepts many modifications to his script (notably the addition of songs, and the transformation of his hero into a heroine) without feeling that he is betraying his original ambition. Thus, the film presents some dangers of both radical modernization and absolute conservatism, and therefore seems to advocate a sort of compromise. In both cases, conventions and traditions allow the characters to avoid ruin and failure although the moral compromise is more problematic in the case of Srikanth.

If the film seems to advocate a balance between tradition and modernization, it mostly stresses the need to preserve a specifically Indian identity against damaging Western influences. In this process of redefinition of national values, the role of women is essential. The film insists, for instance, on the passage from hereditary riches and family power to wealth and power that are acquired personally (by women), although without advocating individualism. As a plate on the front of the house, which is often visible on screen, indicates, Chandrasekhar's estate is called "Lakshmi Nivas," the palace of Lakshmi. In Hindu mythology, Lakshmi is the goddess of wealth, power and beauty. She is traditionally represented on a throne made out of lotus flowers, and holds in her hands, two other Lotus flowers, named "Padma" and "Kamala," like the mother and the youngest sister. Lakshmi is a domestic deity particularly popular among women, who look to her to protect the well-being and prosperity of the family. "Meenakshi" is also the name of a goddess, Sowmya being therefore the only one who is not associated with any mythological or religious figure. When she is hired as a computer engineer in Chennai, she buys a beautiful apartment in a modern building, and several shots feature the plate on her door inscribed only with her own name, "Sowmya." The replacement of "Lakshmi Nivas" with the name of the young woman shows the transition from a traditional household to a family that is taken up in the reality of urban economics, where the responsible, working woman provides for the family.

Like Norland in *Sense and Sensibility*, Lakshmi Nivas becomes corrupted when Padma's brother and sister-in-law take possession. In a series of scenes that are very close to those in Ang Lee's film, the women are gradually expelled by the newcomers. The latter are clearly depicted as vulgar upstarts, who embody the most despicable aspects of modern, capitalist India. Just as John and Fanny Dashwood are likely to bring damage to Norland, notably with their plans for improvement, in the form of cutting down trees and building hothouses, the characters in the Indian film plan to transform the palace into a coffee shop or a restaurant. They discuss these plans in English, while drinking a kind of Coca Cola, which associates them with the nefarious influence of Western capitalism.

These transpositions show how well Austen's narrative structure, and some episodes from Ang Lee's film, are used to address eminently modern questions. An internet user provides a commentary on *Kandukondain* which differentiates it from Ang Lee's film: "While Ang Lee did a commendable job in his treatment of the relationships, one could not identify or even feel for the character because the nature and society in which they were set were too distant. In *Kandukondain*, the characters are real. They are one of us, we are one of them."[17] The word is out: this type of cinematic appropriation manages to accentuate the identification process and to make the story more "real." Here, film adaptation is no longer about adapting a canonical text or textual strategies, but about the appropriation of a framework which can apply to very diverse cultures and contexts. The necessity for women to make their own choices based on a balance of sense and sensibility, and the integration of sentimental relationships in a very realistically depicted socio-economic environment, are two of the main features of the novel which contribute to its universal, a-temporal appeal, now actualized in cinematic adaptations.

By appropriating characters, events and a plot structure from Jane Austen and by integrating them into a very popular Indian cultural form, this film could also embody a compromise with the literary culture of the former colonizing power. *Kandukondain* is thus a very rich cultural object, since it represents the meeting between an author whose image is associated with a very circumscribed idea of Englishness, and a cinema which used to be deemed incomprehensible to a Western audience. Through films such as *Kandukondain*, "Jane Austen" and her stories seem therefore perfectly "real," and relevant to modern-day realities, an entity that allows mediation between apparently contradictory forms or cultures, just as the texts themselves have also been associated with "narrative mediation," examples of "*conceivable* mediation between otherwise incommensurable 'worlds'; of men and women; of realism and romance; of art and popular culture (which expresses itself since the twentieth century as a new film audience for her narratives); and finally of the material and ideational (or spiritual) contexts for understanding literature itself."[18]

"The Perfect Antidote to Life": The Jane Austen Book Club

Directed by Robin Swicord in 2007, *The Jane Austen Book Club* was first a successful novel by Karen Joy Fowler (2004). Both novel and film follow six characters who decide to start an "all Jane Austen all the time Book Club" in modern-day California. The discussions around each of Austen's novels, led by each of the six members of the group successively, structure both works, and a network of echoes and correspondences develop between Austen's characters and the members of the club. "Jane Austen" is presented in the film as a powerful connecting force between these different people, and Austenian texts are used as a sort of behavioral therapy for women whose private lives are under strain—the novels seem particularly relevant to events in their real lives, "just as the horoscope always seems to be about you."[19] Whereas in each chapter, the novel resorts to flashbacks revealing the past of the characters, the film concentrates more on the diegetic present, and on the interweaving between references to Austen and the characters' lives: Sylvia's recent divorce, Jocelyn and Grigg's relationship, Allegra's deceptive girlfriend, Prudie's marital problems and her crush on a high school student, and Bernadette's reminiscences of her several marriages.

Austen's characters, her own life, her "lessons" on love, marriage, and human relationships, are the main topics for discussion, more than her literary technique or ideological position (one character, Prudie, is stigmatized for her pedantic references to Austen's irony and literary techniques: it is clearly not what is at stake here). The limit between fiction and reality is blurred, and Austen's fictional creations become as important to the book club members as real people. This is demonstrated by Jocelyn and Grigg's debate over the "reality" of characters: when he asks her if she has read the science fiction books he recommended, she answers, "I prefer books about real people," to which he ironically answers, "So Elizabeth Bennet is real, but people in science fiction are not?" Austen's characters thus assume a mythic quality because of the way they are perceived by those readers, who "recognize in them the emblematic representation of their desires, fantasies or fears."[20] In the club's discussions, the literary characters also seem to recede slightly; what matters most is the way each member interacts with Colonel Brandon, Fanny Price or Anne Elliot, more than Austen's technique of characterization. This interaction is also often influenced by the cinematic adaptations of the novels: in the film, Bernadette and Prudie get acquainted talking about Rozema's *Mansfield Park*, Prudie and Allegra start fighting because Allegra refers to Ang Lee's *Sense and Sensibility* rather than Austen's, and Bernadette's reference to "an encounter in the woods with Mr. Darcy" certainly bears the mark of Colin Firth's interpretation in the BBC miniseries.[21]

Austen's works are thus considered as almost magical narratives that readers have integrated to their own private lives and beliefs, and where they can find the expression of a symbolical thought in relation to human psyche and concerns. "Jane Austen" thus becomes a sort of solution to the main problems in these mostly female characters' lives; her novels supply answers and moral lessons, provided one knows how to read them. This corresponds to a class of myths described by Northrop Frye:

> Certain stories seem to have a peculiar significance: they are the stories that tell a society what it important for it to know, whether about its gods, its history, its laws, or its class structure. These stories may be called myths in a secondary sense, a sense that distinguishes them from folktales—stories told for entertainment or other less central purposes. They thus become "sacred" as distinct from "profane" stories.[22]

Novel and film also illustrate the phenomenon of sacralization that accompanies such an evolution in the status of the texts. The book club meetings are indeed presented as rituals, centered on the communion around sacred texts as well as food and drink. Any profanation is censored, for instance when Prudie calls the author by her first name, or on the occasions when Grigg admits he has never read *Pride and Prejudice* and reveals that he thinks Austen's novels, which he has purchased in a single volume, may be sequels. Austenian texts are supposed to be *already known* by everyone, part of the collective unconscious; when Bernadette decides to start the book club, the prerequisite is that they should discuss "books that [they]'ve already read," and Austen emerges as the natural choice. Ironically enough, Grigg's naïve assumption that her novels are related as sequels is not so far from reality, when one considers the way the discussions of the different novels often intersect, and how the different heroes are set into competition,[23] or how Austen herself seems to become a fictional character. Jane Austen's texts had already given way to rituals before the age of film, as Kipling's story about Janeites indicates,[24] but cinema has brought the phenomenon to a more significant level, by expanding the range of the audience concerned, in terms of place, gender and social class (as our two examples illustrate, from rural Tamil Nadu to urban California, from the middle-class audience of *The Jane Austen Book Club* to the very popular appeal of Indian cinema).

The bond that "Jane Austen" creates among this "bunch of old women, and married women, and lesbians"[25] (Grigg excluded, of course, as the only man in the group) is materialized in the narrative voice used in Fowler's novel, which expresses itself as "we," while never identifying with a particular member of the group. The connection underlying this "we" in the novel is only based on Jane Austen and her novels, some characters knowing each other before, and others joining the group only on the occasion of the book club. The beginning of the novel makes it clear: the book is not going to be so much about Jane Austen as with the way several characters have appropriated these stories, and incorporated them to their own, private histories. The recurrent use of possessives in the Prologue presents the different faces of "Austen" according to the readers: "Each of us has a private Austen," the first sentence goes, before making a list of the diverse "Austens" we are going to meet: "Jocelyn's Austen wrote...," "Bernadette's Austen was a comic genius...," "Sylvia's Austen was a daughter, a sister, an aunt," and so on (3–5). The "romance" dimension of the novels, and most of all their happy endings, play a central role, sometimes perceived as uplifting and inspiring, or occasionally as dangerously deceptive. In the novel, Allegra claims that science fiction is perfectly innocuous as opposed to Austen, who is "writing the really dangerous books.... Books that people really do believe, even hundreds of years later. How virtue will be recognized and rewarded. How love will prevail. How life is a romance" (141). In the film, the fact that all her novels end with marriage is repeatedly stressed as well, as by Sylvia who laments, "Austen has a way of making you forget most marriages end in divorce." Each character has a specific reason for joining the book club that is linked with sentimental disappointment: Jocelyn has just lost her dog and Bernadette wants to cheer her up; Sylvia has just been left by her husband and the others (including Allegra, her daughter) want to help her get over him; Jocelyn invites Grigg in order to set him up with Sylvia, whereas he joins because he is attracted to her. The film's characters are all younger and more attractive than in the novel, and the happy ending is more absolute than in the source text, even if Fowler's conclusion already stresses the very beneficial effect the Austen book club has had in their lives, notably when Grigg suggests they continue their literary activity with another author: "We'd let Austen into our lives, and now we were all either married or dating. Could O'Brian have done this?" (249) In the film, this proposal takes the form of an idealized final dinner in which all the happy couples plan to convert a newcomer, Bernadette's new husband, who has not yet been "Austenized."

Whatever problem these characters encounter, Austen's texts indeed seem curative as Bernadette predicts: "It's the perfect antidote ... to life!" At the end of the novel, Allegra transforms a "Magic 8 ball" into an "Austen ball," replacing the usual answers with quotations from the novels: "She'd painted it a dark green, and over the old 8, she'd transferred a reproduction of Cassandra Austen's sketch of her sister, set in a framed oval like a cameo.... *Ask Austen* was painted in red on the ribbon" (233–4). This anecdote is dropped from the film, which prefers to develop this theme through another secondary plot concerning Prudie, the prim high school French teacher, and her attraction to Trey, the handsome student. When Prudie is about to yield to her desire and join Trey in a motel, the film represents her standing on one side of a busy street, while Trey waits for her on the other. She gazes at the traffic light which, instead of the traditional "walk" or "don't walk" signs, flashes four words successively: "WHAT / WOULD / JANE / DO?"

References to Austen are thus incorporated into the most trivial aspects of modern life, into the very objects and conventions which regulate our social behavior today, such as traffic lights. The highly effective symbolism of the moment is part of a more general introduction of Austen into modern everyday life in the film, as in the opening sequence which represents all the little disagreements of everyday life in a modern American city (overhearing other people's cell phone conversations, losing a parking ticket, and so on), a sequence placed under the auspices of an Austen quotation: "Is not general incivility the very essence of love?" The sentence, extracted from its original context, takes on a meaning that is very far from its original sense, like most "Austen quotes" that are to be found on commercial artifacts today, such as mugs, sewing kits, and writing paper. Yet, these examples demonstrate that Austen's narratives have become part of modern "mythologies" in the sense defined by Barthes, that is "adapted to a certain consumption, invested with ... a social usage."[26]

Should we then consider this "sacralization" of Austen through film, and through multiple forms of adaptation or appropriation, as actually a debasement, the manifestation of a consumerist culture which deprives the original works of their complex and subtle meaning? The phenomenon is not absolutely new; the novels have long been compared to fairy tales, and audiences have been attracted to the satisfactory closures of these romances as much as to the ironic distance of their style. Beyond their fairy tale quality, however, the realism of Austen's plots and the fact that they are "actualized" by cinema stresses the relevance of these stories in our everyday life, brings them also very close to the notion of myth with regard to the function they serve. As Lévi-Strauss explains, "individual works are all potential myths, but it is their adoption on the collective mode which actualizes, as it were, their mythism."[27] Cinema has greatly accentuated the identification process, and these stories and characters seem more and more to escape their original source to follow a separate destiny. This is not necessarily detrimental to the original work: "nothing demonstrates more certainly the power of a creator than the infidelity or the disobedience of its creature. The more alive it was made, the freer it was made. Even its rebellion glorifies the author: God knows...."[28] The common reluctance to accept new manifestations of "Jane Austen" today, and her multifaceted presence in our contemporary world, partakes of the resistance to the idea of separation between form and content, as Kamilla Elliot explains: "adaptation commits the heresy of showing that form (expression) can be separated from content (ideas)—something both mainstream aesthetic and semiotic theories have resisted or denied."[29] Because of its acute visibility, "Jane Austen" as a cultural mix of literature, film, and individual imagination, can sometimes be felt to eclipse the original texts, the "real" nature of the historical author and her intentions (whatever they may have been) and to substitute for them a vague mythical concept whose "fundamental character," to use Barthes's terms again, "is to be appropriated."[30]

Afterword: On Fidelity

JOHN WILTSHIRE

Nothing is more common among academic film critics than to disparage the notion of "fidelity." "The study of adaptation," argues Brian McFarlane in a widely cited and influential study, "has been inhibited and blurred by ... the near fixation with the issue of fidelity." "Fidelity, it needs to be stressed," he writes, "cannot profitably be used as an evaluative criterion; it can be no more than a descriptive term to designate loosely a certain kind of adaptation."[1] More recently, in an important article Thomas Leitch has declared that "fidelity to its source text—whether it is conceived as success in re-creating specific textual details or the effect of the whole—is a hopelessly fallacious measure of a given adaptation's value because it is unattainable, undesirable, and theoretically possible only in a trivial sense."[2] He adds that "the valorization of fidelity amounts to a valorization of literature as such in face of the insurgent challenge of cinema studies."[3] Or as Erica Sheen puts it: "Fidelity criticism is perhaps most appropriately seen as a rhetoric of possession."[4] Such assertions cut both ways, of course.

In this chapter, I take up the broad debate in the specific, and perhaps special, context of Jane Austen adaptations. The intention of anti-fidelity criticism, it might be argued, is to disenfranchise precisely that audience which shares knowledge with the scriptwriter and director—knowledge of and familiarity with the original "classic" texts. The audience for an Austen film may never have read an Austen novel, but there is a segment of that audience familiar with the books, and upon this segment the film's commercial and possibly critical success can depend. The filmmakers, like this audience, know their source novel well, and their decisions in making the film are very often guided by conscious reference to the source text. The commentaries on their film-making by directors and scriptwriters now common in DVD presentations of movies based on Austen make this plain. In these, allusions to the original novel are ubiquitous—either to validate a production decision through an appeal to the text's authority, to defend a departure by emphasizing the distinct capabilities of film, or to point out gaps which the adaptation has the opportunity to fill. Such commentaries are now part of the reference material which any study of adaptation must consult. The rhetoric of anti-fidelity film criticism seeks to quarantine this knowledge and expertise, rendering it irrelevant or damaging to a just critique of the film itself. What I propose is the reverse: that it actually enhances the appreciation of a film to know the novel from which it ultimately derives—that the reader who knows the novel is thus an ideal "reader" of the film. The paradox is that anti-fidelity criticism is often informed by knowledge of the source, but refuses, on principle, to allow that knowledge any role in understanding, or assessing the film. This disavowal, it might be suggested, puts an argument about adaptation in bad faith.

It may be that Austen adaptations are indeed a special case. The explosion of "Austenmania" in the decade of the nineteen-nineties was preceded but hardly anticipated by what Laura Carroll calls Whit Stillman's "dalliance" with *Mansfield Park* in his *Metropolitan* of 1990.[5] Nineteen ninety-five saw the release of the Ang Lee/Emma Thompson *Sense and Sensibility*, a six-hour BBC miniseries of *Pride and Prejudice*, the cinema release of a British film originally made for television, *Persuasion*, as well as *Clueless*, a teen comedy drawing much of its plot from *Emma*; the next year saw two versions of Austen's *Emma*, one made in Hollywood, one made for British television. Most of the films were presented and received under the banner of Jane Austen's name. *Mansfield Park* lagged behind in 1999. Less than a decade later another, more diverse, cluster of films and television productions marketed under the Austen brand appeared. *Pride and Prejudice* was released in 2005, new versions of *Mansfield Park*, *Persuasion* and *Northanger Abbey* were shown on British television in 2007, and a new three episode *Sense and Sensibility* was produced by the BBC soon after. More para–Austenian products began to appear, like *Becoming Jane* (2006), *The Jane Austen Book Club* (2007), *Miss Austen Regrets* (2008); still more are promised, or threatened. These films are released into a context in which the DVD (accessible as "Chapters") allows the interested viewer to give an attention to them analogous to the attention a reader gives a novel.

Mary Musgrove, in *Persuasion* "had got books from the library and changed them so often" that her stay in Lyme was trifled happily away *(P* II, 2, 141). Circulating libraries, often lending out three volume novels one volume at a time, were the most reliable market for works such as Jane Austen's. A romantic novel was trash, to be consumed, returned and quickly replaced by another. It is rare now to see one of Austen's in its original binding, which declares clearly how ephemeral and disposable the books were intended to be. But her works were quickly recognized as literature, not merely circulating library material; they were books to be purchased and re-read, as William Gifford, the publisher John Murray's aide, understood when he wrote to Murray that he had read *Pride and Prejudice* "*again*," his emphasis signaling how unusual this was.[6] All of them, but especially *Emma*, expect and require a reader who is prepared to dwell on the text; and, as the Cambridge editors of this novel remark, it was "in her bold decision to write a novel that demanded repeated rereadings, that Austen made the most striking claim for her profession."[7] Something loosely similar has now occurred with the films: instead of one screening, a DVD can be viewed many times, slowed down for frame by frame analysis, and thus one of the common critical claims about moving pictures, that they work through perception, whilst novels work through conception (however dubious in the first place) has been further eroded. As Leitch remarks, "the difference between percept and concept may well be more properly a function of rereading, and of a specifically analytical kind of rereading, than of a difference between movies, which are commonly assumed against mounting evidence to be watched only once, and novels."[8] And the DVD now, like the literary novel then, is something to be purchased, with the intention of re-viewing. The result is that far from that "hierarchy of genres," of which David Monaghan writes in the Introduction to this book, and which is so much objected to by anti-fidelity critics, there is now a convergence, if not of genres, certainly of forms.

Released within the same decade or so, these productions, if not in actual competition with each other, are at least in dialogue. The producers cannot but be aware of the other films released under the rubric of Austen, aware that they work within a quite specific genre, or rather species, of film, and quite conscious that their work will be judged (by the most informed of their audience) against the previous versions of the same novel. So the question of adaptation, and the related question of intertextuality, must be inflected differently in the very specific and novel conditions of Austen adaptation. That "each individual adaptation invokes many precursor texts besides the one whose title it usually borrows" is certainly true.[9] But the statement ignores the implicit contractual relationship offered when a film is presented with the same name as a famous novel. This is analogous to the "autobiographical pact" as defined by Philippe Lejeune.[10] If an autobiography's principal figure bears the same name as the author and narrator, there is an implicit contract with the reader that what they are reading is a true story. The audience for a film called *Bride and Prejudice* is cued to expect a variation on Austen's novel; but the audience for a film called *Pride and Prejudice* (even if as may well be the case, they have never read the novel) might reasonably expect that the film would offer some form of reproduction of the text whose name, and therefore whose authority, it bears. The statement also elides the question of differential cultural capital. Unlike most of the novels adapted for film, Austen's novels are in print in many editions; they are widely read and taught in the academy; this cultural capital is drawn upon by the film's backers, and for some, they carry a freight that the film is expected to honor.

Nevertheless, intertextuality must be seen as a marked feature of Austen adaptations. Whether consciously or not, they borrow from and allude to each other, so that the viewer of the whole emerging corpus may detect motifs, gestures, even whole sequences as echoes of a previous film. The clearest example, because the most conscious, is the McGrath *Emma* of 1995, which already signals in the opening sequence its relationship to the 1940 MGM *Pride and Prejudice*. Both movies begin with titles that emphasize the distance of their action from the contemporary world. "It happened in old England" becomes "A time when one's town was one's world," accompanied in each case by folksy sketches of great houses and small villages. There is certainly a tongue-in-cheek quality to these and other effects, such as the recreation of the bantering dialogue of the archery scene between Garson and Olivier (itself deriving from Hugh Thomson's nineteenth-century illustrations for Austen's novels) as an archery contest and exchange of barbs between Gwyneth Paltrow and Jeremy Northam, and in the film's reversion to old Hollywood in its screwball comedy, voice-over sequences, and fabulously artificial settings. It is possible that the director, mimicking the older film, is paralleling *Emma*'s own amused, sardonic and critical relation to the conventions of the romantic novel, but it is imitation, not satire, and perhaps not so much mimicry as homage. Both films carry the message, intrinsic to Austenland, that the past was a sunnier, less demanding place.

Much less clear, and perhaps more intriguing, are those similarities which therefore suggest how a common pool of effects and conventions has developed within the Austen film, as distinct from the Austen novel. Towards the close of the 2008 *Sense and Sensibility*, Colonel Brandon is shown with a tame hawk: he demonstrates his skill with the bird to Marianne, and the bird is then shown flying freely high in the air. Does this scene have any relation to the hawk which so noticeably sits on Colonel Tilney's shoulder, and signals his predatory nature, in the early television version of *Northanger Abbey* (1987)? What relation does it have to the motif of birds trapped and released in the *Mansfield Park* of 1999? Hawking is a period effect, and used in the one case to underline the character's viciousness, in the other to bolster the manliness of his pursuits. But when a motif is so systematically worked as it is in Rozema's film, its fallout will be less easy to define or isolate. In the 1995 *Persuasion*, Anne Elliot comes across a volume of the Navy List and opens it to find a letter in Captain Wentworth's handwriting, a sequence which skillfully communicates her desolate thoughts through the visual image; in the 2008 *Sense and Sensibility*, Elinor Dashwood, traveling towards the isolation of Devon in a coach, opens a volume and reads its dedication in Edward Ferrars's handwriting, an incident which similarly invites the viewer to imagine her desolation. Is one inspired by the other? Elizabeth Bennet surveys nude male statues in the Chatsworth sculpture gallery in a memorable sequence of Wright's *Pride and Prejudice* (2005): is this the reason why a classical nude presides over the setting where Willoughby rebuffs Marianne in the 2008 *Sense and Sensibility*? The very same statue is seen in the garden of Kellynch hall in the *Persuasion* of the previous year. Are these intertextual references or incidental props of Austenland?

Just as the films appear to borrow motifs or ideas from each other (or replicate features of the species), they depend to some extent upon each other for their life as commercial entities. To that degree then, the cinematic Jane Austen who is the subject of this book has been usurped as a source by previous films. Sometimes overtly, as in this 2007 *Persuasion*, they are presented as "By Jane Austen," but in any case they are perceived as authorized through the power of the same cultural icon, less of an author, more a romantic ideal. It is now possible to compare three such versions of *Emma*, four versions of *Pride and Prejudice*, and three versions of *Mansfield Park*. Films prepared for television viewing, to be interrupted every twenty minutes with ads for cellphones, insurance and supermarket bargains (like the ITV products of 2008) or appearing in serial form over several weeks, and made under even more exigent conditions than movies, are not precisely the same art-form, but comparing them is clearly a more viable option than referring them back to a novel. Moving between a film version and a novel (the dyadic activity which invokes "fidelity") becomes something quite different when not one, but two or three versions of the same original, are put into play. If one does compare a film with another, a silent monitor is always present—the third text, that on which both films have ultimately depended—a relation signaled in their titles. The Alexander/Davies *Sense and Sensibility* of 2008 includes a scene in which Willoughby arrives on horseback after Marianne's illness, declares that he genuinely loves her, and asks, in effect, for Elinor's pity. In the earlier Lee/Thompson *Sense and Sensibility* of 1995 Willoughby's return is only discernible in its final sequence featuring the wedding procession, as, in the script's words, "we see, on the far edge of frame, very small, a man sitting on a white horse, watching."[11] No meaningful comparison of the directors' decisions could take place without reference to the chapter in the novel (a remarkable and much discussed scene, as it happens) of which the earlier film incident is a vestigial trace.

More complex issues of intertextuality occur when the issue involves not deleting, but amplifying, reworking elisions or supplying gaps in the original text. Andrew Davies remarks in the DVD commentary on his *Sense and Sensibility* script that "Jane Austen doesn't give us enough" about the men in the novel. This may occur because Austen is working largely from within the consciousness of Elinor Dashwood, and more importantly, because, as Moreland Perkins argues in *Reshaping the Sexes in "Sense and Sensibility,"* Jane Austen attributes characteristics conventionally assigned female to the men in her novel, especially to Edward Ferrars, and vice-versa.[12] Colonel Brandon enters into the text through the medium of Marianne's disparaging comments; "silent and grave" (*SS* I, 7, 40) in these first chapters, he is a shadowy presence for much of the novel. In contrast both recent visualizations feature carefully staged sequences to enhance Brandon's first appearance and to communicate his immediate interest in Marianne. Both employ, very successfully, the distinctive cinematic resources of lighting, music and camera movement. In Lee's film, Marianne is seen at the pianoforte, performing at Barton Park for the Middletons and her family. To the background accompaniment of her singing, a gentleman is shown riding up to the front entrance of the house; then his silhouetted figure, unreadable against the light behind, enters the house; gradually, as the camera tracks back with his progress through the hall, more light intermittently falls on his face, he throws his hat aside, and moves forward, captured by the sound of music from the room he is approaching. Now clearly lit, he stands at the entrance, "silent and grave" indeed, but with intense presence, the camera remaining focused unmovingly on his face for several seconds. The sound of Marianne's singing continues. Elinor looks up and seems to notice the direction of his gaze.

In the three episode television treatment, mindful, as the commentary by the producer, Anne Pivcevic, makes plain, of the earlier successful film, Brandon's relation to Marianne is also figured through music, and the first scene similarly shows him mesmerized, or at least deeply moved, by her playing. In a sequence shot again at Barton Park, cross cutting from Marianne's playing, Brandon is seen at left, intently listening, his face in profile lit from outside the frame. The mise en scène (darkness and candles) fosters the intimacy of the moment. The camera glides round so that the listening Brandon is almost fronting the viewer, and then comes to rest, focusing unmovingly on his face, intent, for several seconds, whilst the sound of Marianne's playing continues off camera. The effect of the movement of the visual image is to suggest that this is a focal moment for the character. A midshot of Elinor and Brandon talking then performs the same function as Elinor's glance in the previous film of linking the two potential lovers. The actors in both portray mingled admiration and conflict in the gentleman's face. In creating these scenes the filmmakers generate a sense of the appropriate relationship between the sexes, and restore the males to their right-ful—or conventional—place. In effect, in their mesmerizing power, they reverse what Perkins argues is the project of the novel.

This later (and longer) version treats Marianne and Brandon's early relationship more fully, and the motif of music solidly establishes the basis of their subsequent companionate marriage. Each treatment has been developed from a single paragraph in *Sense and Sensibility*:

> Marianne's performance was highly applauded. Sir John was loud in his admiration at the end of every song and as loud in his conversation with the others while every song lasted.... Colonel Brandon alone, of all the party, heard her without being in raptures. He paid her only the compliment of attention; and she felt a respect for him on the occasion, which the others had reasonably forfeited by their shameless want of taste. His pleasure in music, though it amounted not to that extatic delight which could alone sympathize with her own, was estimable when contrasted against the horrible insensibility of the others; and she was reasonable enough to allow that a man of five and thirty might well have outlived all acuteness of feeling and every exquisite power of enjoyment [*SS* I, 7, 41–42].

It would be foolish to complain that either of these films is here "unfaithful" to the novel. Nevertheless, admiring the skill with which the film-makers have transformed this moment, one cannot but note how different this many-faceted ironic prose is from scenes filled with piano music played "appassionato" (as Brandon in the 2008 film remarks), and romantic feeling generated by all the artifices of the cinema. The later *Sense and Sensibility*, which displays the isolation of Barton Cottage close to the sea, with recurrent shots of waves crashing against black and jagged rocks, certainly differentiates itself dramatically from the Lee/Thompson film, but in the process takes the tendency, perhaps always present in "heritage" film, towards full-blown romance, and the Romantic, a step further. Willoughby recites lines from "Tintern Abbey" to Marianne, not Cowper. In the new (2007) *Persuasion* (screenplay by Simon Burke, directed by Adrian Shergold) Captain Wentworth comes across Anne Elliot seated at the piano. She is playing the slow movement of Beethoven's "Moonlight" sonata. This, like the Wordsworth, is a moment of intertextuality: more than a reference, it contributes its own aura, devolves its own field of meaning, into the film. Very different kinds of art than Austen's have been melded into hers.

Earlier, Anne has been seen in her room, opening a box of treasures. In a brief gesture borrowed from a painful moment in *Three Colours Blue*, the first of Kieslowsky's trilogy (1993), she runs her finger over the portrait of her dead mother, before turning to a bundle of letters, tied with ribbon. The

viewer is to understand that these are from Wentworth. Like Elinor's opening a volume from Edward Ferrars in *Sense and Sensibility* (2008) this incident again recalls the sequence in the 1995 *Persuasion* (screenplay by Nick
Dear, directed by Roger Michell) in which Anne finds a folded letter amid
the pages of an old Navy List. There is a novel element here, since their proximity in the keepsake box links Anne's two losses—of her mother and Wentworth—together. But since Anne does nothing but look at the pile of letters,
instead of a convincing interiority, little is achieved but a sentimental
reminder of forsaken love.

A comparison of these two *Persuasions* will demonstrate how reference
to their source is an inevitable adjunct to the reading of the films. There are
some striking instances which suggest that the 2007 film is under the influence
of the 1995 version. In that film, in a candle-lit dinner-party scene, Anne,
sitting across from Captain Benwick, listens whilst the bereaved man intones
Byronic verses, and when he declares that she cannot know the depths of his
despair, replies, quietly, "Yes, I can." In the later film, the scene is replicated:
at another candle-lit dinner party (though evidently assisted with studio
lighting), Anne is filmed from above, sitting isolated at the head of the table.
Being adjacent to Benwick, she offers her condolences on the loss of his
fiancée. He replies, "There never was a love like ours, and never will be again."
Anne then responds, "Captain Benwick, you are still young, and I pray you
may one day rally and be happy with another." In the earlier film Anne also
says, "You will rally again." Why do they use the same words? Because the
source of both is a passage in the novel before Anne is actually introduced
to the bereaved sailor:

> The sympathy and good-will towards Captain Benwick was very great.
> "And yet," said Anne to herself, "he has not, perhaps, a more sorrow-
> ing heart than I have. I cannot believe his prospects so blighted for ever.
> He is younger than I am; younger in feeling, if not in fact; younger as a
> man. He will rally again, and be happy with another" [*P* I, 11, 105].

Lifting the sentiment out of Anne's self-communings and inserting it into
each dramatic scene minimizes the self-pity that threatens here to ambush
Austen's conception of the character, and arguably improves on the novel.
But the earlier film, by allowing Anne to listen to Benwick's "You cannot
know the depths of my despair" and responding softly that she can, makes
Benwick's articulated sorrow the vehicle for Anne's unspoken grief. In the
successor version, Anne appears to be merely making politely consolatory
remarks.

These dialogues are about fidelity between men and women, and for the
critic they raise the issue of fidelity between novel and films in an acute form.

The turn this dialogue now takes in the 2007 film brings it to a crunch: "A man does not forget a woman as readily as you forget us," Benwick continues. "I will not allow a woman's nature to be more inconstant than a man's," Anne replies. "And yet you will allow that poetry and novels are against you," says Benwick, "They tell us endlessly of the fickleness of women." Anne: "And are they not all written by men?" The conversation ends with Anne asserting that she "would never suppose that true constancy is known only by women. But one claim I shall make for my sex is that we love longest, when all hope is gone." The film then cuts to Captain Wentworth's handsome, laughing face at the opposite end of the table: all hope is, apparently, gone.

These sentiments have a familiar ring, partly because in the 1995 *Persuasion* they are found in a dialogue towards the end of the film between Anne Elliot and—not Captain Benwick, but—Captain Harville, carried on at the White Hart, in a room occupied by Mrs. Musgrove and Lady Russell chatting, with Captain Wentworth writing a note on Harville's behalf at a nearby table. Here the exchange follows from a miniature of Captain Benwick that Harville holds in his hand. "Poor Phoebe," he says, "She would not have forgotten him so soon." The dialogue proceeds with Anne affirming that "We do not forget you as soon as you forget us. We live at home, quiet, confined, and our feelings prey on us." Harville takes her up: "I will not allow it to be any more man's nature than women's to be inconstant. I believe the reverse...." (an affirmation rephrased and given to Anne in the later film). At this point there is a close-up shot of a vessel falling from Wentworth's table. Harville evidently likes an argument: he resumes with the challenge that "All histories are against you, prose and verse." Anne replies, in more or less the same words as the later film, "But they were all written by men," and like Captain Benwick there, Harville responds with amusement to his antagonist's quick wit. But if Anne has described the situation of women left to brood at home on the past and its losses, Harville matches this with an eloquent account of a sailor's yearning to see his wife and family when he returns from a long voyage. The temperature of the exchange is heightened, and Anne catches the wave of his earnestness with her own response: "I believe you capable of everything great and good.... All the privilege I claim for my own sex, is that of loving longest, when hope is gone."

Transferring bits of this dialogue to a scene between Benwick and Anne is an attempt to repeat the success of the earlier film in deepening the viewer's knowledge of Anne's secret thoughts in a middle stretch of the drama. The sequence in the 1995 film (similarly shot as an intimacy fostered by half darkness) is impressively scripted, lit, photographed and acted. The 2007 film has, not surprisingly, been unable to escape its aura, and seeks, as the

1995 film does, to invest a conversation merely reported in the novel (and that with ironic amusement) with material which dramatically reveals Anne's inner life. The scene in 2007 is thus a hybrid of two precursor texts: the 1995 film, and the 1817 novel. And because the point of the earlier version was that the dialogue was overheard by Wentworth, leading to his passionate declaration of his own constancy, and the resolution of the drama, the 2007 film is left with the problem of finding an alternative ending.

But to compare the films without reference to the novel text which they adapt, as I have so far been doing, is an entirely artificial exercise. Both utilize a key moment in the novel's dialogue:

> "Songs and proverbs, all talk of woman's fickleness. But perhaps you will say, they were all written by men."
>
> "Perhaps I shall.—Yes, yes, if you please, no reference to examples in books. Men have had every advantage of us in telling their own story. Education has been theirs in so much higher a degree; the pen has been in their hands. I will not allow books to prove anything" [*P* II, 11, 254–5].

The effect of Anne's words in what is itself a written text is quite different from "They were all written by men" spoken in a film. In the novel they are relevant to the reader's immanent experience of reading. There is a moment of identification between the character, the author, and the reader. These words feel as if they emanate from a consciousness quite distinct from the position that Anne Elliot has occupied throughout the novel—from a woman who is here in control of, and aware of her control of, the history of which this exchange is a part.

It's not irrelevant to note that Jane Austen herself had trouble in finding the appropriate climax, and had to re-write the last chapters of the novel. Nor is it irrelevant to notice that both film versions draw on her rejected chapter to dramatically heighten the difficulties and misunderstandings that constantly bedevil the lovers' understanding. But what is the nature of the climax she eventually found, and why is it so damaging to the Burke/Shergold film to omit it? It resides in an extended and entirely uncinematic conversation between Anne and Captain Harville. But this conversation is thrilling largely because behind it lies the complex artifice of the previous chapters of the novel. It is because Anne Elliot has not been permitted (and has not permitted herself) to express her feelings, her regrets and broodings, the unavailing constancy of her love, that this opportunity, in which her speech draws on, if it does not directly express, her own experience (as both the reader and Wentworth detect) has so much emotional and intellectual weight. The reader has been made aware of Anne's emotions, but simultaneously taught to recognize that her social position as a gentlewoman makes it impossible for her to speak, or to do anything about them. This secret life, so essential to the novel, is here now released into speech. Suspense is resolved, readerly need is gratified, in this scene.

Moreover, Anne, as I have argued in Chapter 1, is continually presented as the abjected listener, whose inner life is invaded and shaped by scraps overheard from the conversations around her, whilst Wentworth is the life and soul of every gathering he attends. These archetypical male and female positions are now reversed. It is Wentworth, the active, unreflective male, who sits and overhears, and Anne, the normally acquiescent and repressed female, who argues eloquently and convincingly. This scene draws together and resolves the narratological, political and aesthetic strands of the novel; that is why it is a necessary and compelling climax. To omit it, and to replace it with scenes of Anne tearing along the Royal Crescent in Bath and then back again in search of Wentworth as the 2007 film does—to substitute physical intensity for emotional resolution—is more than clumsy or inept. Like the omission of the Portsmouth scenes in the *Mansfield Park* of the same ITV series, it fails, not because it alters the original, but because it overrides a sequence in the source which is not only essential to the plot, or structure, but to the whole emotional trajectory of the work. What can a criticism which responsibly takes the opportunities offered by these films to revisit and review the novels that are their sources, call it, but an act of infidelity?

I would argue then, that the critic of Jane Austen films cannot simply take them on their merits as films. The mere presence of two or more treatments of the same novel impels the viewer towards comparison, and comparison of the films impels the viewer towards the source text. The later films derive as much from the earlier films as they do from the novels: they are hybrid, or even miscengenated works, which derive only in part from the cinematic Jane Austen.

Chapter Notes

Introduction

1. Macdonald and Macdonald, *Jane Austen on Screen*, 260–5, list twenty-six film and television adaptations of Austen's novels up to the year 2000 in their filmography. At least eight more had appeared by mid-2008, not counting two bio-pics and the Austen themed *Jane Austen Book Club*. Several more adaptations are reported to be in production. In all there have been ten adaptations of *Pride and Prejudice* alone.

2. Tallis, "The Realistic Novel," 64.

3. Only Seymour Chatman's "What Novels Can Do" and *Coming to Terms* come close to matching the influence of Bluestone's *Novels into Film* in arguing that novel and film are semiotically distinct.

4. Bluestone, *Novels*, 212.

5. Elliott, *Rethinking the Novel/Film Debate*, 134.

6. Bluestone, *Novels*, 62.

7. Bluestone, *Novels*, 122, 126.

8. Bluestone, *Novels*, 199, 126.

9. Willemen, *Looks and Frictions*, 27.

10. Gard, "A Few Skeptical Thoughts," 10–12.

11. In the current theoretical climate, the fidelity school of criticism, with its tendency to employ a "moralistic and judgmental" (Stam, Introduction, 14) language of betrayal and violation in condemning films for falling short of their linguistic originals, has become almost anathema.

See the final chapter of this book for Wiltshire's nuanced reworking of the concept of fidelity.

12. McFarlane, *Novel to Film,* 27

13. McFarlane, "It Wasn't Like That," 169.

14. Stam, Introduction, 25.

15. McFarlane, *Novel*, 13, 14

16. Vladimir Propp, *Morphology of the Folktale*; Joseph Campbell, *The Hero with a Thousand Faces*.

17. Elliott, *Rethinking*, 12–13.

18. Sound has not received much critical attention in studies of the novel or film, or of the adaptation of novel into film. However, Eisenstein states that "the visual images of Dickens are inseparable from aural images" ("Dickens, Griffith," 211) while Esrock, *The Reader's Eye*, 204, points out that the auditory is one of the sensory modes that comes into play as part of the act of reading. While Elliott's attention in *Rethinking* is focused on words and images, she does indicate that sound can be part of the figuration process that "bridges word and image divides" (217): "Not all imaging is visual: we can imagine sound, taste, smell, and touch" (273). The scarcity of such discussions is hard to explain given the fundamental role of sound in novel and film.

Ariane Hudelet deals extensively with sound in chapters 3 and 4.

19. Quoted by Boyum, *Double Exposure*, 28.

20. Andrew, "The Well-Worn Muse," 12. Other theorists who have identified the perceptual aspects of the reading experience and/or the conceptual dimensions involved in watching films include Cohen, *Film and Fiction*, 4; Scholes, "Narration and Narrativity," 291.

21. Elliott, *Rethinking*, 9.

22. Elliott, *Rethinking*, 221. For Elliott's statement that she is using "a new (yet also old) model of analogy," see 185.

23. Elliott, *Rethinking*, 210, 211.

24. Elliott, *Rethinking*, 212.

25. Elliott, *Rethinking*, 215.

26. Bluestone, *Novel*, 1.

27. Elliott, *Rethinking*, 221.

28. Elliott, *Rethinking*, 215.

29. Kellman, "The Cinematic Novel," 268.

30. Mayne, *Private Novels, Public Films*, 6–9. In describing certain types of novels as "readerly," Mayne is drawing on Barthes' distinction between the readerly (*le lisable*) and the writerly (*le scriptible*). As explained by

Mayne, "The distinction between the readerly and the writerly is primarily a question of the materiality of language, as well as the difference between a referential and transparent use of language, on the one hand, and an engagement in the complexity and polyvalence of linguistic signs on the other" (8). In other words, readerly novels are ones in which language does not draw attention to itself, and therefore does not appear to obstruct the reader's access to the narrative.

31. Elliott, *Rethinking*, 210.

32. Kellman, "Cinematic," 474.

33. Cohen, *Film and Fiction*, 83–7, and Introduction, 21–2. As Kellman points out, neither Woolf ("The Cinematic," 467, 470) nor Proust (470) had a high opinion of film. He is therefore somewhat skeptical of critics who attribute cinematic qualities to their work. Kellman is probably justified in feeling that some critics have been too ready to put cinematic labels on literary techniques. However, he also admits that, for commentators such as Arnold Hauser, the twentieth-century is "The Film Age" (469), a theory given some credence by Henri Bergson's use of a cinematic analogy in "articulating the modernist conception of mind as a function of movement and continuity" (468). Consequently, it is quite possible that Woolf and Proust possessed film sensibilities despite themselves.

34. Eisenstein, "Dickens," 198–237.

35. Lodge, "Thomas Hardy," 246–54.

36. Spiegel, "Flaubert to Joyce," 229–33; McFarlane, *Novel*, 5.

37. Kellman, "Cinematic," 472; Elliott, *Rethinking*, 113–25.

38. Eisenstein, "Dickens," 200–1.

39. Lodge, "Thomas Hardy," 249–54; Spiegel, "Flaubert," 229–33.

40. McFarlane, *Novel*, 12. See also Mayne, *Private Novels*, 8. However, this argument has been challenged by Alain Robbe-Grillet, for whom film is more properly connected with modern novelistic forms such as the *nouveau roman* than the model provided by the nineteenth-century novel ("For a New Cinema," 118). We should note, though, that Robbe-Grillet is advocating a new direction in filmmaking rather than describing the current practices of the mainstream film industry. What this new direction might look like is indicated by Elliott in her unpublished conference paper, "Unfilmable Books," where she demonstrates that writers and directors willing to deviate from conventional filmmaking techniques can make successful adaptations of non-linear and self-reflexive texts such as *Tristram Shandy* and *The Orchid Thief*.

41. "Scenographic" is a term used by Spiegel, "Flaubert," 233, to describe the way in which a scene is presented to the audience in proscenium arch theater.

42. Eco, *The Open Work*, passim.

43. As the failure of film versions of novels such as *Ulysses* and *The Sound and the Fury*, both of which have been described as cinematic, demonstrates, the terms cinematic and adaptable are not always synonymous. However, as note 40 above indicates, it is not so much that such novels are incompatible with the film medium as that they require a more adventurous approach to adaptation than is possible under the self-imposed restrictions of the dominant classic realist style of filmmaking. Given that almost all fiction is adaptable to the film medium but not every novel can justifiably be described as cinematic, it is always dangerous to equate the terms cinematic and adaptable.

44. Hoberg, "The Multiplex Heroine," 122; Heckerling, "High School Confidential," 53.

45. Lauritzen, *Jane Austen's "Emma,"* 69–91.

46. Kaplan, "Mass Marketing Jane Austen," 177–87; Richards, "Regency Romance," 111–26. The quotation is taken from Kaplan, 178.

47. Gay, *Jane Austen and the Theatre*, 162–3; Sutherland, *Jane Austen's Textual Lives*, 342–3; Pucci, "The Return Home," 139.

48. A cross section of the many critics who see Austen's narrator as posing problems for filmmakers includes Hannon, "Austen Novels," 28–9; Hoberg, "The Multiplex," 109; Sales, "In Face of," 194; Troost and Greenfield, Introduction, 7. For discussions of problems relating to the interiority of Austen's novels, see Morrison, "*Emma* Minus Its Narrator," 2; Troost, "Filming Highbury," 7. Critics who point to the difficulties encountered by filmmakers because of Austen's lack of detailed description include Groenendyk, "The Importance of Vision,"11; Murphy, "Books, Bras," 26.

49. The process of making a film adaptation of a novel involves a transition from a telling to a showing medium (see Hutcheon, *A Theory of Adaptation*, 22–5) that usually but not always renders the narrator redundant. Filmmakers who employ narrators have done so with varying degrees of success. McGrath's use of both omniscient and first-person narrators in his adaptation of *Emma* is ineffective because it is intermittent and, like the film in general, lacks the irony of Austen's narrator. By contrast, Cher's first-person narration in *Clueless* is much more prominent and Heckerling is often successful in playing off Cher's

voice against the film's action for ironic effect. However, there are many resources other than narrative voice available to filmmakers who want to replicate Austen's ironic tone including dramatic irony, a technique frequently used by Austen herself (See Carroll, "A Consideration of Times," 171 for a discussion of Whit Stillman's ironic use of the camera in *Metropolitan*, a loose updating of *Mansfield Park*). Similarly, as Bazin has pointed out, while they cannot depict thought and feeling directly, films have a "thousand ways" of manipulating their "outward signs" to reflect "inner reality" ("In Defence of Mixed Cinema," 18). Belton, for example, provides numerous examples of cinematic devices employed in the 1995 adaptation of *Pride and Prejudice* to communicate the complex feelings Elizabeth experiences after reading Darcy's second letter ("Reimagining Jane Austen," 191–3). As for the third problem, it is difficult to see how lack of description makes Austen's novels either more or less adaptable unless we posit a filmmaker totally lacking in visual imagination. Indeed, Bluestone even goes so far as to argue that the descriptive gaps in Austen's novels serve as opportunities rather than problems for filmmakers (*Novels*, 120).

50. Karounos, "Ordination and Revolution," 715–36.

51. Said, "Jane Austen and Empire," 88.

52. Despotopoulou, "Fanny's Gaze," 569–83; Wiltshire, "*Persuasion*," 183–6; Sodeman, "Domestic Mobility," 787–800; Spence, "The Abiding Possibilities," 625–36.

53. Dussinger, *In the Pride*, passim; Monaghan, *Jane Austen*, passim.

54. Young, "Feeling Embodied," 81, 85–6; Despotopoulou, "Fanny's," 575; Sales, *Jane Austen*, 114.

55. Gilbert, "What the Ear Has," 126–36, describes *Mansfield Park* as Austen's quietest and noisiest novel, while Sodeman, "Domestic," 800, comments on the part played by noisy exteriors in providing privacy for Anne Elliot and Captain Wentworth in *Persuasion*.

56. Wiltshire, "(De)colonising *Mans-field Park*," 313.

57. Mise en scène was originally a theatrical term meaning literally "putting into the scene." Its use in film, as Wiltshire indicates in chapter 1, can be quite complex but the term can be broadly defined as the arrangement of objects and characters within the frame. The term mise en scène is therefore employed in film studies for discussions of space and composition.

58. Elliott, "Unfilmable Books."

Chapter 1

1. Southam, *Jane Austen: The Critical Heritage*, 159.

2. Cronin and McMillan, *Emma*, 587 n.1.

3. Elliott, *Rethinking the Novel/Film Debate*; Byrne, *Jane Austen and the Theatre*; Gay, *Jane Austen and the Theatre*.

4. "To accord cinematic properties to the novel before/cinema even existed forges a problematic and mythological anachronistic aesthetic history" (Elliott, *Rethinking*, 113–14).

5. As in the sub-title of Giddings and Sheen, *The Classic Novel: From Page to Screen*.

6. Wood, "New Criticism." Quotation taken from Gibbs, *Mise-en-scène*, 57.

7. Gibbs, *Mise-en-scène*, 60.

8. See, for instance, Branigan, *Point of View*. Branigan's approach "does not assume that a text is a communication involving the psychological experiences of characters and spectators" (211); see also Wilson, *Narration in Light: Studies in Cinematic Point of View*.

9. See Cohn, *Transparent Minds*, passim, for a discussion of this topic.

10. Booth, *The Rhetoric of Fiction*, 247.

11. Booth, *The Rhetoric*, 256.

12. Byrne, *Jane Austen*, 123.

13. Monaco, *How To Read a Film*, 186ff.

14. Quoted Gibbs, *Mise-en-scène*, 57.

15. Cohen, *Film and Fiction*, 23.

16. Gregory, *A Father's Advice*, 26

17. Miller, *The Secret of Style*, 71.

18. Miller, *The Secret*, 68.

19. The film's handling of sound is interesting: Mrs. Croft and Mrs. Musgrove's chatter virtually disappears from the soundtrack when the camera focuses on Harville and Anne talking earnestly at the window. It thus loses the novel's suggestion of Wentworth's capacity to hear Anne despite the ambient sounds. The 2008 film omits the scene altogether: I discuss this in Chapter 9.

20. Tanner, *Jane Austen*, rev. ed., 219.

21. Perkins, *Film as Film*, 72.

Chapter 2

1. Strangren and Nordau, *Movies: A Language in Light*; Wilson, *Narration in Light*. Though Wilson discusses Ophuls' *Letter from an Unknown Woman* (1948) extensively, he never comments on the film's period lighting. This is cited as typical of much film criticism.

2. Section VI "Light" in Arnheim, *Art and Visual Perception*, 302–29. "Night is not the negative result of withdrawn light, but the

positive arrival of a dark cloak that replaces or covers the day" (304).

3. Blühn and Lippincott, *Light! The Industrial*, 25.

4. "The Alchymist, in Search of the Philosopher's Stone, Discovers Phosphorus" celebrates a discovery which led to Boyle's experiments and the discovery of the nature of combustion (Egerton, *Wright of Derby*, 84). "Arkwright's Cotton Mills by Night" (c1782–8) is a plate on 199, 198–200. "The Alchymist" may be viewed at: www.derby.gov.uk/Leisure Culture/MuseumsGalleries/The_Alchymist. htm. Other Wright paintings are to be found at www.wga.hu.

5. Nicholson, *Joseph Wright*, 39.

6. Fraser, "Joseph Wright of Derby," 15–24; see also Uglow, *The Lunar Men*.

7. Blühn and Lippincott, *Light*, 80.

8. Schivelbusch, *Disenchanted Night*, 20.

9. See, for instance, Le Faye, *Jane Austen: A Family Record*, 185. When she visited Carlton House in November 1814, Austen would certainly have passed through Pall Mall (225). "The walk, Pall-Mall! Might every evening boast/ A head illumined for each illumin'd post!" declares a contemporary satire published that year. Quoted in Bluhn and Lippincott, *Light!*, 128, fn. 2, from the anonymous *An Heroic Epistle to Mr. Windsor* (London, 1808).

10. Bluhn and Lippincott, *Light!*, 102. Frederick Accum's *A Practical Treatise on Gas Light* was published in London in 1815.

11. Bachelard, *La flamme d'une chandelle*, 90. "L'ampoule électrique ne nous donnera jamais les rêveries de cette lampe vivante qui, avec de l'huile, faisant de la lumière. Nous sommes entrés dans l'ère de la lumière administrée.... Nous ne sommes plus que le sujet méchanique d'une geste méchanique."

12. In his famous "Elegy Written in a Country Churchyard" (1751).

13. Cowper, *The Task* (1785), Book IV "The Winter Evening," ll. 212–310; S. T. Coleridge, "Frost at Midnight" (c.1798).

14. *A Sicilian Romance* features "A Grotto in the Gulf of Solerno" (1780); *The Romance of the Forest* features 'Virgil's Tomb by Moonlight' (detail), 1782.

15. O'Dea, *The Social History of Lighting*, 2, quoted in Blühn and Lippincott, *Light!* 14.

16. Burney, *Cecilia*, 124.

17. Austen, "The Watsons," in Chapman, *The Works of Jane Austen*, vol. 6, *Minor Works*, 344.

18. Schivelbusch, *Disenchanted*, 137.

19. The sequence discussed is *Mansfield Park*, II,1, 208–14.

20. LoBrutto, *Stanley Kubrick, A Biography*, 378. This account of lighting in *Barry Lyndon* is based on LoBrutto's Chapter 16, "Candlepower," 376–408: further page references to this book are given in brackets after the quotation. Nelson gives a fine and detailed reading of the film in his *Kubrick: Inside a Film Artist's Maze*, 166–194. His account, which focuses on its "contrary tendencies of verbal narration and visual narrative" (183) and attends closely to the film's music, has almost nothing to say about its lighting.

21. Monaco, *How to Read a Film*, 83–4.

22. Wickre, 'Pictures, Plurality and Puns," 165–184. Wickre notes that "the candlelight scenes … demonstrate the dramatic tenebrism and halolike effects also found in Chardin or the dramatically lamp-lit paintings of Wright of Derby" (171).

23. The scene describing "sun-shine in a town" in *Mansfield Park* (III, 15, 508) is an exception.

24. Higson, *English Heritage, English Cinema*, 38. In *Adaptation Revisited*, Sarah Cardwell finds "slow-paced style and 'heritage' content" (134) typical of Austen adaptations. See also Vincendeau, *Film/Literature/Heritage*, especially Section I, "'A New Genre,'" 3–52.

25. In a later garden, a statue of the Borgese gladiator may be seen.

26. Nelson, *Kubrick*, 173.

27. Thompson, *Jane Austen's Sense and Sensibility*, 50–1.

28. Lascelles, *Jane Austen and her Art*, 16–17.

29. *Shirley*, Chapter 12. Page references are given in brackets after quotations.

30. Southam, *Jane Austen: The Critical Heritage*, 127.

31. Woolf, *To the Lighthouse*, 257.

32. See Samuelian, "'Piracy is Our Only Option,'" 148–158. Fuller, "Cautionary Tale," 77–80, gives an excellent short account of *Sense and Sensibility* with a different emphasis on Lee's direction.

33. The art director may have intended an allusion to Wyatt's well-known monument to Princess Charlotte in St. George's Chapel, Windsor. The sculpture of the dead princess, covered in a shroud, is surrounded by four wholly draped mourning figures: the furniture in the scene is arranged to suggest a similar panoply of grief. The Princess died in 1817, the year of *Persuasion*'s publication.

34. This scene may be compared with the attempt to imitate it in the 2007 ITV production. For further discussion, see Chapter 9.

35. McGann, *Byron: The Complete Poetical Works*, III, 382. The poem, privately published, found its way into *The Champion* of April 14, 1816.

36. Harris, "'Domestic Virtues and National Importance,'" 196.

37. Schivelbusch, *Disenchanted*, 221.

Chapter 3

1. Thomas Leitch, for instance, refers to this tendency to consider the lack of visual details or elaborate description as an "uncinematic" quality, according to which it would be "a hopeless endeavor to adapt Jane Austen's novels to film because their visual texture is so remarkably thin" ("Twelve Fallacies," 61).

2. "The designation of novels as 'words' and of films as 'images' is neither empirically nor logically sustainable: rather, it participates in ancient representational rivalries" (Elliot, *Rethinking the Novel/Film Debate*, 14).

3. Recent works on the question of sound in film include notably Michel Chion's books, such as *L'audio-vision*, *La voix au cinéma* or *La toile trouée*.

4. For Tony Tanner, this notion of communication is central to Austenian writing: "dialogue is as crucially revealing in her novels as her own voice…. Almost exclusively the characters define themselves in their speech—or free indirect speech, which Jane Austen uses so often and so brilliantly" (*Jane Austen*, 41).

5. Penny Gay herself acknowledges that Austen's texts offer "the sort of detail that only in the twentieth century was it possible to represent theatrically, in the realistic formats and observant lenses of film and television" (*Jane Austen and the Theatre*, 163). For Paula Byrne, "The building bricks of Austen's novels were also dramatic scenes. This is one reason why they adapt so well to film representation" (*Jane Austen and the Theatre*, xii-xiii). And Kathryn Sutherland explains, "The obvious dramatic qualities of Austen's art have ensured her regular adaptation from the late nineteenth century: encounters and incidents structured as scenes in a play (the opening of *Pride and Prejudice*, the action in the grounds of Sotherton in *Mansfield Park*), brisk dialogue, strong characterization (including excellent comic cameos), a reliance on dramatic entrances and exits (Sir Thomas Bertram's return from Antigua), her fine use of stage business (Frank Churchill fiddling with Mrs. Bates's spectacles)" (*Jane Austen's Textual Lives*, 342).

6. My translation of "le point d'écoute," a term coined by Michel Chion (*L'audio-vision*, 79–82).

7. For instance Howard S. Babb, *Jane Austen's Novels*, K.C. Phillips, *Jane Austen's English*, or Norman Page, *The Language of Jane Austen*.

8. Harriet Smith could also be included: we find in her lines the same techniques which make her speech a corporeal manifestation rather than a coherent discourse. Whether she is expressing her impatience to understand a charade or whether she is telling about her encounter with Mr. Martin, we find the same accumulation of dashes or exclamations, untimely changes of topics, interjections, repetitions. Harriet is even described as a pretty little animal, whose happiness can reside exclusively in physical well-being: "To be in company, nicely dressed and seeing others nicely dressed, and to sit and smile and look pretty, and say nothing, was enough for the happiness of the present hour" (*E* II, 8, 237). We could also mention examples from other novels such as Miss Steele's repetitions and interjections (*SS* III, 2, 311–13).

9. In her chapter entitled "Speaking Commas" (*Jane Austen's*, 266–313), Kathryn Sutherland proposes a thorough study of how punctuation was initially used by Austen as a rhythmical tool, "which often runs counter to grammatical sense but which can be closer to the inflections of language as spoken and heard," a use that has been "corrected," notably by Chapman who mistook this "formally endorsed punctuation (punctuation signalling graphically the text's aural dimensions)" for "textual corruption" (296).

10. We hear Miss Bates rather than we listen to her: "*To hear* is a physiological phenomenon, *to listen* is a psychological act" (Barthes, *L'obvie et l'obtus*, 217. My translation).

11. This expression is inspired by Norman Page's description of the Harvilles' reaction after Louisa's accident in *Persuasion*, as "fragments of free indirect speech" (*The Language*, 128–9).

12. My translation of "point d'écoute," an expression coined by Michel Chion, *L'audio-vision*, 59. For a detailed analysis of this passage, see also Sutherland, *Jane Austen's*, 306–7.

13. "A physical reaction … may be given through typographical devices stressing the absence of words, so the presence of other methods of communication. A work such as Richardson's *Clarissa* is full of lacunae, asterisks, dashes and disturbed or aberrant typography, indicating emotion beyond words" (Todd, *Sensibility*, 6). We could also have concentrated on Anne's violent emotion when she sees Wentworth again at Uppercross, which is transmitted through her physical reaction. In the very rhythm of sentences, in the tone, the reader perceives her physical confusion before the meaning of the words themselves. There is no first person, no formalized discourse, but the very texture and form of the language rep-

resents the interior confusion of the heroine, a phenomenon studied in Wiltshire, *Jane Austen and the Body*, 89.

14. "When her mother went up to her dressing-room at night, she followed her, and made the important communication. Its effect was most extraordinary; for on first hearing it, Mrs. Bennet sat quite still, and unable to utter a syllable. Nor was it under many, many minutes that she could comprehend what she heard" (*PP* III, 17, 419).

15. This term is notably used by Vladimir Nabokov in his analysis of *Mansfield Park*: "She makes apt uses of participles (such as *smiling, looking*, etc.) in descriptions of attitude and gestures, or of phrases like *with an arch smile*, but introducing them in a parenthetical way, without *he* or *she said*, as if they were stage directions" ("*Mansfield Park*," 56–60).

16. Expressions used, among many others, for Wentworth ("his half averted eyes, and more than half expressive glance" [*P* II, 8, 202)]), Miss Bingley ("His sister was less delicate, and directed her eye towards Mr. Darcy with a very expressive smile" [*PP* I, 9, 48]), or Willoughby ("'I understand you,' he replied, with an expressive smile, and a voice perfectly calm" [*SS* III, 8, 360]).

17. "The female body also became an organism peculiarly susceptible to influence. Women were thought to express emotions with their bodies more sincerely and spontaneously than men; hence their propensity to crying, blushing and fainting" (Todd, *Sensibility*, 19).

18. Anne Elliot is clever and sensitive enough to be able to interpret this language of the emotions. All along the novel, she has proved that she could "read" Wentworth's expression (at the Musgroves' for instance, when his real opinion about Dick Musgrove is perceptible in "a certain glance of his bright eye, a curl of his handsome mouth" [*P* I, 8, 73]), as well as Mr. Elliot's and Captain Benwick's. Not all characters boast this ability to decipher and interpret visual signs adequately.

19. We could draw a long list of such examples where an emotion, a question, a confirmation, are expressed by the body rather than by words, such as Emma's surprise when she learns that Harriet is finally going to marry Robert Martin: "her eyes, in eager gaze, said, 'No, this is impossible!' but her lips were closed" (*E* III, 18, 514), or Fanny Price's expression when she walks with Edmund after refusing Henry Crawford's marriage proposal: "She assented to it rather by look than word" (*MP* III, 4, 400). When Wentworth sees Anne at Bath again, he offers his help silently: "[Captain Wentworth], by manner rather than

words, was offering his services to her" (*P* II, 7, 192).

20. "For this rare phenomenon to happen, for music to burst into language, you need of course a certain *physique* of the voice (by *physique* I mean the way the voice stands in the body—or the body stands in the voice)" (Barthes, *L'obvie*, 251. My translation).

21. Director Roger Michell indeed regrets the sound uniformity of many adaptations: "I was repulsed by the idea of people in Jane Austen speaking in the same voice. It seemed absolutely absurd so I've tried to get as many varieties as possible" (Davies, "To Kiss or Not to Kiss?"). *Persuasion* thus distinguishes itself with its rich mix of accents (Ciaran Hinds's Irish twang, Corin Redgrave's Somerset intonations) and with its desire to favor expression and spontaneity over absolute intelligibility.

22. *Pride and Prejudice*, which runs 301 minutes, is the only exception; the other adaptations of the 1990s and 2000s all have a standard length of two hours or less.

23. The treatment of characters like Harriet Smith and Mrs. Elton also relies on the interpretation of actresses more than on choices of mise en scène. Juliet Stevenson's interpretation of Mrs. Elton in *Emma* insists more on the vulgarity of the character than on her boring side. All her lines are perfectly intelligible, and her pedantry is essentially linked during her first visit to Hartfield with her monopolizing conversation. After every question asked by Emma, the newly-weds start answering at the same time, but Mr. Elton is systematically forced to give way to his more assertive wife. The latter can therefore display her wonderful vulgarity, speaking with her mouth full, snapping her fingers in the middle of a sentence or cleaning her teeth with her tongue.

24. An example could be his answer to Miss Bingley after she has described him as a "man without fault": "that is not possible for anyone ... but it has been my study to avoid these weaknesses which expose strong understanding to ridicule."

25. At Pemberley, this conversation goes on in a similar manner for a few moments, and Darcy repeats his initial question: "Excuse me.... Your parents are in good health?," and then his question "Where are you staying?" and subsequent reaction, "Oh yes, of course," are pronounced almost as a single syllable. In Lee's *Sense and Sensibility*, Hugh Grant also sometimes resorts to a lack of intelligibility, notably in the way he erases the last syllable in his pronunciation of "Miss Dashwood."

26. A contact which Elizabeth refuses in Kent, when she immediately turns the conver-

sation to Jane's presence in London, a topic which crystallizes their confrontation.

27. His voice furthermore contrasts with those that surround it, notably Mrs. Jennings and Sir John's whose sonorous and rambling voices pour out sentences almost without pause, in a continuous flow.

28. Sutherland, *Jane Austen's*, viii.

29. "Indices sonores matérialisants," an expression used in Chion, *L'audio-vision*, 98–9.

30. Mosier, "Clues for the Clueless," 240.

31. As when Emma and Mr. Knightley help Mr. Woodhouse into his armchair at the beginning of the film.

32. In the same logic one could quote Tom's sonorous belching or retching, or the sound of the laudanum as Lady Bertram pours it into a little glass.

33. *Sense and Sensibility* punctually resorts to these sound clues, with body noises during the ball; cutlery sounds during meals at Norland, which reinforce the cold feelings between John and Fanny and the rest of the family; and the cracking of the chairs whenever Edward sits down, an embodiment of his uneasiness, notably in London.

34. Although, as in this instance, there are published scripts of some Jane Austen adaptations, I have chosen to rely on my own transcriptions of the films because there are sometimes variations between the script and dialogue in the film. I have followed the same practice in my other chapters.

35. Woolf, The Captain's Death Bed, 184–5. Quoted in Wiltshire, Recreating Jane Austen, 34.

Chapter 4

1. Locke, *Essay Concerning Human Understanding*, II, 1, 105–6.

2. In a similar way, once Wickham's true nature is revealed, Jane Bennet regrets this ambivalence: "Poor Wickham; there is such an expression of goodness in his countenance! such an openness and gentleness in his manner" (*PP* II, 17, 250).

3. Tanner, *Jane Austen*, 75–102.

4. See also John Wiltshire's interpretation: "The secret problematic at the novel's heart, that Willoughby did not write the letter he wrote, that Marianne's intuition is correct, that the face and body do give proofs of affection, undoes (and deliberately undoes—this is not a deconstructive reading) the sovereignty of sense… . [T]here is a language of the body which cannot lie" (*Jane Austen and the Body*, 50–1).

5. "Like Henry Crawford in *Mansfield Park*, [Willoughby] has a gift for role-playing which is indicated in a passing allusion to his prowess at reading parts in plays, though he doesn't stay long enough with Marianne to finish reading his part of *Hamlet*. (One guesses that he had perhaps arrived at the part where Hamlet inexplicably rejects Ophelia)" (Tanner, *Jane Austen*, 93).

6. Elizabeth explains this difficulty at the Netherfield ball: "I do not get on at all. I hear such different accounts of you as puzzle me exceedingly" (*PP* I, 18, 105).

7. When Elinor blames Marianne for not confiding in her enough, her sister retorts: "Our situations then are alike. We have neither of us any thing to tell; you, because you do not communicate, and I, because I conceal nothing" (*SS* II, 5, 193).

8. In his essay on *Pride and Prejudice*, Tony Tanner stresses the questioning on knowledge, and the relationship between the novel and Locke's ideas: "Locke pointed out how, because of 'settled habit,' often 'we take that for the perception of our sensation which is an idea formed by our judgment.' This fairly accurately sums up Elizabeth's earlier reactions to Darcy. She identifies her sensory perceptions as judgments, or treats impressions as insights" (Tanner, 105–6).

9. For instance, Elizabeth's first impressions of Mr. Collins and Lady Catherine turn out to be true, but she is wrong about Wickham and Darcy.

10. Knox-Shaw, *Jane Austen and the Enlightenment*, 11–12.

11. Mosier, "Clues for the Clueless," 246.

12. Sales, "In Face of All the Servants," 195

13. Braudy, "Acting: Stage vs. Screen," 248–51.

14. Kettle, "Emma," 113.

15. Directors and release dates are, respectively, Akira Kurosawa, 1950; John Ford, 1962; Orson Welles, 1941; Alfred Hitchcock, 1945; Bryan Singer, 1995 and David Lynch, 2001.

16. Hutcheon, *A Theory of Adaptation*, 57.

17. Ian Watt compares the construction of the identity of the novelistic characters to Locke's definition of "identity": "'an identity of consciousness through duration in time,' the individual was in touch with his own continuing identity through the memory of his past thoughts and actions" (*Rise of the Novel*, 21).

18. The same technique is used when Elizabeth learns about Lydia's elopement. She then "sees" some of Wickham's expressions again, and tries to interpret them in the light of this shocking evolution. One of Darcy's sentences from the letter also comes back to her—"She

was then but fifteen ... years old"—when she associates Lydia's story to Georgiana's. The use of the same intonation, the same pause before the end of the sentence, provides a link between this passage and the reading of the letter: both "happen" within the heroine's consciousness.

19. Baridon, *Les Jardins*, 816–17.

20. "'I don't think there's a chance of people getting the detective story, or even realizing there's a lot of clues being dropped, on the first reading of the book because they don't know it's a detective story,' says Andrew [Davies]. 'Jane Austen never told anybody! So you have to read the book twice to get all the clues.' For the adaptation, Andrew had to look at ways to give the audience a fair chance of picking up those clues, without giving too much away." Birtwistle and Conklin, *The Making of "Jane Austen's*, 12–13.

21. See for instance the ending of *Northanger Abbey*, but we could also include the reference to Emma's answer to Mr. Knightley's proposal ("What did she say?—Just what a lady always does" [III, 13, 470]), or the ironical comment of the narrator about Edmund Bertram's change of feelings for Fanny in *Mansfield Park* ("I purposely abstain from dates on this occasion ... . I only intreat every body to believe that exactly at the time when it was quite natural that it should be so, and not a week earlier, Edmund did cease to care about Miss Crawford, and became as anxious to marry Fanny, as Fanny herself could desire" [*MP* III,17, 544]).

22. The only other occurrence of the mirror motif appears metaphorically in *Mansfield Park*, when Fanny Price's warm sisterly feelings fuels Henry Crawford's admiration: "her manners were the mirror of her own modest and elegant mind" (*MP* II, 12, 341). We could also include the card game "Speculation" played by the Bertrams and Crawfords since it metaphorically reveals the nature of the different characters around the table.

23. We could think, among many others, of Welles's *The Lady from Shanghai* (1948), or Michael Powell's *Peeping-Tom* (1960), not to mention the numerous adaptations of myths or fairy tales in which the mirror plays an important role, as in Jean Cocteau's *Orphée* (1950) or Walt Disney's *Snow-White* (1937).

24. The film, like the mirror, reflects while revealing a fundamental absence and it is this absence, as Christian Metz says, which lies at the heart of filmic pleasure (*Le Signifiant Imaginaire*, 61–81).

25. A motif which has influenced all sorts of representations in Western culture, from the numerous paintings of Venus at her mir-

ror (by Veronese, Velasquez, Rubens, among others) to commercials for beauty products, not to forget *Snow White* or *Alice in Wonderland*. On this motif, see the catalogue of the exhibition *On Reflection*, curated by Jonathan Miller at the National Gallery. See also Baltrusaitis, *Le Miroir*, 281.

26. A few seconds earlier, another short sequence is structured by a large mirror, when Julia warns her sister Maria about openly flirting with Henry Crawford while engaged to Rushworth. The two sisters talk to their respective reflections in the mirror in front of Maria, an object which already associates the Bertram sisters with appearances and vanity.

27. A term used by C.S. Lewis, "A Note on Jane Austen," 27.

28. For a close study of the passage, see also Anne-Marie Paquet-Deyris, "Mise en scène de l'intériorité," 3.

29. A transposition of the novel's picture gallery.

30. Fanny's last line, uttered when they reach Norland, illustrates the way she subtly reverses the situation:

JOHN: They will have five hundred a year among them as it is—

FANNY:—and what on earth can four women want for more than that? Their housekeeping will be nothing at all—they will have no carriage, no horses, hardly any servants and will keep no company. Only conceive how comfortable they will be! ... they will be much more able to give *you* something.

31. In the novel, the conversation is quite long (*SS* I, 2, 9–15), but screenwriter Emma Thompson chooses to retain only the minimum, and relies on Ang Lee's images to represent visually what the story and dialogues confirm only later.

32. "In this incomparable rationalisation of meanness and selfishness we have an unexcelled example of Jane Austen's comprehension of the power of language to make black appear white" (Tanner, *Jane Austen*, 92).

33. Trilling, *Emma and the Legend*, 152.

34. Such as studies by Beatrice Battaglia or Peter Knox-Shaw, who went so far as to see Austen as an ancestor of Joyce (Battaglia, *Jane Austen*, 39; Knox-Shaw, *Jane Austen*, 14).

35. Other recent films are entirely based on this unreliability of images: the story of *The Usual Suspects* (1995) is radically reconfigured in the final seconds of the film by the discovery of the true identity of the "narrator"; the "truth" investigated in the first half of *Mulholland Drive* (2001) is destroyed by the reversals of identity of the second half; each new se-

quence of *Memento* (2000) comes to question the previous one.

36. And before them, Tony Richardson's *Tom Jones* (1963) or Karel Reisz's *The French Lieutenant's Woman* (1981) are good examples of such a technique.

37. "Nous ne sommes pas assez subtils pour apercevoir l'écoulement probablement absolu du devenir; le permanent n'existe que grâce à nos organes grossiers qui résument et ramènent les choses à des plans communs, alors que rien n'existe sous cette forme. L'arbre est à chaque instant une chose neuve; nous affirmons la forme, parce que nous ne saisissons pas la subtilité d'un mouvement absolu" (my translation). Barthes, *Le Plaisir du Texte*, 96.

Chapter 5

1. Todd, *The Cambridge Introduction*, 66.

2. George Bluestone's treatment of the film in *Novels into Film* praises it for finding "analogies" or "equivalents" of Austen's "meanings." The deletion of the Pemberley sequence is passed over as one "scene" which is "either too meditative or fails to advance the story line" (140).

3. Belton, "Reimagining Jane Austen," 180.

4. Belton, "Reimagining," 193.

5. Wiltshire, "Mrs. Bennet's Least Favorite," 179–187.

6. Le Faye, *Jane Austen's Letters*, 203.

7. First published as "The Controlling Hand: Jane Austen and 'Pride and Prejudice,'" *Scrutiny* 13 (1945): 99–111. My quotation is taken from the reprint in Watt, *Jane Austen*, 68.

8. Le Faye, *Jane Austen's*, 202. Just before this, Austen has complained that "a 'said he' or a 'said she' would sometimes make the Dialogue more immediately clear."

9. Fergus gives an illuminating reading of the three-way conversation in I, 10, revealing how little Elizabeth really understands about the relationship of the two men (*Jane Austen*, 109–115).

10. Hacking, *Rewriting the Soul*, 259. Hacking's is a modern clinical/philosophical examination of the vicissitudes of memory in the context of multiple personality disorder.

11. The music is adapted from one of Bach's Brandenburg concertos, played here by unaccompanied strings.

12. "How stark you look in your portrait. But I remember your warmth, and would soften that look," thus deleting any reference to the smile, which is also absent from the por-

trait. Troost emphasizes the correspondence between the style of the painting in 1995 and the film's depiction of an informal, "natural" Darcy. "Elizabeth gazes at his romantic portrait as Darcy dives into a lake in an attempt to cool his ardour." (Troost, "Filming Tourism, Portraying Pemberley," 492).

13. Hopkins, "Mr. Darcy's Body," 111–21.

14. Stewart, *Domestic Realities and Imperial Fictions*, 71.

15. Fraiman, *Unbecoming Women*, 85.

16. Sheen, "'Where the Garment Gapes,'" 22–3.

17. Fergus, "Two *Mansfield Parks*," 70.

18. "Music which peaks at the full display of certain objects suggests that they should be regarded as emotional foci. Clearly this choice of foci is ideologically significant, but of equal concern is the objects' aesthetic and emotional significance" (Cardwell, 141).

19. Polhemus, *Erotic Faith*, 40.

20. I am indebted to my colleague Dr. Kay Souter's discussions of *Pride and Prejudice*.

Chapter 6

1. Kirkham, *Jane Austen: Feminism*, on the topic of gender; Johnson, *Jane Austen: Women, Politics*, on sexuality; Smith, "My Only Sister Now," on incest; and Castle, "Sister-Sister," on lesbianism; James Thompson, *Between Self and World*, on ideology; and Said, "Jane Austen and Empire," on colonialism.

2. White, Introduction, 1–3.

3. See, for example, Johnston's fine analysis of the ways in which the radical aspirations of Thompson/Lee's *Sense and Sensibility* are undercut by "the film's absorption in its own picturesque quality" ("Historical Picturesque," 174).

4. Johnson, Introduction, 5–6.

5. Herlevi, "*Mansfield Park: A Conversation.*"

6. Moussa, "*Mansfield Park* and Film," 257.

7. Herlevi, "*Mansfield Park.*"

8. Wiltshire, *Recreating Jane Austen*, 136.

9. For discussions of Austen's Burkeian Conservatism, see Butler, *Jane Austen, passim;* Duckworth, *The Improvement of the Estate, passim;* Karounos, "Ordination and Revolution," 715–36.

10. Burke, *Reflections on the Revolution*, 106.

11. See Sales, *Jane Austen and Representations*, 87–113, and Tanner, "The Quiet Thing," 142–75, for discussions of this group of overactive and disruptive characters. It might be noted that there are characters in most of

Austen's novels that represent the flaws inherent in either excessive mobility or extreme passivity. Her overactive characters include John Thorpe, the rude and boorish boy racer who tries to impress Catherine Morland with his carriage driving prowess in *Northanger Abbey*, and Mrs. Elton in *Emma*, who is both obsessed with "exploring" (II, 14, 295) the countryside by barouche-landau and a great admirer of a brother-in-law who often "flies about" and "twice in one week … went to London and back again[from Bristol] with four horses" (II, 18, 331). Austen is equally critical of impetuous characters such as Marianne Dashwood in *Sense and Sensibility* and Louisa Musgrove in *Persuasion*. Both are brought near to death by their willful insistence on straying off the beaten path. Apart from Lady Bertram, Austen's most passive characters are Mr. Woodhouse in *Emma* and Mr. Bennet in *Pride and Prejudice*. Woodhouse feels threatened by traveling half a mile to attend a Christmas party at Randalls (I, 13, 116) and warns Frank Churchill about the dangers he will encounter in walking the few hundred yards from Hartfield to the Bates' house (II, 5, 210), while Mr. Bennet frequently retreats to his study to avoid coping with family responsibilities.

12. For discussions of the long-ways country dance and its function in Austen's novels, see Adams, "To Know the Dancer," 55–65; Elsbree, "Jane Austen and the Dance," 113–36; Mansell, *The Novels of Jane Austen*, *passim*; Monaghan, *Jane Austen: Structure*, *passim*, Stovel, "Every Savage Can Dance," 29–49; Alison Thompson, "The Felicities of Rapid Motion," 1–6; and Wilson, "Dance, Physicality, Social Mobility," 55–75.

13. Richardson, *Social Dances*, 29. The style of dancing at provincial balls was probably a good deal less refined. The crude romping that characterizes the Meryton ball in Joe Wright's *Pride and Prejudice* (2005) may reflect reality more accurately than the highly choreographed dances in other film versions of Austen's novels.

14. Alison Thompson, "Felicities," 3.

15. The approach and rejection pattern around which parts of *Pride and Prejudice* are structured provides an excellent example of the influence of dance patterns on the structure of Austen's novels (Monaghan, *Structure*, 68–80). A good example of ballroom etiquette as a gauge of a character's morality is provided by the contrast between John Thorpe's and Henry Tilney's attitudes to the prior invitation convention in *Northanger Abbey*. Performance on the dance floor is particularly significant in providing evidence of Mr. Collins' unsuitability as a life partner for Elizabeth Bennet. By so

"often moving wrong without being aware of it," he transforms their two dances together into exercises in "mortification" (*PP*, I, 18, 101).

16. Beddell, "Slow Down, You Move," 4.

17. See Aragay, "Possessing Jane Austen," 177–85, for a summary of the fidelity debate and its relevance to Rozema's *Mansfield Park*. See note 24 for further discussion of the fidelity question.

18. See Pawl, "Fanny Price," 296, and Karounos, "Ordination," 728–9, for discussions of Mrs. Norris's motives for confining Fanny to the periphery of the Bertram family.

19. Tanner, "The Quiet," 156, 157.

20. See Delaney, "A Sort of Notch," 533–47, for an excellent discussion of the complex factors involved in defining a person's social position in Austen's England.

21. Most critical discussions of Rozema's *Mansfield Park* have dealt with themes of entrapment and escape (Parrill, "Not the Bluebird," 186–92; Troost and Greenfield, "The Mouse that Roared," 193–200). However, they have generally focused on the slavery motif and Rozema's overt use of flight imagery, and have not considered the extent to which the motif is imbedded in the film's visual style. Neither have previous critics compared Rozema's use of movement to Austen's.

22. These words do not appear in the published script but are spoken immediately after "and her aunt tried not to cry" (Rozema, *Jane Austen's "Mansfield Park*," 70.) Subsequent references to Rozema's script will be cited parenthetically in the text of the essay.

23. In "Jane Austen, Anti-Jacobin," 18–25, Stove identifies Austen's stance in "Love and Freindship" as anti-Jacobin.

24. Moussa, "*Mansfield Park*, 256. In proposing that Rozema is free to treat her source materials as she wishes, I am implicitly rejecting the often challenged but persistent notion that adaptations, particularly of canonical works, should remain faithful to the originating text. This stance—commonplace amongst the general public and film reviewers, but also frequently adopted by professional critics who approach adaptation from a primarily literary perspective—has, as Kamilla Elliott argues (*Rethinking the Novel/Film*, 127–8), too often forestalled productive discussion of the interplay between films and the works upon which they are based.

The fidelity argument and, more specifically, the idea of the existence of authoritative original texts, has been debunked with great effectiveness by Sara Martin and John Wiltshire, writing on Shakespeare and Austen adaptations respectively. As each points out, far from being authoritative originals that enjoy a privileged status above the realm of intertextual relations, the works of even such iconic authors as Shakespeare and Austen are "themselves adaptations of miscellaneous sources" (Martin, "Classic Shakespeare for All," 49) and are engaged in precisely the same process of "rework[ing], rearrang[ing], and recylc[ling]" (Wiltshire, *Recreating*, 3) as their adaptors. So far as Wiltshire, in particular, is concerned, the fidelity argument not only founders on the question of "faithful to what?" but demonstrates a fundamental misunderstanding of the very process of literary creation: "Redesigning and plundering the creations of the past ... , rather than their preservation, is a process so continuous and endemic, that it is arguable that this is the central motor of artistic development" (3). Aragay takes a similar position by arguing that the fidelity argument is fundamentally flawed by its assumption that the originating text has one "true meaning" (178) to which adaptors are obliged to remain faithful.

In the final chapter of this book, Wiltshire offers further thoughts on the fidelity issue.

25. Johnson, Introduction 10; Wiltshire, *Recreating*, 135.

26. The phrase "wild beast" is taken from a letter written by Jane Austen. Its attribution to Fanny Price thus serves to reinforce the connection Rozema is trying to forge between her character and the free-spirited author. However, as Wiltshire points out, Rozema—like the biographer David Nokes, who may have influenced her understanding of Austen—is "wildly misreading Austen's letter" (*Recreating*, 136).

27. This scene takes what Duckworth calls Rozema's "Brontification" of Austen to the edge of unintentional parody (Rev. of *Mansfield Park*, 567).

28. Johnson, Introduction, 8.

29. For a discussion of Jane Austen's acceptance and then, after a night of anxious self examination, rejection of Harris Bigg-Wither's marriage proposal, see Tomalin, *Jane Austen: A Life*, 180–2.

30. I am not at all sure how Rozema intends the viewer to regard Fanny's marriage to Edmund. While his roles as friend and literary agent are plausible enough, Edmund is not convincing as a sexual partner, as indicated by the sardonic manner in which Fanny speaks of his expression of love for her. In this respect at least, I suspect that Rozema has failed to reconcile the demands of Austen's plot to her own subversive agenda. Had she been a little bolder, Rozema might have invented an alternative lover for Fanny. In keeping with the hints of lesbian attraction between Fanny and Mary Crawford offered earlier in the film, Rozema might even have made this lover female.

Chapter 7

1. Spring, who does not believe that Sir Walter Elliot is representative of his class, has disputed the historical accuracy of the argument that the gentry was in decline early in the nineteenth century. However, he neither explains why Austen offers no examples of responsible gentry in *Persuasion* nor why she does not finally reintegrate Anne Elliot into landed society ("Interpreters of Jane Austen's," 65–8). We might also note that Spring's positive assessment of the gentry's social and economic situation becomes questionable during the period following the end of the Napoleonic Wars, in the early part of which the action of *Persuasion* is set. See Todd and Blank, Introduction, xxxii-iv.

2. For a discussion of movement and stasis in Dear and Michell's *Persuasion* that takes a rather different direction from my own, see Favret, "Being True to Jane Austen," 72–80. Sodeman, "Domestic Mobility," *passim*, offers an excellent discussion of Austen's response to contemporary debates surrounding travel and mobility in *Persuasion* and *Sanditon*.

3. See *Pride and Prejudice* (I, 5, 21; I, 11, 63) for discussions of the difference between vanity and justifiable pride.

4. Lynch, Introduction, xxi.

5. Tanner, *Jane Austen*, 209.

6. For an excellent discussion of themes of professionalism and domesticity and their connection to the navy in *Persuasion*, see Cohen, "Persuading the Navy Home," *passim*.

7. Wiltshire points out that "the word [instantly] is habitually tagged to [Wentworth's] gestures, movements, and actions" ("*Persuasion*: Pathology," 193).

8. Blackwell, "A Slender Girl," *passim*, argues that Anne Elliot's wasted physical condition results from her anorexic response to the loss of Wentworth.

9. See Medalie for a thorough discussion of contingency in *Persuasion* ("Only as the Event," *passim*).

10. See Southam, "'Manoeuvring' in Jane Austen," *passim*, for other examples of this particular movement motif in *Persuasion* and earlier novels. While the focus of my analysis is movement, the concert scene also clearly provides an excellent example of Austen's ability to manipulate a group of characters within a defined space, an aspect of her art clearly analogous to what is called mise en scène in film.

11. See Sodeman, "Domestic," 800, for an astute discussion of the ways in which the proposal scene and the conclusion of the novel demonstrate Austen's reconfiguration of domesticity as egalitarian, mobile, and public. While Sodeman's argument is persuasive, I do not feel that it takes sufficient account of the value given in the novel to the improvised domestic interior spaces created by the Harvilles and Crofts.

12. References to Nick Dear's *Persuasion: A Screenplay* will be cited parenthetically in the text of this chapter.

13. Wallace, "Filming Romance: *Persuasion*," links the ordinary seaman in these two scenes to Sir Walter's servants as members of an "underclass, ... overworked, possibly mistreated, and probably discontented" (139). This is reading a lot into the sailors' "set faces" (139) and ignores the more affirmative picture communicated by camera movement and editing.

14. Dear and Michell may be picking up on Anne Elliot's comment in the novel that, during the Crofts' tenure at Kellynch, "the parish [was] to be so sure of a good example, and the poor of the best attention and relief" (II, 1, 136). However, there is no further indication in *Persuasion* that wealthy sailors such as the Crofts and Wentworth have any interest in assuming the role of landed gentlemen.

15. Gottlieb makes a similar point when he argues that the "broad circling movement of the camera that dominates the latter part of the film especially ... offers a commentary on society at large" ("*Persuasion* and Cinematic Approaches,"107).

16. Hoberg offers the following eloquent description of Lady Dalrymple: "the lacquered, mummified Lady Dalrymple, a hollowed-out title, who fittingly stands mute for the entire production" ("Her First and Her Last," 156). It should be noted, though, that Lady Dalrymple, as she does in the novel, speaks once in the film when she comments on Wentworth's "fine" (*P*, II, 8, 204; Dear, 75) appearance during the concert.

17. I do not give much credence to Wallace's suggestion that, by including footage from *The Mutiny of the Bounty*, Michell intends to associate Wentworth with the brutal Captain Bligh ("Filming Romance," 140).

18. Favret, "Being True to Jane Austen," 74, and Wiltshire, *Recreating Jane Austen*, 94, offer illuminating analyses of the significance of the white sheets.

19. Rzepka, "Making It," *passim*, offers a decisive rebuttal to Auerbach's argument in "O Brave New World," that Anne will in future join Wentworth on active service, by pointing

out that—unlike the childless Mrs. Croft, who has gone to sea with the Admiral on a number of occasions, and does seem to offer a plausible model for a new type of professional woman—Anne possesses nurturing qualities that destine her for motherhood and something approximating traditional domesticity. Rzepka, 99, and Lynch, Introduction, xvii, further point out that Austen would not have anticipated a recall to active service for Wentworth because she would have known when she wrote *Persuasion* that the navy was not remobilized following Napoleon's escape from Elba.

20. The scenes set in the Harvilles' lodgings at Lyme utilize tight framing, a warm fire and candlelight to convey warmth and domesticity. However, the actual living space is extremely rough and lacks any visual evidence of Captain Harville's ability to use skills learned in the navy "to turn the actual space to the best possible account, to supply the deficiencies of lodging-house furniture" (I, 11, 106). The connection between the navy and domesticity is completely broken in the recent ITV *Persuasion*. Here Harville lacks family and home and, for all the viewer knows, may well live on the beach where he meets the visitors from Uppercross.

21. In the novel, Anne's leadership qualities are most fully revealed by her response to Louisa's fall from the Cobb. However, I believe that in the film the earlier scene discussed here is more effective in giving visual expression to Anne's abilities.

22. Wallace, who calls them "egregious lapses of register" ("Filming Romance," 131), objects to scenes in which Anne displays such behavior. Thus, she argues that in rushing across the Pump Room to greet the Crofts (132), Anne comes to resemble Lydia Bennet. However, her argument is based on the assumption that Dear and Michell's film either intends to be or should be a direct copy of Austen's novel.

23. I find little merit in Wallace's argument that Wentworth "barely acknowledges [Anne's] presence" ("Filming Romance," 139) and that she is "irrelevant" (140) to life on board ship.

24. Gottlieb, "*Persuasion*" (109), briefly notes stylistic similarities between the two films while Favret, "Being True" (76), compares Ada's "drowning" in *The Piano* to Louisa's fall from the Cobb. In addition, the low angle underwater shot of the bottom of Admiral Croft's tender is an obvious reference to the similar shot of the ship's tender that carries Ada ashore on her arrival in New Zealand.

Chapter 8

1. Apart from the numerous television adaptations released in 2008, and the two biopics (*Becoming Jane* and *Miss Austen Regrets*), other films are also reported to be in production, such as Finna Torres's *Sense and Sensibilidad*, and a hip hop musical version of *Emma* produced by Screen Gems. http://www.cinematical.com/2008/04/08/emma-goes-hardcore-remixed-into-hip-hop. June 2008.

2. Austen is also now perceived through the filter of the many film adaptations that have been made of her novels, and her "public persona," however difficult to define, is also shaped by the cinematic recreations of her works. Austen is now associated, in the public imagination, with both literature and film. Several major websites, including the "The Republic of Pemberley" were created just after the beginning of Austenmania, to discuss films and novels as if they formed one single corpus. Today the imagination linked with Austen includes ball scenes, carriage rides, not to forget Mr. Darcy diving into the pond—this scene itself has become mythical. One would need to be a sociologist, with years of field research and interviews, to map the collective image of Jane Austen that exists today, a sort of mix of texts, films, commonly received ideas, clichés and personal experience.

3. Sutherland, *Jane Austen's Textual Lives*, 315.

4. Sutherland, *Jane Austen's*, 315. Austen has always been the source for theatrical adaptations, public readings, or Regency era celebrations, but the phenomenon seems to have expanded dramatically thanks to the film adaptations from 1995 onwards, accompanied, or followed, by a multitude of rewrites, sequels, prequels, not to mention the flourishing of biographies, Jane Austen experiences, balls, tours of England, and so on. There is already an Austen dice game (the winner is the player who gets married first, mentioned in Hutcheon, *A Theory of Adaptation*, 50) and a book of which you are the hero (Webster, *Lost in Austen*). No doubt Austenian video games will also soon be developed.

5. "[T]he power of Austen's novels rests not only in their presentation of plausible 'romantic' narratives, but in their articulation, as no other texts of her time do, of the challenges faced in the formation of a self—specifically and particularly the formation of a female self.... They come furthermore with the authority of history." Wiltshire, *Jane Austen, Introductions*, 115.

6. "Jameson notes that we have experienced a critical shift from the question of *what* literary works *mean* to the question of *how* they work. I am interested in the purpose of literary works: what are they *for*?" Tauchert, *Romancing Jane Austen*, 9.

7. John Wiltshire tackles the question of the "universality" of Austen, and already tries to answer the paradox "how does such an insular, even isolationist writer appeal to readers and critics of quite different cultural traditions?" Wiltshire, *Jane Austen*, 111.

8. To clarify the term "myth," see Barthes' *Mythologies*, Northrop Frye's *The Great Code*, or Joseph Campbell's *The Hero with a Thousand Faces*. Cinema makes a substantial contribution to the establishment of this mythical dimension today because of its very wide audience, as Bruno Bettelheim indicates: moving pictures are the art form best suited for "the task of giving us myths ... to live by in our time." Bettelheim, "The Art of Moving Pictures," 83.

9. It is difficult to know to what extent the filmmakers are familiar with Austen's novel, which they do not credit. In an interview, when asked if he consciously chose Austen, director Rajiv Menon's remarks leave us in doubt as to his precise reading of the novel: "I found the idea of honour, family, sibling rivalry and the ability to hold pain and not talk about it, interesting. The characters belonged largely to that time. Money was not an issue, nor was success. In fact successful people were looked down upon. Honour and loyalty were important. Two things that were taken up to adapt to modern days while making the film." Menon, *The Hindu*.

10. Tanner, "Secrecy and Sickness," 75–102; Johnson, *Jane Austen, Women, Politics and the Novel*, xix.

11. Wiltshire *Jane Austen*, 115.

12. Wiltshire, *Jane Austen*, 115.

13. Chennai (whose former name was Madras) is the center of the Tamil Film industry, which differs from the dominating Hindi industry, located in the Mumbai studios, commonly called "Bollywood."

14. Nasreen Kabir associates the importance of the mother-son relationship in Indian films with the social importance of producing a male heir: "the birth of a male child is the only way a mother can get any respect in society." Kabir, *Bollywood*, 18–19.

15. An expression used by Henry Tilney in his comparison between marriage and dancing (*NA* I, 10, 74).

16. My reference to the film uses the subtitles from the DVD, which are unfortunately of poor quality.

17. http://us.imdb.com/Comments Show?0242572 June 2008.

18. Tauchert, *Romancing*, 11.

19. Ebert, Review of *The Jane Austen Book Club*.

20. Huet-Brichard, *Littérature et Myth*, 29. My translation.

21. This blurring of the frontier between fiction and reality also evokes Bridget Jones's confusion between Colin Firth and Mr. Darcy. When "Darcymaniac" Bridget sees pictures of Colin Firth in a magazine, she gets confused over the actor/character divide: "Feel disoriented and worried, for surely Mr. Darcy would never do anything so vain and frivolous as to be an actor, and yet Mr. Darcy *is* an actor. Hmmm. All v. confusing. " Fielding, *Bridget Jones's*, 247–8.

22. Frye, *The Great Code*, 32.

23. This connection between the works, the fact that they seem to combine into a larger framework, evokes Frye's definition of myth as necessarily part of a mythology: "some sense of a *canon* relates them to one another: a myth takes its place in a mythology, an interconnected group of myths, whereas folktales remain nomadic, traveling over the world and interchanging their themes and motifs." Frye, *The Great Code*, 33.

24. In Kipling's story, "The Janeites," a secret society of officers read Austen in the trenches, and reading her after the war is over reminds them of wartime camaraderie.

25. Fowler, *The Jane Austen Book Club*, 163. Further references to the novel are included in parentheses in the text.

26. Barthes, *Mythologies*, 194. My translation.

27. Levi Strauss, *L'Homme nu*, 560. My translation.

28. Valéry, *Mon Faust*, 7–8. My translation.

29. Elliot, *Rethinking the Novel/Film Debate*, 133.

30. Barthes, *Mythologies*, 204. My translation.

Chapter 9

1. McFarlane, *Novel to Film*, 194, 166. Actually, McFarlane's position is more complex than this suggests: see, for instance, 197.

2. Leitch, "Twelve Fallacies in Contemporary." Cited from *Expanded Academic ASAP*. Gale, 9. See also Leitch, *Adaptation and its Discontents*, 153: "the quest for fidelity is always a fetish" and *passim*.

3. Leitch, "Twelve Fallacies," 10.

4. Sheen, Introduction, 1–13, 3.

5. Carroll, "A Consideration of Times," 169.

6. Smiles, *A Publisher and his Friends*, I, 282.

7. Cronin and McMillan, "Introduction," lvii.

8. Leitch, "Twelve Fallacies," 7.

9. Leitch, "Twelve Fallacies," 11.

10. Lejeune, "The Autobiographical Pact," 3–30.

11. Thompson, 155.

12. Perkins, *Reshaping the Sexes, passim*.

Bibliography

Primary Sources

NOVELS

The Cambridge Edition of the Works of Jane Austen. General Editor, Janet Todd. Cambridge: Cambridge University Press, 2005–08: *Northanger Abbey*, edited by Barbara M. Benedict and Deidre Le Faye, 2006; *Sense and Sensibility*, edited by Edward Copeland, 2006; *Pride and Prejudice*, edited by Pat Rogers, 2006; *Mansfield Park*, edited by John Wiltshire, 2005; *Emma*, edited by Richard Cronin and Dorothy McMillan, 2005; *Persuasion*, edited by Janet Todd and Antje Blank, 2006.

The Works of Jane Austen. Editor R. W. Chapman. Vol. 6, *Minor Works*. London: Oxford University Press, 1954.

FILMS AND TELEVISION SERIALS ON DVD

Barry Lyndon. Screenplay and directed by Stanley Kubrick. Peregrine/Hawk Films, distributed by Warner Bros., 1995.

Emma. Screenplay by Denis Constanduros. Directed by John Glenister. BBC, 1972.

_____. Screenplay and directed by Douglas McGrath. Miramax, 1996.

The Jane Austen Book Club. Screenplay and directed by Robin Swicord. Mockingbird Pictures, 2007.

Jane Austen's Emma. Screenplay by Andrew Davies. Directed by Diarmuid Lawrence. ITV, 1996.

Kandukondain, Kandukondain (English title *I Have Found It*). Adaptation of *Sense and Sensibility*. Screenplay and directed by Rajiv Menon. Sri Surya Films, 2000.

Mansfield Park. Screenplay and directed by Patricia Rozema. Miramax, 1999.

Miss Austen Regrets. Written by Gwyneth Hughes. Directed by Jeremy Lovering. BBC, 2008.

Persuasion. Screenplay by Nick Dear. Directed by Roger Michell. BBC, 1995.

_____. Written by Simon Burke. Directed by Adrian Shergold. ITV, 2007.

Pride and Prejudice. Screenplay by Aldous Huxley and Jane Murtin. Directed by Robert Z. Leonard. MGM, 1940.

_____. Screenplay by Fay Weldon. Directed by Cyril Coke. BBC, 1980.

_____. Screenplay by Andrew Davies. Directed by Simon Langton. BBC, 1995.

_____. Screenplay by Deborah Moggach. Directed by Joe Wright. Focus Features, 2005.

Sense and Sensibility. Screenplay by Emma Thompson. Directed by Ang Lee. Mirage/Columbia, 1995.

_____. Screenplay by Andrew Davies. Directed by John Alexander. BBC, 2008.

Secondary Sources

Adams, Timothy Dow. "To Know the Dancer from the Dance: Dance as Metaphor of Marriage in Four Novels of Jane Austen." *Studies in the Novel* 14, no.1 (1982): 55–65.

Andrew, Dudley. "The Well-Worn Muse: Adaptations in Film History and Theory." In *Narrative Strategies: Original Essays in Film and Prose Fiction*, edited by Syndy M. Conger and Janice R. Welsch, 9 17. (Macomb): Western Illinois University, 1980.

Aragay, Mireia. "Possessing Jane Austen: Fidelity, Authorship, and Patricia Rozema's *Mansfield Park* (1999)." *Literature/Film Quarterly* 31, no. 3 (2003): 177–85.

Arnheim, Rudolf. *Art and Visual Perception: A Psychology of the Creative Eye*, 2nd ed. Berkeley: University of California Press, 1974.

Auerbach, Nina. "O Brave New World: Evolution and Revolution in *Persuasion*." *ELH* 39, no. 1 (1972): 112–28.

Babb, Howard S. *Jane Austen's Novels: The Fabric of Dialogue*. Columbus: Ohio State University Press, 1962.

Bachelard, Gaston. *La flamme d'une chandelle.* Paris: Presses Universitaires de France, 1961.

Baltrusaitis, Jurgis. *Le miroir: révélations, science-fiction et fallacies.* Paris: Elmayan/Seuil, 1978.

Baridon, Michel. *Les jardins.* Paris: Robert Laffont, 1998.

Barthes, Roland. *Mythologies.* Paris: Seuil, 1957.

_____. *L'obvie et l'obtus.* Paris: Seuil, 1982.

_____. *Le plaisir du texte.* Paris: Seuil, 1973.

Battaglia, Beatrice, ed. *Jane Austen Oggi e Ieri.* Ravenna: Longo Editore, 2002

Bazin, André. "In Support of Mixed Cinema." In *Film And/As Literature,* edited by John Harrington, 13–21. Englewood Cliffs, NJ: Prentice Hall, 1977.

Beddell, Geraldine. "Slow Down, You Move Too Fast." *The Observer Review,* 4 February 2001, 4.

Belton, Ellen. "Reimagining Jane Austen: The 1940 and 1995 Film Versions of *Pride and Prejudice.*" In Macdonald and Macdonald, *Jane Austen on Screen,* 175–96.

Bettelheim, Bruno. "The Art of Moving Pictures." *Harper's,* October 1981, 80–3.

Birtwistle, Sue, and Susie Conklin. *The Making of "Jane Austen's Emma."* London: Penguin, 1996.

Blackwell, Bonnie. "A Slender Girl and a Thin Plot: Starvation and Spectacle in *Persuasion.*" *Lit: Literature Interpretation Theory* 15, no. 2 (2004): 153–80.

Bluestone, George. *Novels into Films.* Berkeley: University of California Press, 1957.

Blühn, Andreas, and Louise Lippincott. *Light! The Industrial Age 1750–1900.* London: Thames and Hudson, 2000.

Booth, Wayne C. *The Rhetoric of Fiction.* Chicago:University of Chicago Press, 1961.

Boyum, Joy Gould. *Double Exposure: Fiction into Film.* New York: New American Library, 1985.

Branigan, Edward. *Point of View in the Cinema : A Theory of Narration and Subjectivity in Classical Film.* Mouton: Amsterdam, 1984.

Braudy, Leo. "Acting: Stage vs. Screen." In *Film and Literature,* edited by Timothy Corrigan, 248–51. Upper Saddle River, NJ: Prentice Hall, 1999.

Brontë, Charlotte. *Shirley.* 1849. Edited by Herbert Rosengarten and Margaret Smith. Oxford: Clarendon Press, 1979.

Brower, Reuben. "The Controlling Hand: Jane Austen and *Pride and Prejudice.*" *Scrutiny* 13 (1945): 99–111.

Burke, Edmund. *Reflections on the Revolution in France.* 1790. Edited by Conor Cruise O'Brien. London: Penguin, 1986.

Burney, Frances. *Cecilia, or Memoirs of an Heiress.* 1782. Edited by Margaret Anne Doody and Peter Sabor. London: Oxford University Press, 1988.

Butler, Marilyn. *Jane Austen and the War of Ideas.* Oxford: Clarendon Press, 1975.

Byrne, Paula. *Jane Austen and the Theatre.* London: Hambledon, 2002.

Byron, George Gordon. *The Complete Poetical Works.* Edited by Jerome McGann. Oxford: Clarendon Press, 1980.

Campbell, Joseph. *The Hero with a Thousand Faces.* Princeton, NJ: Princeton University Press, 1968.

Cardwell, Sarah. *Adaptation Revisited: Television and the Classic Novel.* Manchester: Manchester University Press, 2002.

_____. "*Pride and Prejudice* (1995)." In *Adaptation Revisited,* 133–59.

Carroll, Laura. "A Consideration of Times and Seasons: Two Jane Austen Adaptations." *Literature/Film Quarterly* 31, no. 3 (2003): 169–76.

Castle, Terry. "Sister-Sister." *London Review of Books,* 5 August 1995, 3.

Chatman, Seymour. *Coming to Terms: The Rhetoric of Narrative in Fiction and Film.* Ithaca, NY: Cornell University Press, 1990.

_____. "What Novels Can Do That Films Can't (and Vice Versa)." *Critical Inquiry* 7, no.1 (1980): 121–40.

Chion, Michel. *La voix au cinéma.* Paris: Cahiers du Cinéma, 1982.

_____. *La toile trouée, la parole au cinéma.* Paris: Cahiers du Cinéma, 1988.

_____. *L'audio-vision.* Paris: Nathan, 1990.

Cohen, Keith. *Film and Fiction.* New Haven: Yale University Press, 1979.

_____. Introduction. In *Writing in a Film Age,* edited by Cohen, 1–44.

_____, ed. *Writing in a Film Age: Essays by Contemporary Novelists.* Niwot: University Press of Colorado, 991

Cohen, Monica F. "Persuading the Navy Home: Austen and Married Women's Professional Property." *Novel* 29, no. 3 (1996): 346–66.

Cohn, Dorrit. *Transparent Minds: Narrative Modes for Presenting Consciousness in Fiction.* Princeton, NJ: Princeton University Press, 1978.

Cronin, Richard, and Dorothy McMillan, eds. *Emma.* Cambridge: Cambridge University Press, 2005.

Davies, Tristan. "To Kiss or not to Kiss?" *Daily Telegraph,* 7 January 1995, 12.

Dear, Nick. *Persuasion: A Screenplay.* London: Methuen, 1996.

Delaney, Paul. "'A Sort of Notch in the Donwell Estate': Intersections of Status and

Class in *Emma.*" *Eighteenth-Century Fiction* 12, no.4 (2000): 533–47.

Despotopoulou, Anna. "Fanny's Gaze and the Construction of Feminine Space in *Mansfield Park.*" *Modern Language Review* 99, no. 3 (2004): 569–83.

Duckworth, Alistair M. *The Improvement of the Estate: A Study of Jane Austen's Novels.* Baltimore: The Johns Hopkins University Press, 1971.

_____. Rev. of *Mansfield Park*, written and directed by Patricia Rozema. *Eighteenth-Century Fiction* 12, no. 4 (2000): 565–71.

Dussinger, John. *In the Pride of the Moment: Encounters in Jane Austen's World.* Columbus: The Ohio State University Press, 1990.

Ebert, Roger. Review of *The Jane Austen Book Club.* 21 September 2007. http://roger ebert.suntimes.com/apps/pbcs.dll/article?AID=/20070920/REVIEWS/709200 302

Eco, Umberto. *The Open Work.* Cambridge: Harvard University Press, 1989.

Egerton, Judy, ed. *Wright of Derby.* London: Tate Gallery, 1990.

Eisenstein, Sergei. "Dickens, Griffith, and the Film Today." In *Film Form: Essays in Film Theory*, edited and translated by Jay Leyda, 195–255. New York: Harcourt Brace Jovanovich, 1949.

Elliott, Kamilla. "Unfilmable Books." Paper presented at the Association of Literature on Screen Studies inaugural conference, De Montfort University, Leicester, September 11, 2006.

_____. *Rethinking the Novel/Film Debate.* Cambridge: Cambridge University Press, 2003.

Elsbree, Langdon. "Jane Austen and the Dance of Fidelity and Complaisance." *Nineteenth-Century Fiction* 15, no. 2 (1960): 113–36.

Esrock, Ellen. *The Reader's Eye: Visual Imaging as Reader Response.* Baltimore: The Johns Hopkins University Press, 1994.

Favret, Mary A. "Being True to Jane Austen." In *Victorian Afterlife: Postmodern Culture Rewrites the Nineteenth-Century*, edited by John Kucich and Dianne F. Sadoff, 64–82. Minneapolis: University of Minnesota Press, 2000.

Fergus, Jan. *Jane Austen and the Didactic Novel.* London: Macmillan, 1983.

_____. "Two *Mansfield Parks*: Purist and Postmodern." In Macdonald and Macdonald, *Jane Austen on Screen*, 69–89.

Fielding, Helen. *Bridget Jones's Diary.* London: Picador, 1996.

Fowler, Karen Joy. *The Jane Austen Book Club.* New York: Marian Wood, 2004.

Fraiman, Susan. *Unbecoming Women: British*

Women Novelists and the Novel of Development. New York: Columbia University Press, 1993.

Fraser, David. "Joseph Wright of Derby and the Lunar Society." In *Wright of Derby*, edited by Egerton, 15–24.

Frye, Northrop. *The Great Code: The Bible and Literature.* New York: Harcourt Brace Jovanovich, 1982.

Fuller, Graham. "Cautionary Tale." In *Film/Literature/Heritage*, edited by Vincendeau, 77–81.

Gard, Roger. "A Few Sceptical Thoughts on Jane Austen and Film." In Macdonald and Macdonald, *Jane Austen on Screen*, 10–12.

Gay, Penny. *Jane Austen and the Theatre.* Cambridge: Cambridge University Press, 2002.

Gibbs, John. *Mise-en-scène: Film Style and Interpretation.* Wallflower Books: London, 2002.

Giddings, Robert, and Erica Sheen, eds. *The Classic Novel: from Page to Screen.* Manchester: Manchester University Press, 2000.

Gilbert, Deidre. "What the Ear Has to Offer: A Soundscape of *Mansfield Park.*" *Persuasions* 28 (2006): 126–36.

Gottlieb, Sidney. "*Persuasion* and Cinematic Approaches to Jane Austen." *Literature/Film Quarterly* 30, no. 2 (2002): 104–10.

Gregory, John. *A Father's Advice to his Daughters.* Sherborne: Goadby, 1776.

Groenendyk, Kathi L. "The Importance of Vision: *Persuasion* and the Picturesque." *Rhetoric Society Quarterly* 30, no.1 (2000): 9–28.

Hacking, Ian. *Rewriting the Soul: Multiple Personality and the Sciences of Memory.* Princeton, NJ: Princeton University Press, 1995.

Hannon, Patrice. "Austen Novels and Austen Films: Incompatible Worlds?" *Persuasions* 18 (1996): 24–32.

Harris, Jocelyn. "'Domestic Virtues and National Importance': Lord Nelson, Captain Wentworth, and the English Napoleonic War Hero." *Eighteenth-Century Fiction*, 19, nos.1–2 (2007): 181–205.

Heckerling, Amy. "High School Confidential." *Rolling Stone*, 7 September 1995, 53.

Herlevi, Patty-Lynne. "*Mansfield Park*: A Conversation with Patricia Rozema." 11 February 2000. www.nitrateonline.com/2000/fmansfield.html.

Higson, Andrew. *English Heritage, English Cinema: Costume Drama Since 1980.* Oxford: Oxford University Press, 2003.

Hoberg, Tom. "Her First and Her Last: Austen's *Sense and Sensibility* and *Persuasion*, and Their Screen Adaptations." In

Lupack, *Nineteenth-Century Women at the Movies*, 140–66.

_____. "The Multiplex Heroine: Screen Adaptations of *Emma*." In Lupack, *Nineteenth-Century Women at the Movies*, 106–28.

Hopkins, Lisa. "Mr. Darcy's Body: Privileging the Female Gaze." In Troost and Greenfield, *Jane Austen in Hollywood*, 111–21.

Hudelet, Ariane. "Incarnating Jane Austen: The Role of Sound in the Recent Film Adaptations." *Persuasions* 27 (2005): 175–84.

Huet-Brichard, Marie-Catherine. *Littérature et mythe*. Paris: Hachette, 2001.

Hutcheon, Linda. *A Theory of Adaptation*. London: Routledge, 2006.

Johnson, Claudia L. Introduction. In Rozema, *Jane Austen's "Mansfield Park,"* 1–10.

_____. *Jane Austen: Women, Politics and the Novel*. Chicago: University of Chicago Press; 1988.

Johnston, Susan. "Historical Picturesque: Adapting *Great Expectations* and *Sense and Sensibility*." *Mosaic* 37 no.1 (2004): 167–84.

Kabir, Nasreen. *Bollywood: The Indian Cinema Story*. London: Channel 4 Books, 2001.

Kaplan, Deborah. "Mass Marketing Jane Austen: Men, Women and Courtship in Two Film Adaptations." In Troost and Greenfield, *Jane Austen in Hollywood*, 177–87.

Karounos, Michael. "Ordination and Revolution in *Mansfield Park*." *SEL: Studies in English Literature 1500–1900* 44 no. 4 (2004): 715–36.

Kellman, Steven G. "The Cinematic Novel: Tracking a Concept." *Modern Fiction Studies* 33, no. 3 (1987): 467–77.

Kettle, Arnold, "*Emma*." In Watt, *Jane Austen*, 112–23.

Kipling, Rudyard. "The Janeites." In *Debits and Credits*, edited by Kemp, 119–40. Harmondsworth: Penguin, 1987.

Kirkham, Margaret. *Jane Austen: Feminism and Fiction*. Totowa, NJ: Barnes and Noble, 1983.

Knox-Shaw, Peter. *Jane Austen and the Enlightenment*. Cambridge: Cambridge University Press, 2004.

Lascelles, Mary. *Jane Austen and Her Art*. 1939. Oxford: University Press, 1965.

Lauritzen, Monica. "Jane Austen's 'Emma' on Television: A Study of a BBC Classic Serial." *Gothenburg Studies in English* 48. Gothenburg, Sweden, 1981.

Le Faye, Deirdre. *Jane Austen's Letters*. 3rd ed. Oxford: Oxford University Press, 1995.

_____. *Jane Austen: A Family Record*. 2nd ed. Cambridge: Cambridge University Press, 2004.

Leitch, Thomas. "Twelve Fallacies in Contemporary Adaptation Theory." *Criticism* 45, no. 2 (2003): 149–72.

_____. *Adaptation and its Discontents. From "Gone with the Wind" to "The Passion of the Christ."* Baltimore: The Johns Hopkins University Press, 2007.

Lejeune, Phillipe. "The Autobiographical Pact." In *On Autobiography*, edited and with a foreword by John Paul Eakin, translated by Katherine M. Leary, 3–30. Minneapolis: University of Minnesota Press, 1988.

Lévi-Strauss, Claude. *L'Homme nu*. Paris: Plon, 1971.

Lewis, C.S. "A Note on Jane Austen." In Watt, *Jane Austen*, 25–34.

LoBrutto, Vincent. *Stanley Kubrick, A Biography*. New York: Da Capo Press, 1999.

Locke, John. *An Essay Concerning Human Understanding*. 1689–1700. Edited by Peter Nidditch. Oxford: Clarendon Press, 1975.

Lodge, David. "Thomas Hardy and Cinematographic Form." *Novel* 7, no. 4 (1974): 246–54.

Lupack, Barbara Tepa, ed. *Nineteenth-Century Women at the Movies: Adapting Classic Women's Fiction to Film*. Bowling Green, KY: Popular Press, 1999.

Lynch, Deidre Shauna. Introduction. In Jane Austen, *Persuasion*, edited by James Kinsley, vii–xxxiii. Oxford World's Classics. 2nd ed. Oxford: Oxford University Press, 2004.

Macdonald, Gina, and Andrew F., eds. *Jane Austen on Screen*. Cambridge: Cambridge University Press, 2003.

Mansell, Darrell. *The Novels of Jane Austen: An Interpretation*. New York: Macmillan, 1973.

Martin, Sara. "Classic Shakespeare for All: *Forbidden Planet* and *Prospero's Books*, Two Screen Adaptations of *The Tempest*." In *Classics in Film and Fiction*, edited by Deborah Cartmell, I.Q. Hunter, Heidi Kaye, and Imelda Whelehan, 34–53. London: Pluto Press, 2000.

Mayne, Judith. *Private Novels, Public Films*. Athens: University of Georgia Press, 1988.

McFarlane, Brian. "It Wasn't Like That in the Book." *Literature/Film Quarterly* 28, no. 3 (2000): 63–69.

_____. *Novel to Film: An Introduction to the Theory of Adaptation*. Oxford: Clarendon Press, 1996.

Medalie, David. "'Only as the Event Decides': Contingency in *Persuasion*." *Essays in Criticism* 49, no. 2 (1999): 152–69.

Menon, Rajiv. Interview by Chitra Mahesh, *The Hindu*, 18 January 2002. http://www.hinduonnet.com/thehindu/fr/2002/01/18/stories/2002011801320100.htm June 2008.

Metz, Christian. *Le signifiant imaginaire*. Paris: Christian Bourgeois, 1977.

Miller, D. A. *Jane Austen, or The Secret of Style*. Princeton: Princeton University Press, 2003.

Miller, Jonathan. *On Reflection*. London: National Gallery Publications Ltd., 1998.

Monaco, James. *How to Read a Film*. 3rd ed. New York: Oxford University Press, 2000.

Monaghan, David. *Jane Austen: Structure and Social Vision*. London: Macmillan, 1980.

Morrison, Sarah. "*Emma* Minus Its Narrator: Decorum and Class Consciousness in Film Versions of the Novel." *Persuasions On-Line*, no. 3 (1999): 1–8. http://www.jasna.org/PolOP1/Morrison.html.

Mosier, John. "Clues for the Clueless." In Macdonald and Macdonald, *Jane Austen on Screen*, 228–53.

Moussa, Hiba. "*Mansfield Park* and Film: An Interview with Patricia Rozema." *Literature/Film Quarterly* 32, no. 4 (2004): 255–60.

Murphy, Olivia. "Books, Bras and Bridget Jones: Reading Adaptations of *Pride and Prejudice*." *Sydney Studies in English* 31, no. 2 (2005): 21–38.

Nabokov, Vladimir. "*Mansfield Park*." In *Vladimir Nabokov: Lectures on Literature*, edited by Fredson Bowers, 55–60. London: Weidenfeld and Nicolson, 1983.

Nelson, Thomas Allen. *Kubrick: Inside a Film Artist's Maze*. Bloomington: Indiana University Press, 2000.

Nicholson, Benedict. *Joseph Wright of Derby: Painter of Light*. London: Paul Mellon Foundation for British Art, 1968.

O'Dea, William. *The Social History of Lighting*. London: Routledge and Kegan Paul, 1958.

Page, Norman. *The Language of Jane Austen*. London: Blackwell, 1972.

Paquet-Deyris, Anne-Marie. "Mise en scène de l'intériorité dans *Pride and Prejudice* de Joe Wright." *Cercles, Occasional Papers Series* (2007): 53–8. <http://www.cercles.com/occasional.html>.

Parrill, Sue. "Not the Bluebird of Happiness: Bird Imagery in the Film *Mansfield Park*." *Literature/Film Quarterly* 31, no. 3 (2003): 186–92.

Pawl, Amy J. "Fanny Price and the Sentimental Genealogy of *Mansfield Park*." *Eighteenth-Century Fiction* 16 no. 2 (2004): 287–315.

Perkins, Moreland. *Reshaping the Sexes in "Sense and Sensibility."* Charlottesville, VA: University of Virginia Press, 1998.

Perkins, V. F. *Film as Film: Understanding and Judging Movies*. Harmondsworth, UK: Penguin, 1972.

Phillips, K.C. *Jane Austen's English*. London: André Deutsch, 1970.

Polhemus, Robert. *Erotic Faith: Being in Love from Jane Austen to D.H. Lawrence*. Chicago: University of Chicago Press, 1990.

Propp, Vladimir. *Morphology of the Folktale*. Translated by Laurence Scott. Austin: University of Texas Press, 1968.

Pucci, Suzanne R. "The Return Home." In *Jane Austen and Co: Remaking the Past in Contemporary Culture*, edited by Suzanne R. Pucci and James Thompson, 133–155. Albany: State University of New York Press, 2003.

Radcliffe, Ann. *A Sicilian Romance*. 1790. Edited by Alison Milbank. Oxford University Press: London, 1993.

_____. *The Romance of the Forest*. 1791. Edited with an Introduction by Chloe Chard. Oxford University Press: London, 1986.

Richards, Paulette. "Regency Romance Shadowing in the Visual Motifs of Roger Michell's *Persuasion*." In Macdonald and Macdonald, *Jane Austen on Screen*, 111–126.

Richardson, Philip J. S. *The Social Dances of the Nineteenth Century in England*. London: Herbert Jenkins, 1960.

Robbe-Grillet, Alain. "For a New Cinema." In Cohen, *Writing for a Film Age*, 112–20.

Rozema, Patricia. *Jane Austen's "Mansfield Park": A Screenplay*. New York: Talk Miramax Books, 2000.

Rzepka, Charles. "Making It in a Brave New World: Marriage, Profession, and Anti-Romantic Ekstasis in Austen's *Persuasion*." *Studies in the Novel* 26, nos.1, 2 (1994): 99–121.

Said, Edward W. "Jane Austen and Empire." In *Culture and Imperialism*, 80–97. New York: Knopf, 1994.

Sales, Roger. *Jane Austen and Representations of Regency England*. London: Routledge and Kegan Paul, 1994.

_____. "In Face of All the Servants: Spectators and Spies in Austen, with Special Reference to the 1995 Adaptation of *Persuasion*." In *Janeites: Austen's Disciples and Devotees*, edited by Deidre Shauna Lynch, 188–205. Princeton, NJ: Princeton University Press, 2000.

Samuelian, Kristin Flieger. "'Piracy is Our Only Option': Postfeminist Intervention in *Sense and Sensibility*." In Troost and Greenfield, *Jane Austen in Hollywood*, 159–76.

Schivelbusch, Wolfgang. *Disenchanted Night: The Industrialisation of Light in the Nineteenth Century*. Translated by Angela

Davies. Berkeley: University of.California Press, 1988.

Scholes, Robert. "Narration and Narrativity in Film." *Quarterly Review of Film Studies* 1, no. 3 (1976): 283–96.

Sheen, Erica. Introduction. In Giddings and Sheen, *The Classic Novel*, 1–13.

_____. "'Where the Garment Gapes': Faithfulness and Promiscuity in the 1995 BBC *Pride and Prejudice*." In Giddings and Sheen, *The Classic* Novel, 14–30.

Smiles, Samuel. *A Publisher and His Friends, Memoir and Correspondence of the Late John Murray*, 2 Vols, London: John Murray, 1891.

Smith, Johanna M. "'My Only Sister Now': Incest in *Mansfield Park*." *Studies in the* Novel 18, no.1 (1987): 1–15.

Sodeman, Melissa. "Domestic Mobility in *Persuasion* and *Sanditon*." *SEL: Studies in English Literature 1500–1900* 45, no. 4 (2005), 787–814.

Southam, B. C. *Jane Austen: The Critical Heritage*. London: Routledge and Kegan Paul, 1968.

_____. "'Manoeuvring' in Jane Austen." *Women's Writing* 11, no.3 (2004): 463–76.

Spence, Jon. "The Abiding Possibilities of Nature in *Persuasion*." *SEL: Studies in English Literature 1500–1900* 21, no. 4 (1981): 625–36.

Spiegel, Alan. "Flaubert to Joyce: The Evolution of a Cinematographic Form." *Novel* 6, no. 3 (1973): 229–43.

Spring, David. "Interpreters of Jane Austen's Social World: Literary Critics and Historians." In *Jane Austen: New Perspectives*, edited by Janet Todd, 53–72. New York: Holmes and Meier, 1983.

Stam, Robert. "Introduction: The Theory and Practice of Adaptation." In *Literature and Film: A Guide to the Theory and Practice of Film Adaptation*, edited by Robert Stam, 1–52. Oxford: Blackwell, 2005.

Stewart, Maaja. *Domestic Realities and Imperial Fictions: Jane Austen's Novels in Eighteenth-Century Contexts*. Athens: University of Georgia Press, 1993.

Stove, Judy. "Jane Austen, Anti-Jacobin." *The New Criterion* 23, no. 5 (2005): 18–25.

Stovel, Nora. "'Every Savage Can Dance': Choreographing Courtship." *Persuasions* 23 (2001): 29–49.

Strangren, Richard L., and Martin F. Nordau. *Movies: A Language in Light*. Englewood Cliffs, NJ: Prentice Hall, 1984.

Sutherland, Kathryn. *Jane Austen's Textual Lives: From Aeschylus to Bollywood*. Oxford: Oxford University Press, 2005.

Tallis, Raymond. "The Realistic Novel Versus the Cinema." *Critical Quarterly* 27, no. 2 (1985): 57–65.

Tanner, Tony. *Jane Austen*. London: Macmillan, 1986. Rev.ed. Basingstoke: Palgrave, 2007.

_____. "Secrecy and Sickness: *Sense and Sensibility*." In *Jane Austen*, 75–102.

_____. "The Quiet Thing': *Mansfield Park*." In *Jane Austen*, 142–75.

Tauchert, Ashley. *Romancing Jane Austen: Narrative, Realism, and the Possibility of a Happy Ending*. Basingstoke: Palgrave, 2005.

Thompson, Alison. "The Felicities of Rapid Motion: Jane Austen and the Ballroom." *Persuasions On-Line* 21, no.1 (2000). http://www.jasna.org/pol102/thompson.html.

Thompson, Emma. *Jane Austen's "Sense and Sensibility": The Screenplay and Diaries*. London: Bloomsbury, 1995.

Thompson, James. *Between Self and World: The Novels of Jane Austen*. University Park: Pennsylvania State University Press, 1983.

Todd, Janet. *The Cambridge Introduction to Jane Austen*. Cambridge: Cambridge University Press, 2006.

_____. *Sensibility: An Introduction*. London: Methuen, 1986.

_____, and Antje Blank. Introduction. Jane Austen, *Persuasion*. In *The Cambridge Edition of the Works of Jane Austen*, xxi–lxxxii.

Tomalin, Claire. *Jane Austen: A Life*. London: Viking, 1997.

Trilling, Lionel. "Emma and the Legend of Jane Austen." In *Jane Austen's Emma*, edited by David Lodge, 148–69. London: Macmillan, 1968.

Troost, Linda. "Filming Tourism, Portraying Pemberley." *Eighteenth-Century Fiction* 18, no. 4 (2006): 477–98.

_____. "The Mouse that Roared: Patricia Rozema's *Mansfield Park*." In *Jane Austen in Hollywood*, 2nd ed., edited by Linda Troost and Sayre Greenfield, 188–204. Lexington, KY: University of Kentucky Press, 2001.

_____, and Sayre Greenfield. "Filming Highbury: Reducing the Community in *Emma* to the Screen." *Persuasions On-Line*, no. 3 (1999): 1–7. http://www.jasna.org/persuasions/online/opno3/troost_sayre.html.

_____. "Introduction: Watching Ourselves Watching." In Troost and Greenfield, *Jane Austen in Hollywood*, 1–12.

_____, and _____, eds. *Jane Austen in Hollywood*. Lexington, Ky: University of Kentucky Press, 1998.

Uglow, Jenny. *The Lunar Men: The Friends Who Made the Future, 1730–1810*. London: Faber and Faber, 2002.

Valéry, Paul. *Mon Faust.* Paris: Gallimard Folio, 1988.

Vincendeau, Ginette, ed. *Film/Literature/Heritage: A Sight and Sound Reader.* London: British Film Institute, 2001.

Wallace, Tara Ghoshal. "Filming Romance: *Persuasion.*" In Macdonald and Macdonald, *Jane Austen on Screen,* 127–43.

Watt, Ian, ed. *Jane Austen: A Collection of Critical Essays.* Englewood Cliffs, NJ: Prentice-Hall, 1963.

_____. *The Rise of the Novel.* 1957. London: Hogarth Press, 1987.

Webster, Emma Campbell. *Lost in Austen: Create Your Own Jane Austen Adventure.* New York: Riverhead Books, 2007.

White, Laura Mooneyham. Introduction. In *Critical Essays on Jane Austen,* edited by Laura Mooneyham White, 1–10. New York: G.K. Hall, 1998.

Wickre, Bille. "Pictures, Plurality and Puns: A Visual Approach to *Barry Lyndon.*" In *Depth of Field: Stanley Kubrick, Film, and the Uses of History,* edited by Geoffrey Cocks, James Diedrick, and Glenn Perusek, 165–84. Madison: University of Wisconsin Press, 2006.

Willemen, Paul. *Looks and Frictions: Essays in Cultural Studies and Film Theory.* Bloomington: Indiana University Press/BFI, 1994.

Wilson, Cheryl A. "Dance, Physicality, and Social Mobility in Jane Austen's *Persuasion.*" *Persuasions* 25 (2003): 55–75.

Wilson, George M. *Narration in Light: Studies in Cinematic Point of View.* Baltimore: The Johns Hopkins University Press, 1986.

Wiltshire, John. "Decolonising *Mansfield Park.*" *Essays in Criticism* 54, no. 4 (2003): 303–22.

_____. *Jane Austen and the Body.* Cambridge: Cambridge University Press, 1992.

_____. *Jane Austen: Introductions and Interventions.* Delhi: Macmillan India, 2003.

_____. "Mrs. Bennet's Least Favorite Daughter." *Persuasions* 23 (2001): 179–187.

_____. "*Persuasion*: The Pathology of Everyday Life." In *New Casebooks: "Mansfield Park" and "Persuasion,"* edited by Judy Simons, 183–204. Basingstoke: Macmillan, 1997.

_____. *Recreating Jane Austen.* Cambridge: Cambridge University Press, 2001.

Wood, Robin. "New Criticism" *Definition* 3 (1960–1): 9–11.

Woolf, Virginia. *The Captain's Death Bed and Other Essays.* New York: Harcourt, Brace, 1950.

Young, Kay. "Feeling Embodied; Consciousness, *Persuasion,* and Jane Austen." *Narrative* 11, No. 1 (2003): 78–92.

Index

Ackerman, Rudolph 41
Adams, Timothy Dow 180n.12
Andrew, Dudley 8
Aragay, Mireia 180n.17, 181n.24
Argand, Ami 41, 45
Arnheim, Rudolf 173–4ch.4n.2
Auerbach, Nina 182n.19
Austen adaptations: Austenmania 2, 93, 148, 161; candlelight in 48; character revelation in 80–1; difficulties in creating 13, 172n.48; DVD commentaries 160–1, 165; fidelity approach to 160–1, 171n.11, 180–1n.24; intertexuality amongst 162–4; mirrors in 86; as modern appropriations 149–50; narrators in 172–3n.49; number of 5, 161, 171n.1; as readings of novels 96; recent and forthcoming 183n.1; revisionist treatments in 111; romanticized 55; sound in 68, 70–2, 74–5, 171n.18; undecidability of 93; versions of *Pride and Prejudice* 96; *see also* individual films
Austen, Jane, fictional works: alternate language in 57, 58, 59, 62–4, 65, 71, 175n. 8, 9, 175–6n.13, 176n.18, 19; author's opinion of *Pride and Prejudice* 100; as cinematic 12–16, 36–7, 63, 67, 77, 118, 138, 148; as conservative 112; contemporary dimension 111–12, 113–14, 150–9; country dance, role of 112–13; early reputation 162–3; instability of texts 148–9; irony in 66–7, 85; landed gentry, role of 131; mirrors in 86, 178n.22; narrative point of view 19, 24; overhearing in 27–8, 29–30, 37; perception and judgment in, 76–7, 79, 85–6, 92–3; reinventions of 149, 183n.2; visual elements 17–27, 36–7, 57, 72; *see also* individual works
Austen, Jane, life: industrialized light, experience of 41, 174n.9

Babb, Howard 175n.7
Bach, Johann Sebastian: *Brandenburg Concertos* 179ch.5n.11
Bachelard, Gaston 41–2
Baltrusaitis, Jurgis 178n.25
Baridon, Michel 178n.19

Barry Lyndon (1975 film): contrasted with *Sense and Sensibility* (1995 film) 51; as heritage film 48; lighting compared with *Persuasion* (1995 telefilm) 52, 53; lighting techniques 39, 46–8
Barthes, Roland 7, 68, 93, 158, 159, 171n.30, 175n.10, 179n.37, 183n.8
Battaglia, Beatrice 178n.34
Bazin, André 173n.49
Becoming Jane (2006 telefilm): recent Austen films amongst 161
Bedell, Geraldine 180n.16
Belton, Ellen 97, 173n.49
Bergson, Henri 172n.33
Bettelheim, Bruno 183n.8
Birtwistle, Sue 178n.20
Blackwell, Bonnie 181n.8
Blank, Antje 181n.1
Bluestone, George 6–9, 173n.49, 179ch.5n.2
Blühn, Andreas 174n.3, 7, 9, 10, 14
Booth, Wayne 19–20
Brandenburg Concertos 179ch.5n.11
Branigan, Edward 173n.8
Braudy, Leo 81
Bridget Jones's Diary 184n.21
Brontë, Charlotte: *Shirley* 50
Brower, Rueben 101
Burke, Edmund 112–13
Burney, Fanny: *Cecilia*, lighting in 43–4
Butler, Marilyn 80, 179ch.6n.9
Byrne, Paula 173n.3, 12, 175n.5
Byron, George Gordon 42, 54

Campbell, Joseph 7, 185n.8
Cardwell, Sarah 174n.24, 179n.18
Carroll, Laura 161, 173n.24
Castle, Terry 179ch.6n.1
Cecilia, lighting in 43–4
Chatman, Seymour 6, 171n.3
Chion, Michel 71, 175n.3, 6, 12, 177n.29
cinematic novel, definitions of 9–12
Clueless (1995 film) 12, 111, 161; narrator 172–3n.49
Cohen, Keith 10, 171n.20, 173n.15
Cohen, Monica F. 181n.6